Louis Agassiz Fuertes

Louis Fuertes with a trained Peregrine Falcon.

Photograph by A. A. Allen.

LOUIS AGASSIZ
FUERTES

His life briefly told and his correspondence

edited by MARY (FUERTES) BOYNTON

New York • OXFORD UNIVERSITY PRESS

1956

Printed in the United States of America

FOR M.S.F.

Preface

IN COPYING THE LETTERS or passages therefrom I have omitted salutations, closings, and signs at the beginning and end to show that the letters as printed are not complete. Elisions within a single letter are indicated by three dots. The punctuation of the letters and the spelling of bird names have been normalized.

The following persons named in the text (or their heirs) offered letters for my use, or gave permission to quote from letters received by Louis Fuertes, or both: Gladys Thayer Reasoner, John Paul Young, A. K. Fisher, Frank M. Chapman, William A. Maxon, Vernon Bailey, Courtenay Brandreth, Frances H. Allen, Gilbert Grosvenor, George M. Sutton, William C. Strunk Jr., Katharine Finch, George Sarton, Wilfred H. Osgood, Carl Burger, Conrad Roland, Allan Brooks, T. G. Pearson, Joseph Grinnell, Martin D. Hardin, H. W. vanLoon, James E. Baum Jr. The passage from Thayer's father's journal came, with much other assistance, from Thayer's biographer, Nelson C. White. Vernon Bailey, Hugh Breckenridge, William Strunk Jr., and Alfred M. Bailey sent reminiscences written especially for my use; R. Wolcott Hooker contributed a paper composed by him for a memorial service. I am grateful to them and to Alden Hadley and George Sutton for permission to quote from their articles previously printed. Correspondence with former officials of the United States Biological Survey, now the Fish and Wild Life Department, was placed at my disposal by Rachel Carson, who also informed me of the large collection of Fuertes paintings in the Service's possession and helped in listing them.

May I here express my thanks to all who sent letters, information about pictures, and personal reminiscences that did not find their way into the text. Everything was useful in establishing proportion and emphasis, and only limitations of space excluded much that I wish could have been retained.

To R. C. Murphy and other members of the Department of Birds of the American Museum of Natural History, to the staff of the Cornell University Library, and most of all to A. A. Allen and Elsa G. Allen I am grateful for unfailng kindness throughout the long period during which this manuscript was in preparation. I do not name all the friends and members of my family who have read the manuscript at various stages in its preparation and given me valuable help. I thank them, and in particular I thank Paul Slud for carefully checking the manuscript in its final form, and David Kennedy-Fraser for reading the proofs. For any errors or infelicities that may remain in the published book the author alone is responsible.

Trumansburg, N. Y.   M.F.B.
November, 1955

Foreword

IN THE HISTORY of ornithology in North America, a few names stand out as the architects and builders of a science that has achieved great popular appeal.

Some are the names of the pioneers who explored the new continent and collected and named its birds. Some are the names of the curators in great museums who came later and brought orderly sequence into bird classification. Some are the names of writers who familiarized themselves with all the birds and produced manuals or guides for common use. A few are those of educators who through the written or spoken word have passed on to the next generation the knowledge and the skills attained by their predecessors. A very few are of artists, skilled in the portrayal of birds, who illustrated their own books or those of others with lifelike paintings of the birds described.

The name of Louis Agassiz Fuertes stands out among these as the greatest artist of wild bird portraits that has ever lived.

This in itself is sufficient reason for a book dealing with his life and achievements. But when one realizes that he became the best-beloved of all Cornell alumni, the most talented member of the Savage Club, the most useful and public-spirited member of his community, there can be no question that the possessor of such a rare combination of gifts is worthy of perpetuation in book form.

Many of Louis' friends are still living for he died relatively young and at the time nearly every boy and girl of scout age in his home city of Ithaca claimed him as a friend—'Uncle Louis.' And each of them has the fondest memories of some experience in Louis' studio or of meeting him on the street or after a lecture.

This host of friends, as well as ornithologists and bird-lovers the world over who revere his memory and cherish his bird portraits, will welcome this book from the hand of his own daughter. And they will welcome her publication of his correspondence with those who may have influenced his life or who, in turn, received great inspiration from him.

In all his letters, as well as in the every day events of his life, one is impressed with the sincerity and the humility and the genius of this charming man.

During the last three years of his life he was a lecturer in ornithology at Cornell University where it was my privilege to be associated with him more closely, perhaps, than in the preceding twenty years of our friendship. Students flocked to his lectures on bird coloration and never thought of taking notes. So vivid was his personality, so original his vocabulary, so humorous his metaphors and so warm his human understanding, they went away inspired.

During my fifty years at Cornell, I have at no other time nor in any other classroom seen such a spontaneous response from students and from colleagues as that which followed Louis Fuertes' lectures. His early death robbed Cornell of one of the greatest teachers it has ever known as well as the greatest bird artist.

Now read what Mary Fuertes Boynton has to say about her father and his friends.

ARTHUR A. ALLEN
Professor of Ornithology, Emeritus,
Cornell University

Contents

List of Illustrations

The frontspiece is published through the courtesy of A. A. Allen. The other illustrations are from original life studies by Louis Agassiz Fuertes owned by the American Museum of Natural History and published with permission.

Introduction

FOR THIRTY YEARS, from the end of his formal education at Cornell University in 1897 until his death in 1927, Louis Agassiz Fuertes produced drawings and paintings of birds that are unique in their lively likeness to the individuals whose portraits they are.

In addition to his dominant love for birds Louis Fuertes received other good gifts at birth. The seeing eye was one, an excellent physical organ that never failed and served for the closest work as well as for the farthest sight. He would say, 'Here comes an eagle,' and after a moment other eyes would be able to discern a speck where he was looking, presently they could tell it was some kind of bird, and after a while an eagle would circle into the range of their ability to identify it. 'At the moment [of seeing some particularly interesting bird] not a line would be drawn or a note written, but so indelibly and distinctly was what he had seen etched on his memory that it could later be visualized as clearly and faithfully as though the original were before him.' This is what Frank M. Chapman wrote, and in another place he illustrates it. 'I recall being with Fuertes when in Glen Alpine near Lake Tahoe he for the first time saw a living Dipper. The bird's distinctive form, poses, and gestures entranced him as he watched it through his binoculars, but not a single sketch was made. Nevertheless, later, when describing the experience, sketches, showing the bird's characteristic actions, rolled from his pencil as readily as though the bird were still before him.' And Vernon Bailey says, 'One morning at sunrise in our base camp in a gulch of the Chisos Mts., a Mearns Quail came and sat on a rock and preened and strutted and spread its hooded crest within four or five feet of his nose. When it had gone he burst out of his sleeping bag and fairly danced with joy as he ran for pencil and paper and worked for an hour on sketches of the quaint bird.'

Another gift was the hearing ear, and with it the ability to reproduce by voice or whistle just what he heard. He was a sensitive instrument, alive to everything beautiful, joyful, pitiful, or absurd, and response for him was action. A bird seen called forth a drawing, one heard, a whistled imitation of its song. Things beautiful made him rejoice, or 'gloat' as he said, with whatever friend was at hand, or long for one to gloat with if he was alone. Things pitiful drew from him quick tears, or alms, or help. Things absurd were translated at once into anecdote or imitation delivered with exquisite and delightful skill.

His gifts were fostered by sympathy and perfected by training. Life offered him the best of mentors and teachers, opportunity to travel widely and collect those images of bird life with which his mind became stored, a family and the means to support it, and a wealth of friends, with the result that he became a full man, able to pour forth delight for those among whom he lived.

To even the generality of his time he was known as the leading painter of bird pictures, for his drawings were reproduced in government and state publications, magazines with a wide circulaton, as well as in ornithological books and journals. A great many people heard him lecture on birds and give imitations of bird-calls and songs, and show slides illustrative of his journeys. One member of such an audience, a student at Smith College, wrote to her mother: 'He was a marvelous mimic, could mimic the song of a White-throated sparrow until (I shall have to admit) the tears came to my eyes.'

To Cornellians of his and succeeding generations he was 'Louis,' to the students of the 1920's and to children he was 'Uncle Louis.' To them all his studio was a place they could come to for information or for talk (Louis could paint and listen at the same time) whenever they wanted. He was formally connected with Cornell as a resident lecturer only for the last five years of his life, but during those years and the decades before he supplied the light touch, the bright spark to many and many a university gathering, class reunion, or undergraduate club meeting. Boys brought their families to the studio, fathers pestered him with letters asking him to help their sons find a room or keep off 'probation,' the generations within his own fraternity did not come and go too quickly to become his friends.

To the community of Ithaca also he was one who would enliven any meeting or promote any cause that lay within the circle of his interests—wild life conservation, the Boy Scouts, the war effort, local service organizations—by painting a poster, writing a letter, conducting bird-walks, singing in a chorus or giving a talk. 'Every cause into which he threw himself was molded into something more attractive and more directly applicable to human needs, and was deflated of all its bunk and preciousness. Hyprocrisy could not stand up against his clearness of vision and his choicest weapon, a laugh,' wrote the editor of the Cornell Alumni News. He was not one of the pompous men who are apt to pervade civic affairs, and he had little to do with them, as with the sentimentalists among bird-lovers.

To the neighborhood where he lived he was the repository for dead, injured, strange, or simply found animals, insects, and birds. He was the one who could answer questions about wild life, the husband at home during the day willing to replace fuses, thaw frozen water-pipes, unplug drains, move pianos. Chapman said, 'He was a master hand with tools, who could mend anything'—and did.

He had a success with children that is rare as it is simple; he was deeply interested in all sorts of things they liked, and met them on common ground. He teemed with ways to entertain them, making animal noises or playing a drawing game in which the child would mark five dots on a piece of paper, in any arrangement, choose one

: xvii :

for the head, and then Uncle Louis would use the other four for hands and feet, and draw them into a picture of a man doing something.

To certain children, Boy Scouts, and Cornell under-graduates who had a flair for nature-study, as well as to several young men particularly interested in learning to paint pictures of birds, he was their best teacher. He taught most effectively by example, though what he considered important precepts are written into some of his letters. He was so in love with his subject, and so full of it, that he could not fail, but inspired his pupils as he himself was inspired by Audubon to 'go and do likewise.'

His close friends were many. I place first those artists and ornithologists who perfectly shared his enthusiasm: Abbott and Gerald Thayer, Frank Chapman his companion on 60,000 miles of expedition trails, Wilfred Osgood, Allan Brooks. But their bonds were hardly closer than those between him and his neighbors on Cornell Heights, his boyhood friends, his classmates, fraternity brothers, fellow hunters, artists, entertainers professional and amateur, men with whom he had done business. All were devoted to him, and delighted in his 'rare personal charm which made his mere presence a source of joyous possibilities.' (Thus Dr. Chapman again.)

The letters of which this book is composed deal with a variety of subjects. They are concerned with art, particularly the art of representing the appearances of birds alive in nature; with ideas in the field of natural history; with experiences of travel in remote, beautiful, and fascinating parts of North America, Mexico, South America, and Africa. They are written to (and from) some of the brilliant men of his generation as well as to the members of his own family. They tell the story of an unusual and abundantly productive life. They are full of fun. Chiefly they are worth reading because they are like Louis Fuertes himself.

Louis Agassiz Fuertes

1

Parents and Boyhood

Louis Agassiz Fuertes was born in Ithaca, New York, on February 7, 1874. He owed his name not to any family connection with Louis Agassiz but to the fact that his father was a lively admirer of eminent men just older than himself. He had been uncertain whether to name his new little son 'Louis Agassiz' or 'Ezra Cornell'; possibly because the great Swiss naturalist and teacher had died in December, 1873, the baby was given his name.

Louis was one of those children that now and then appear with a dominant interest in birds and animals that can in no way be accounted for. He and his sister Kippy (Mary Katharine) had their zoo under the front porch, and were from early childhood collectors of all kinds of natural specimens, alive and dead. But in a big and busy family the occupations of the two youngest children went largely unnoticed until forced upon the attention of their elders by the presence of a live owl tied by the leg to the kitchen table, a dead chickadee kept too long in the little coat pocket, or a skunk in the domestic zoo, for there were three older brothers and another sister, and parents perhaps more than normally interested in their own affairs.

The father, Estevan Antonio Fuertes, had joined the faculty of the five-year-old Cornell University as Professor of Civil Engineering the year before Louis was born. A son of the governor of the military hospital in Puerto Rico, he received there an old-world education which he completed at Rensselaer Polytechnic Institute, emerging (as he modestly stated) with the degrees of B.Ph., Ph.D., M.D., Civil Engineer, in addition to many diplomas, prizes, and decorations. He was well known as a consulting engineer before he went to Cornell. While there he was instrumental in building the department of Civil Engineering into a college that sent trained men to many distant countries. In person he was courteous, sociable, tender, severe, and temperamental, and though he had left Puerto Rico for good before he was thirty years old, to the end of his life he retained a strong Spanish accent in his speech and in his manner.

On December 21, 1860, he had married Mary Stone Perry of Troy, New York, of New York State Dutch and Connecticut Yankee parentage. Mrs. Fuertes was an accomplished pianist, continuing to play during the years when she was bearing and rearing her children. Even when she was an elderly grandmother, nearly blind, she performed with vigor and delicacy, playing minor scales, Spanish dances, and certain favorite portions of the piano music of Bach, Scarlatti, Beethoven, Chopin. Thus, there was a father busy with the regular duties of his profession, extra work he enjoyed, and the society of his friends and colleagues; a mother who was a serious musician adored by her children, (who yet may have been almost jealous of her love for music); and four sons and two daughters with differing tastes, diverse activities. The family was together only at meal times and on musical occasions, when the piano and flute of the parents were enthusiastically supported by the children's voices. Louis had a remarkable ear for music and a good voice from the time he was a very small boy.

His experience was in part like that of any American child brought up in a college town with easy access to the country. Throughout a normal boyhood, however, his special interest in birds and their pictures is clearly to be seen. Some understanding person noticed this interest and, taking advantage of an astonishing turn of fortune that had placed in the town library one of the original elephant folio sets of Audubon's Birds of America, led Louis to these great picture books and made arrangements whereby he was allowed to look his fill, with a librarian at hand to turn the pages for him.

Louis said later that for ten years or more these pictures were his daily bread, that even when he was a child he understood that Audubon was inspired by the same love of the form and beauty of birds that he himself was feeling. Louis could not help drawing pictures of birds, and soon was copying the live bird rather than his own or anybody else's representation of it. The distinguished horticulturist Liberty Hyde Bailey, who came to Cornell when Louis was fourteen, recalled seeing him at that age with some bird of prey tied by the leg, drawing it. Louis wrote of himself in an article that was published in The Amateur Sportsman for September, 1910:

About 1888, when fourteen years old, L.A.F. made his first essay at painting a bird from 'the flesh,' in his boyhood home at Ithaca, N. Y. It was a male red crossbill—the first he had ever seen—and the strange coppery brown of its plumage, its unbelievably queer bill, its sturdy little figure, all claimed something that had never before been fully awakened. So, to fasten these peculiar qualities in his mind where they could be retained, he followed the method that first suggested itself, and which he has followed ever since: he drew and painted it to the best of his power. It was a clumsy thing, crudely painted—awkwardly drawn, standing on one foot on a drab branch of impossible anatomy—but it was a beginning. And certainly it was a wise one, for it resulted in the production of a life's interest for the boy, which could not be diverted.

So it was not the natural ability to draw which established this boy in the work of painting birds, but rather the opposite: his anxiety to learn accurately developed him in his crude and unlearned handling of his mediums.

In another place he wrote that he had 'always painted and drawn, at first as a means of study; later the cart turned around and pulled the horse, which has been backing up ever since.'

When Louis was in his teens, his father asked Professor Bailey to come to his house on a particular day when Louis was not at home. His father pulled out drawers in which lay pictures of birds drawn and colored by Louis. He displayed them with some concern, and asked: 'What would you do with a boy like that?' 'Let him go!' was the answer. Mr. Bailey was fond of Louis, and it is likely that his obvious interest in him and these words to his father were the first manifestations of positive encouragement in his life's work that Louis received. Even so Professor Fuertes, watching his youngest son do the usual things boys do, was not willing to take seriously the unusual concern with birds. He did not dare to let him really go his own way, because he could not see how this interest in birds and in drawing pictures of them could lead to a secure and honorable livelihood. At this time in America there was probably no man earning his living by painting pictures of birds. Audubon, who died long before, in 1851, had never succeeded in business, and had had laboriously to solicit money for the publication of his enormously expensive folio volumes. Elliott Coues' Key to North American Birds, a standard work that appeared first in 1872, was profusely illustrated with pen-and-ink diagrams by Coues and Dr. Shufeldt and with reproductions of the work of several European artists. Ernest Seton Thompson, who made good drawings of birds, was a writer first of all, and Robert Ridgway was a professional ornithologist who drew pictures of birds to supply a need, but not to earn a living. Obviously Louis had a gift, an innocent source of pleasure, but he must choose some work, engineering or architecture, recognizable as a profession.

The Fuertes family spent the winter of 1892-3 abroad. Louis enjoyed this as his first experience of bird-life outside of New York state; his father saw only that he was not behaving like a serious student of history at Dr. Keller's school in Zürich.

In the autumn of 1893 he entered Cornell University in the College of Architecture. Fraternity 'rushing' must have been upon him at once, bringing trouble, for his older sister was married to a member of the Alpha Delta Phi fraternity, which he joined, but his boyhood friends were all pledged to join Psi Upsilon. His connection with his fraternity was always happy in the extreme, and of course he did not lose his old friends, but simply added to their

Childhood painting of a Screech Owl

English Sparrow
Passer domesticus

Louis Agassiz Fuertes

number by joining a different group. At a service in the Alpha Delta Phi house in October, 1927, R. Woolcot Hooker said:

I am told that as an undergraduate Louis had the ability of a Pied Piper of Hamelin in attracting others to him. It is a happy picture which has been painted to me of Louis coming down the hill whistling, wandering in one door of the house and out another, followed by a group of boys for a jaunt to town—all whistling now —life had become a lark.

Louis' grades must have troubled his father, a Cornell dean, although seen from this distance the transcript of his record is something of a joke. His grades ranged from 35, 44, 53 in Philosophy, Mathematics, and Chemistry to 100 in Drawing. Fortunately he was allowed to earn a good many hours' credit in this last subject and in such studies as Vertebrate Zoology and Physiology which he managed fairly well.

The note-books in which he recorded his lectures are illustrated with likenesses, cartoons, and caricatures of people (not infrequently the professor) and amazingly sure and suggestive sketches of birds, each species perfectly distinct and individual though only indicated with a few pencil strokes. There is an occasional raccoon, and the drawings of fishes that he made as part of his zoology work are of an excellence that must have astonished Professor Comstock, unless, as seems likely, his teachers already were aware of his particular gifts. His mother had written in a letter of 1892 (quoted by F. M. Chapman in The Auk, January, 1928, p. 5):

Louis is getting to be quite a celebrity. The Christian Association had his drawings of birds on exhibition the other night. At present he is showing them to Dr. Wilder, who asked him to make some plates of animals for a collection in the museum. Louis feels important.

It was, according to his own statement, wanting to know that impelled him. He kept lists of birds seen from the time he was fifteen, perhaps earlier. In the note-book of 1889 that contains the first of these lists there are nine pages on which he had re-grouped Audubon's birds by families, listing the volume and page number of each plate. In 1891, when he was seventeen, he had become an associate member of the American Ornithologists' Union; if he had been able to study Ornithology as such at Cornell he might not have learned more than he taught himself in this subject, although the physical sciences he did study formally were genuine and essential education. There is a story, certainly true to type, that he went out the window of a lecture room while the class was in progress, taking the most direct route to identify an unfamiliar bird song.

2

Elliott Coues

．．．．．．．．．．．．．．．．．．．．．．．．．．．．．．．．．

THE CORNELL MUSICAL CLUBS were accustomed to take trips during the Christmas holidays, giving concerts in several cities where they were entertained by alumni and parents of the boys. As a member of the Glee Club, Louis went on such a trip in December, 1894, in spite of the fact, as his sister Sally said, that 'Father disapproved because Louis was so young and unaware of the temptations of great cities. But the boys were urgent and Father was pleased to see their attachment to Louis.' Charles Henrotin, another member of the Glee Club, had seen Louis' bird pictures and said he had an uncle who lived in Washington, where they were going, who was 'crazy about birds,' too, and probably would like to see those pictures. His name was Elliott Coues, and would Louis like to meet him? There was no one Louis would rather meet. There was no one who could have helped him more than Elliott Coues could and did.

Louis took his portfolio along, and 'Chuck' Henrotin was as good as his word. Louis said that after this first interview with Coues he never thought of adopting any other profession than that of bird portraiture—but it was not going to be easy to persuade his father that there was such a profession, let alone that he was fit to follow it. Louis must have explained his father's position to Mr. Coues, who then sent some word (now lost) to Professor Fuertes under cover of this first letter to Louis.

ELLIOTT COUES TO L.A.F.

Washington, D. C., Dec. 31, 1894.

I will ask you to hand the enclosed to your father, whose full name and address I do not know.

Two of Audubon's granddaughters have been spending the afternoon here, and were very much pleased with your paintings.

I will be glad to look over the rest of them, which you said you would send.

Coues was the brilliant figure among leading ornithologists of his time. 'There was a vividness, a fire in this man's personality that made his presence felt even when he was silent. Every word in the dictionary seemed to be at his command, and one had the comfortable assurance that he would choose the right one. He was an eloquent, brilliant, finished speaker.' Thus wrote Frank M. Chapman, in his Autobiography of a Bird-Lover. Coues was born in 1842 and served as surgeon in the army in the west, using the opportunity to collect specimens and enlarge his knowledge of American birds. He wrote abundantly on birds and animals, and during the last years of his life he was engaged in editing the journals of the early explorers of the continent.

Beginning immediately after his first meeting with Louis Fuertes, Elliott Coues became his sponsor and champion, and he continued until the end of his own life to give advice, encouragement, and opportunity to this unknown, modest young man. Louis disclaimed any credit for this kindness by saying that Coues 'badly needed an illustrator just as I got ripe.' That is true, but it is not the whole truth. The letters Coues wrote and Louis preserved, tied in a bundle apart from his other correspondence, reveal what the older man saw in Louis besides an uncanny ability to get the likeness of a bird on paper.

In the summer of 1895 Louis went abroad as a member of the musical clubs accompanying the Cornell crew to a meet at Henley. The boys were prepared to take England by storm, but their crews were badly beaten and American college songs were neither understood nor enjoyed in England. This experience, which was not pleasant, was redeemed through the kindness of Professor Morse Stephens, who took the disappointed boys to a meeting of the London Savage Club. Here they were given a really good time that led ultimately to the foundation of a Cornell Savage Club on the pattern of its London original. This undergraduate organization has survived, the only one in the United States, I believe, as a group of boys with musical or dramatic ability who entertain the professional actors, dancers, or musicians who may be performing in Ithaca. For many years it has been a source of pleasure for its members and their guests.

From England Louis went rapidly through Holland, Belgium, France, and Germany; this much (and very little else) can be learned from a college essay he wrote on The Advantages of Travel. A sketch-book shows better the use he made of the opportunity.

Mr. Coues had written him twice before he left, and wrote again in October urging him to attend the meetings of the American Ornithologists' Union to be held in Washington. Louis did not go, but the following letter shows the way in which he was represented there.

ELLIOTT COUES TO L.A.F.

Washington, D. C., Nov. 14, 1895.

According to my promise I brought your name prominently before the American Ornithologists' Union by exhibiting about fifty of your best paintings and talking about them. You would have felt proud and pleased if you had been present to see how well they were received, and how highly they were praised by many besides myself. I hope you are persevering under competent instruction in certain points of technique, and that in the end the result will be that I can bring out for you a very handsome volume of colored plates, and thus secure for you a permanent reputation.

Following this debut Louis received queries about his work from Frank M. Chapman who was looking for an artist to illustrate his forthcoming Bird-Life, from Miss Florence Merriam who had a book on western birds to be illustrated, and from Walter Adams Johnson who was about to launch a new ornithological magazine, The Osprey. Dr. Chapman finally gave his commission to Ernest Seton Thompson, but Louis made pen-and-ink drawings for Miss Merriam's A-Birding on a Bronco and lent several pictures to Mr. Johnson for The Osprey. This was during his junior year at college; at the beginning of the fall term of his senior year Mr. Coues wrote as follows:

ELLIOTT COUES TO L.A.F.

Cranberry, N. C., Sept. 14, 1896.

You will no doubt soon receive from the Macmillan Company of New York a very important letter, in regard to making about one hundred drawings of birds for a work which they will publish, and of which I am one of the authors; and if you send me the letter, I shall be in position to advise you how to reply to it. The publishers' choice lay between you and an artist of recognized ability and secure reputation; and I have such confidence in you that I have secured the offer for you. If this proposed arrangement can be made, and the result prove satisfactory, you will have been fairly started on the road to fame and fortune.

The work was Citizen Bird, a book for children by Mabel O. Wright and Elliott Coues; arrangements were made, and on October 8 one hundred and eleven pictures were ordered to be ready for the printer by February.

From October to February is five months, one hundred and fifty days. There were more than a hundred pictures to be drawn and painted by a young man in college with a 'thesis' to write before he could graduate. Louis was on the staff of the college magazine of humor, The Widow, which he had helped create and to which he contributed six or seven cartoons in the course of the year, and he had also assumed the leadership of the Glee Club. He was out of favor with his father who did not believe in his chosen work and knew Louis was a poor student. At the same time Mr. Coues was writing and insisting and repeating, 'Never mind your school work. What matters is what you are doing for me.'

Mrs. Margaret Sumner Fuertes recalls a lunch-time at the Fuertes house before she was engaged to be married to Louis. He had received a check in payment for the first consignment of pictures completed for Mr. Coues. At the table Louis opened the envelope, looked at the check, and passed it to his mother, saying nothing. She looked at it and passed it around the table. When it came to Professor Fuertes, he handed it to the young lady sitting on his right without glancing at it. But after lunch he took her aside. 'What was the amount of that check, Madge?' he asked. Piqued by his refusal to admit Louis' success, she gave him only a spirited 'Don't you wish you knew!'

ELLIOTT COUES TO L.A.F.

Washington, D. C., Oct. 16, 1896.

I suppose you have received your notification of the next Ornithological Congress, at Cambridge, Nov. 9-12. Under existing circumstances this is an event of some importance to your affairs, and you should not fail to present yourself. Let nothing interfere with this. Better also bring with you about fifty of the best things you have in your portfolio, to show, and in all ways appear in your new role of an ornithological artist whose services have been secured by one of the great publishing houses of this country and England.

It would take a week from his classes and precious days from his painting, but this year Louis did attend the meetings, this year and almost every subsequent year of his life. I doubt that any later meeting held so much of interest and excitement as this first, an account of which may be found in The Auk for January, 1897, pp. 84-6. On Tuesday, the first day of public sessions, with Miss Audubon present, Elliott Coues exhibited recently discovered manuscript journals of J. J. Audubon. Louis Agassiz Fuertes exhibited and explained his bird pictures. F. M. Chapman gave a talk on Yucatan. On the second day F. M. Chapman displayed some bird drawings by E. E. Thompson. [His name occurs also as Ernest E. Thompson, Ernest Seton Thompson, and Ernest Thompson Seton.] The business of the afternoon is given in the words of the Secretary, Jno. H. Sage:

The feature of the afternoon session was the open-air talk by Mr. Abbott H. Thayer, demonstrating his theory of the principles of protective coloration. Mr. Thayer placed three sweet potatoes, or objects of corresponding shape and size, horizontally on a wire a few inches above the ground. They were covered with some sticky material, and dry earth from the road on which they stood was sprinkled over them so that they would be the same color as the background. The two end ones were then painted white on the under side, and the white color was shaded up and gradually mixed with the brown of the sides. When viewed from a little distance these two end ones, which were white below, disappeared, while the middle one stood out in strong relief and appeared much darker than it really was. Mr. Thayer explained that terrestrial birds and mammals which are protectively colored have the under parts white or very light in color, and that the color of the under parts usually shades gradually into that of the upper parts. This is essential in order to counteract the effect of the shadow, which otherwise, as shown by the middle potato, makes the object abnormally conspicuous and causes it to appear much darker than it really is. In the case of Mr. Thayer's experiment some of the witnesses could hardly believe that the striking difference in the visibility of the three potatoes was entirely due to the coloring of the under side, and Mr. Thayer was asked to color the middle one like the two others in order that the effect might be observed. Mr. Thayer complied with the request, painting the under side of the middle potato white, and shading the white up into the sides as in the case of the others. The effect was almost magical. The middle potato at once disappeared from view. A similar experiment was tried on the lawn. Two potatoes were painted green to resemble the green of the grass above which they were suspended. One was painted white on the underside and at once became invisible when viewed from a little distance, while the other showed plainly and seemed very dark, the shadow, superadded to the green of the under side, making it remarkably conspicuous. The experiments were an overwhelming success. Discussion followed . . . by Drs. Merriam, Coues, and [J. A.] Allen, Messrs. Phelps, Chapman and Fuertes, the Chair

[D. G. Elliot] and the Author. The thanks of the Union were tendered Mr. Thayer.

On the third day certain questions were raised by E. H. Forbush; C. Hart Merriam gave a talk. Almost every one of the men who participated in these sessions of the 1896 A.O.U. meeting at Cambridge became prominent in Louis Fuertes' life. Elliott Coues, Frank Chapman, and Abbott Thayer are in the very foreground. Dr. Merriam's sister, Miss Florence Merriam, (later Mrs. Vernon Bailey) was the first person to employ him as an illustrator for a book, and she and Mr. Bailey were very good friends to him always. Dr. Merriam procured for Louis his first opportunity to go on an extended scientific expedition, the Harriman Alaska Expedition of 1899, and E. H. Forbush was the author of the Birds of Massachusetts for which Louis was painting the illustrations at the end of his life.

ELLIOTT COUES TO L.A.F.

Washington, D. C., Nov. 21, 1896.

I think you have every reason to be gratified by recent events, and am sure you had a good time in Cambridge and N. Y. Don't let this success turn your head, but just go ahead and work hard, remembering that this is but the beginning of your career, in which final success can only be achieved in the good old-fashioned way of hard work, and plenty of it, to the very best of your ability. I suppose no young man ever had a better opening; it remains with yourself to fill it, and prove that I have not said too much about you.

You did not say whether you had seen the article which appeared in the N. Y. Nation of Nov. 12 regarding your work.

'We notice this booklet mainly to call attention to some of the pictures it contains. About a year ago we had occasion to speak of some artistic work done by Mr. Louis Agassiz Fuertes, a student at Cornell University, whose paintings of birds were much admired when exhibited before the A.O.U. at its last meeting in Washington. He is self-taught, and his technique is still crude, he needs disciplining to keep him from straining for effect; but his power is unmistakable, and we miss our guess if he does not become a great artist in birds in due course, if he perseveres. Thus far his genius overreaches his talent; but his pictures are better than Audubon's were to begin with, and we suspect that the mantle has fallen upon Mr. Fuertes. . . . Ability to draw a live bird instead of a stuffed one, from the very first, is an accomplishment rare enough to deserve more than passing comment.'

The article from which the paragraph above was taken was in fact a review of Miss Merriam's book, in the issue of November 19. Of course, it had been written by Mr. Coues himself.

3

Abbott Thayer

A s a junior in college Louis had been thinking and writing about the coloration of birds, probably reading about it too. Abbott Thayer, the artist-naturalist who conducted the demonstration with painted sweet potatoes, had published articles on the subject in The Auk for April and October. Perhaps Louis had read them; at the session after Thayer's demonstrations he offered some ideas of his own. Apparently he had suggested that the bright colors of a male bird may serve to divert attack from the concealingly colored female and young.

Mr. Thayer's letter below is the first of a wonderful series, treasured by Louis, and it marks the opening of a truly formative relation with Mr. Thayer and his family, with whom Louis spent nearly three years, first as a student of painting, but soon more nearly as one of Thayer's own children. We cannot separate the threads of personality and assign responsibility for each trait, but Louis was surely born with his love of birds and beauty and people, with his longing to learn and his willingness to work, with his sense of fun and his right knowledge of how to live. The volumes of Audubon were an influence that changed him, by helping to bring his abilities into focus; the interest and confidence placed in him by Coues showed him what his life's work could be and started him off upon it. But at mid-career, in 1917, Louis says of his time spent with the Thayers: '[They were] my happiest and most uplifting days. Where would I be now—and what—if I had not had them.' And later, in a letter to Mrs. Thayer:

I wonder if Uncle Abbott ever knew how much he has been to me; how much more I learned from him than he ever taught me consciously, how much more important than his lessons in painting were his lessons in living. . . . No gratitude save that felt and hallowed through a long life could ever be an adequate expression of that priceless gift you all so richly gave me, a young stranger with a peculiar hunger that could nowhere else have had such food.

In the letters given here, the relations begin.

ABBOTT THAYER TO L.A.F.
[On the way to Scarborough, N. Y.]
Dec. 15, 1896.
[In pencil]
What you said at the A.O.U. in Cambridge struck me instantly as looking like a new truth. If you are ever passing Scarborough with time to stay over a train or two, I should greatly enjoy receiving you at our house, and we could talk these charming things over. As to this thought of yours; I could even imagine Nature's protecting certain species, by actually sacrificing in extreme cases a percentage of their males to hawks, since the latter do get, in any case, one sex or the other. Are there not generally more males than females?

Do you know whether any proportion of partridges and sandpipers, for instance, are caught by the animals they try to lure away from their young? I mean caught while feigning illness? If this be a risk they run, it would seem to harmonize with the risk that bright colors appear to bring upon the males (I mean it would seem to tend to support your theory) to divert attack, as you said, from the young.

For all I know you are are already rich in data to support your suggestion.

: 18 :

I have many very interesting vistas in my mind, vistas opened by discovering that law of protective coloration, and a great appetite to show the things to naturalists. I hope you may consent to visit me, as I proposed.

ABBOTT THAYER TO L.A.F.

Scarborough, N. Y., Dec. 25, [1896.]
When I at last noticed in the report of the A.O.U. that you had shown bird pictures I realized for the first time in my unbecoming self-absorption that you are an artist, and since I had clean missed this fact my letter very likely had a stupid sound—

I feel an intense interest in bird pictures, i.e. always, a great hope to see some wonderful ones, and I wish I had seen yours.

On the cover of The Osprey *for March, 1897, there is a reproduction of a drawing of a screech owl signed L.A.F. The frontispiece carries a full-page picture of a rough-legged hawk by the same artist, and on the inner pages there are smaller cuts of the cover screech owl, long-billed marsh wrens, and a snowy owl. Page 91 carries a photograph of Louis Agassiz Fuertes and a letter to the editor of* The Osprey, *by Elliott Coues, which reads in part:*

I am happy to respond to the request for an expression of my opinion regarding Mr. Fuertes' ability to draw and paint birds. It is always a pleasure to me to give praise where it is deserved, and it should be no less a duty than a pleasure to everyone to recognize genius, because that is a rare and precious gift, something over and above mere talent. . . . I say deliberately, with a full sense of the weight of my words, that there is now no one who can draw and paint birds so well as Mr. Fuertes; and I do not forget Audubon himself when I add that America has not produced an ornithological artist of equal possibilities.

ABBOTT THAYER TO L.A.F.

Scarborough, N. Y., Mar. 24, 1897.
I got to-day a copy of the Osprey with the rough-legged buzzard, owl and marsh wren in it—and I can't wait to praise them—this is

my first sight of your work and you know one learns not to expect much beforehand in our line, there is so much bird painting of the Ernest Thompson grade—

Yours are the true thing and I take immense pleasure in looking forward to seeing more and more. The loose fluffy feathers on your hawk envelop a real flesh and blood bird and are very real feathers. Go on and make more and more exquisitely real and dainty representations, I want to see your colorings. Bird colors—the changeable element all over them—are so ravishing to do.

My own boy of 13 is hard at it, and doing birds that I should like to show you—

How much I sh'd like to see your paintings—

I am off for North Carolina for three weeks, tomorrow, then I shall be here three more before I go to Dublin.

I can't say how peculiarly I should enjoy the company of a man doing such work as you. Is it impossible for you to come to Dublin, N. H. for this summer? I am deeply interested. Half my life's passion is birds and pictures of them.

ELLIOTT COUES TO MRS. E. A. FUERTES

Washington, D. C., Mar. 29, 1897.

I am naturally much pleased to receive your letter. We 'understand.'

I fully believe Louis is too sensitive and honest a character to be spoiled by what has been said, or I would have refrained from giving him in public even his just dues. His letter to me to-day contains some expressions that I like, regarding his absorbing interest in his work, which he says is the last thing he thinks of at night, etc. That is what I should expect, if he is on the right track, and there seems to be no danger of turning his head while it is so full of what he wants and intends to do. Then there is a naïveté about his apology for not thanking me more properly—he has been too busy, he says, with 'a mixture of examinations, laboratory reports, and bird-painting.' That is delightful!

I am sure that real genius can never be stayed or thwarted—the most we can do is to guide it a little, in its modes of expression.

This I have tried to do in the present case. I saw his *possibilities*, two years ago, when he had not then drawn a single picture quite fit to print, and undertook to discipline him into the necessary technique. The result thus far is fully up to my expectations—yet I regard it as only a beginning.

If the present series of 111 pictures turn out as I expect, I can probably secure him a contract worth several thousand dollars cash. Both fame and fortune seem to be within his grasp, if I can guide him along the way now opened. I have had the handling of a good many boys who wanted to do this or that in science, but had no means, and I have uniformly told them that the *first* thing was to secure a means of livelihood, which they could not hope for in science at the outset; and to come to me again, in the matter of ornithology, when they had become self-supporting in some 'practical' trade, business or other occupation. With Louis it is different. If things turn out as I expect, the thousand dollars or so he will put in his pocket for this work is very little in comparison with what he will be able to earn soon. He should be independent of the world from the start; if his work goes on as it should, he could command more than a *fair* price for the productions of his pencil and brush. I have sometimes fancied his father not altogether pleased, or even satisfied, and imagined he had other plans for his son's future. But if Louis' gifts be what I believe them, he will never make anything of himself except along the lines of their exercise and development—never attain to more than 'respectable mediocrity' (which for me means dead failure!) in any other direction. I weighed my words in the *Osprey*, in saying that this country has not before seen Louis' equal in the *possibilities* of zoological art (I did not say *actualities*, as yet; good as his pictures already are, I regard them as indicative only of what he may attain to, if he keeps on as he has begun.)

I hope he is not getting hurried or worried about his present press of work. It is urgent, to be sure, as we are printing the text of the book rapidly, and shall be done before he gets all his pictures made to go with it. But I wish you would see that he does not overwork. Far better let the work wait a little, than have a single picture in it that shows signs of haste or carelessness. Every one should be as good as he can possibly make it, and he must take his own time.

As soon as he has finished with this contract, and graduated from college, I hope he will be able to take a long rest, go off in the woods, and get fresh inspiration from contact with nature. Do you know, I can see a difference between the pictures he makes of birds he knows alive, and those he has only dead specimens of to work from? I should like to have him turned loose for the summer, with his field glass, pencils and sketch book. There is nothing like it, for the end we have in view.

On the second of May, Louis did go to Scarborough to show Mr. Thayer his colored studies from live birds. From letters written long afterward we catch glimpses of the day. In 1901 Louis wrote, homesick, from Texas, of his love for the Thayers stored up by those years since he 'came to Scarborough in the rain and began it all.' Mr. Thayer's daughter Gladys was a little girl of eleven when Louis first appeared; forty years later she still remembered when Louis had taken her by the hand to go looking for hepaticas in the woods.

The upshot of the visit was this letter written after a week, and the next written two days later, containing an invitation and an offer that Louis could not do otherwise than gratefully accept.

ABBOTT THAYER TO L.A.F.

Scarborough, N. Y., May 9, 1897.

I'm going to talk to you like a Dutch Uncle! I wish you lived (more than I suppose you to) in art circles—and had heard me spoken of as an authority; since my words would then have additional weight. Somewhere in you there is a strain of very pure art yet [crossed out] and it would respond wonderfully to some pure training such as I can give you.

I want to get hold of you and swiftly develop your powers. The eye-sense is susceptible, in a young painter, of infinite development, exactly comparable to the rectifying the ear of a young musician. At first he bows his violin a little flat or sharp on every note. Your talent makes me itch to train it, the more because it runs to my beloved birds.

I trust you won't fear my influence as hostile to your individuality. I have never feared in my own case, but submitted wholly to the Ecole des Beaux Arts training, knowing that if one has the *gift*, it is a spring gushing out from his center, and no more to be permanently colored or muddied than a spring of water.

I want to get you to Dublin [N. H.] and have you paint birds under my criticism as long as you can arrange to. I am asking my father to send you some clippings which he dotingly collects. I don't remember ever doing such a thing before, but I want to influence you.

Yet I am not sure that you yet know that the highest art-purity is needed in your birds. If so you will ultimately believe it. All that true training does is to purify one's powers, till they no longer *refract the truth* in its passage through.

ABBOTT THAYER TO L.A.F.

[On the way to Dublin, N. H.]
May 11, 1897.

[Written in pencil on a torn-off corner of brown wrapping paper.] My dear Fuertes, (Here you begin to experience my characteristic railroad epistles) I am on my way up to Dublin—I omitted to say (what I suppose is, however, obvious) that of course the pleasure of teaching you would be the only form of pay that I could accept.

You will be amazed, at the end of even a few months of pure abstract exercise of your sight-power, to see how much nearer you can come to the delicate charm of a bird,—no, it can't be *promised* that a few eye-opening months may not at first simply unnerve you by showing you the rocks under your keel—but this I know; that the young man who did those colored studies from live birds has too fine a gift to have a right to hold back from training. It is just as with a wing-shot. He may be very gifted in shooting without putting the gun to his shoulder, but he can't develop that method to so high a score as the man who *aims* may develop *his*. One must freely turn his back on *knacks* and let his full powers be brought to bear. In this case the powers are those of sight—and every art student goes on to realize that at first this sense was only germal. The best thing for you would be to draw from some beautiful antique marbles, i.e. casts awhile.

I send you this at the risk of scaring you away with so much ardor and talk. I am bird-crazy and that's the truth.

By 1897 Mr. Thayer had painted many of his important canvases: The Virgin and The Virgin Enthroned, (now in the Gellatly Collection in Washington, D. C.), the mural design of Florence and the Arts at Bowdoin College, Caritas, (now the property of the Boston Art Museum), and many landscapes and portraits. He was a founder and president of the Association of American Artists; one of his pictures usually had the place of honor at the Society's annual exhibition. He often won prizes and was paid as much as forty thousand dollars for his large works. He was much in demand as a teacher and as a painter of portraits.

Abbott Thayer was right in assuming that Louis Fuertes did not move much in 'art circles.' It is not likely that Louis appreciated Thayer's position among artists, but he did know one of his pictures: a portrait of Susan Sage with her pony which hung in the Sage mansion in Ithaca, where Louis and Kippy Fuertes had seen and admired it, the only original fine painting known to them.

ELLIOTT COUES TO L.A.F.

Washington, D. C., May 15, 1897.

I have your letter and the 4 plates, which latter go to Mr. Brett to-day. A couple more, and you will have filled the bill. I am sure you have worked hard and faithfully, as well as successfully, and now hope you will soon take a good long rest and outing, which you need. Don't undertake any more drawing for the present. I am pleased with what you say of Mr. Thayer. Nothing could be more agreeable or more desirable for you this summer, than to be in such relations with him. Let me know when you graduate. With regards to your parents.

Louis graduated in June. His 'thesis' on the coloration of birds (illustrated with water-color paintings by him and with actual feathers attached to some pages) was accepted by Professor J. M. Hart with a grade of 80. Presently he went up to Dublin, New Hampshire, for the summer. Mr. Thayer lived with his family in a large summer cottage at the foot of Mount Monadnock.

Mrs. Thayer, formerly Miss Emma Beach, was a distinguished painter of flower pictures and a beloved step-mother to the three children of Kate Bloede Thayer, Abbott's first wife and her friend. In 1897 Mary (called Je-je) was twenty-one, Gerald (Gra) was thirteen, and Gladys (Galla) was eleven.

Excerpts from Mr. William Henry Thayer's journal, included with the permission of Nelson C. White, may be used to explain somewhat the background into which Louis Fuertes was moving. Miss Mary Amory Greene of Boston, one of Thayer's pupils, had a summer residence in Dublin. She asked Mr. Thayer to spend his summers there,

. . . offering to build a cottage for him on her land [writes Mr. Thayer's father] and fit up a studio for his pupils. . . . He had a considerable following of pupils, and Miss Greene fitted up an old barn on the south shore of the lake for a studio for them. . . . Miss Greene has built a studio for his own use, near his house, and a stable. . . . She has been a devoted friend in every way. He gladly accepted her offer to manage his business correspondence which was often neglected because he had used up his eyesight in painting, and she collects his pupils' fees and arranges his classes.

The reference to Mr. Thayer's eyesight helps account for the appearance of his letters; he wrote them with his eyes closed, for rest. His passion for birds also gave an intense man the best kind of recreation. The summer after the death of the children's mother (from melancholia and tuberculosis) his father wrote:

[Abbott] has been relieving his mental oppression all summer by fishing or shooting or tramping the woods. His shooting was for getting new specimens for Gerald, who already has a considerable collection of birds which they have skinned and preserved. [So Gerald at eight was an ornithologist and collector. Also all the children were early travelers. Mary was born in Paris.] Abbott and his family spent the summer of 1894 in Europe. . . . They went to St. Ives, Cornwall, via London—for the sake of the society of Thomas Millie Dow and his family, who were spending the summer at St. Ives. They passed a very pleasant two months in that retired place, which was much like an island . . . with all the pleasures such a situation brings—great numbers of birds of great interest to Abbott and Gerald. . . . For several years Gerald has been studying birds industriously, and they had already made a considerable collection of American specimens.

The man who drove Louis from the station to the Thayers' house hinted that they were a queer wild lot; why, he said, the children had never even learned to read and write. They did not go to school —the reason behind the driver's remarks—but they wrote beautifully, letters full of acute observation of nature, people, and books. Mary was a lover of animals, Gerald a passionate ornithologist, and Gladys an enthusiast for the out-of-doors in general, for flowers and little children in particular. Gerald and Gladys in their time became first-rate painters; what they were not, then or later, was worldly. These years of their childhood were lived in a paradise— 'Thayeryland,' it was called by the young people like Louis who were privileged to share it. Some of their many cousins—the Whitings, Richard Fisher, Barry Faulkner—were likely to be there; there was a succession of art students; and usually Mr. and Mrs. George de Forest Brush with their increasing family of children were living near by and sharing the kind of life the Thayers enjoyed. They studied, they painted, they talked, they read Stevenson out loud, they listened to classical music (often that of Beethoven) played for them on the piano, they tramped the woods and climbed the mountain on foot, on skis, on snowshoes.

When they had given up their house in Scarborough and moved to Dublin to live permanently (in 1901) summer and winter, they slept outdoors and ate all their meals on a covered porch, attended by one or two Irish girls (who served also as models for Mr. Thayer, as the children all did). They were blessed by the saving presence of Mrs. Thayer. To the Thayer children she was 'Addie'; to Louis and his sister Kippy who soon joined the group she was 'Aunt Emma.' She managed the household, she maintained the peace and comfort of them all, and she dipped into her own private fortune whenever funds were low, which was not seldom.

Kippy Fuertes says, 'Thayeryland was Eden—almost quite complete, even to the serpent which was devised along with paradise! Abbott's horrible moods were it.' 'He was intensely vital, and lived normally at heights which I reached only occasionally, and then only for short periods,' wrote Frank M. Chapman. One to whose house Thayer had come as a stranger and spent a night, answering the query how he had liked his guest, responded, 'I felt as if I were entertaining an angel.'

We have the feeling, from these and other scraps of testimony given by persons who knew him, that Mr. Thayer was a kind of messenger from heights few of us reach and that he painted for us what he saw there. 'I want the image of one I worship to become visible for all time to this world—voilà tout!' he wrote to Royal Cortissoz. And what did he worship? What did he paint? Sleeping babies, children, young women with angels' wings, a child with a rose, a bowl of roses, a child and an angel, Mount Monadnock, an angel with Mount Monadnock.

Gladys Thayer, the late Mrs. David Reasoner, gave the following account of this first summer Louis Fuertes spent as Abbott Thayer's pupil, in a letter of November 10, 1941, to M. F. Boynton:

It was an instantaneous friendship. . . . He boarded in the village and we saw him about every day. We youngsters gloried in his fun-making company, as we all did in his brilliant work. The Coues Citizen-Bird book had just come out, with what I think were his first illustrations. He delighted impromptu out-door audiences by his uncanny ability to summon long-missing (?) 'bird neighbors' which some of these folks lamented had not been around for years! We all had great wood-walks, camping, etc. . . . Of course my dad, (who worshipped his astounding power of putting the very soul into the birds or animals which he re-created with such speed) did give him regular criticisms on his work. It was usually restricted to 'values' of light and shade, my dad pointing out how the picture would be improved by 'flattening' as artists call it. We youngsters would often have to run for the salt cellar, some of whose contents Papa would thinly sprinkle over the painted bird!

While applying himself to a picture-task in his room, (using sometimes a freshly-shot bird, of whatever kind, to guide him in his miraculous rendering of the bird in life, sometimes a duck or other bird bought in a New York market) no sound would be heard during the two or three morning hours while he worked. When a sudden blast of melodious whistling filled the house, we could be sure the picture was finished, and he would soon bring it down.

Many were the walks, and campfires in the twilight woods, that we enjoyed with him.

ELLIOTT COUES TO L.A.F.

Salem, N. Y., July 22, 1897.

I have yours of the 15th, forwarded from Washington as I am spending a month with the Audubon family, going over old journals and other MSS which Miss A. will soon publish in two handsome volumes.

It is well that you are an alumnus—an A.B., or B.S., or whatever it is. But that is not a circumstance to your accomplishment in *Citizen-Bird*, through which you have made, at a single bound, a reputation that most artists struggle painfully for during many weary years of working and waiting for recognition and mere livelihood. The book was out on the 14th, and is a phenomenal success at the start, with a sale averaging 500 copies a day. We expect to do still better as trade revives in the fall. This great hit is mainly due to your pictures, which I consider the finest series of 108 bird portraits ever printed in black and white. The book sells on sight—almost everybody that sees it wants a copy, and it is sure to be immensely popular.

My private criticism is, that the drawings have not been reduced by uniform scale. Thus, the bluebird is as big as the robin, the sapsucker bigger than the flicker on the opposite page, and all the water birds are reduced out of all proportion. But that is neither your fault nor mine, and few persons will observe it. The book is beautifully printed, and the pictures come out brilliantly. The printers have taken great care to produce the impression.

I am glad you are having such a fine time with Mr. Thayer and his son, on your vacation, in such a pleasant place, amidst congenial artistic environment.

Now, what are you going to do next? I am rather sorry to hear you have made those promises to Scribners, or any one else. Please make no more, without consulting me. I do not want you to make yourself too common, at anybody's order, for mere pot-boilers, or to scatter your forces. You must concentrate yourself on the great work we have in prospect, of which I gave you some intimation when you were in Washington. Only in this way will you fulfill your destiny, and do your genius justice. It would be a crime against nature, and a sin upon your own soul, if you did not at once gather your forces for a splendid accomplishment.

As soon as your outing is over, and you are ready to go to work, I want you to make for me five of the most perfect paintings of which you are capable, as specimens of what you can do in colors. With these under my arm, I can go to N. Y., and probably make the arrangements I have in mind—a plan which, if successful, will make you rich as well as famous. But meanwhile, you must reserve yourself, and do no more small side jobs.

Elliott Coues to L.A.F.

Salem, N. Y., July 28, 1897.

I see by your letter that you are nervous and overwrought, and not getting the rest and recreation you need during your vacation. Do not undertake those pictures for Cheney at present; and do not complete your Scribner contract any faster than you feel like; and especially, do not take upon yourself to make any promises to anybody—not even to me. The great work I have in view for you can wait—in any event, even if all my plans should mature, it would be at least a year before we should come to the beginning of it. Meanwhile, enjoy yourself, and take things perfectly easy; live as much as you can out of doors, letting your inspiration come as it pleases, not forcing it, and not *studying* art, or anything else. Make the most of your summer, in the way of ease, indolence and recreation, and you will feel all right soon.

I go to Portland, Maine, soon, to be there some time, and when you get ready, or feel just like it, come there to see me, and we will talk things over quietly.

Apparently Mr. Coues did not wait for Louis to come to Maine but went himself to Dublin to see how his protégé was being treated.

ELLIOTT COUES TO L.A.F.

Portland, Maine, Aug. 6, 1897.

Besides being personally agreeable, my visit to Dublin, where you insisted on making me your guest, relieved my mind and I have now no fear about you. If our friend Thayer thought I 'wanted to pick you before you were ripe,' as he told me, I thought he wanted to fly away with you. But that is all right now, and I am more than satisfied with things as they are.

It is delightful that they hit upon this figure of speech and it is extraordinary, too, that neither of the older men did what the other feared, that the young man kept his balance, and that Mr. Coues came to stay in Dublin on the friendliest of terms with Mr. Thayer. Later on, when Louis was much too busy and well-grounded to be aware of it, there were some jealousies playing around him; the Thayers and Chapman pulled apart from each other, though never away from Louis, but at this critical time the solid understanding between Thayer and Coues was great good fortune for Louis.

ELLIOTT COUES TO L.A.F.

Portland, Maine, Aug. 14, 1897.

Miss Audubon writes me she has invited you to Salem. *Don't fail to go there.*

Citizen Bird is an immense success. There is a chorus of applause in the newspaper notices. One of the very best of all has just appeared, in *N. Y. Times* of the 7th inst. I copy the part relating to you, as it is only your just due.

From *The New York Times*, Aug. 7.

'If the text of *Citizen Bird* gives the spirit of its subject with exceptional charm and veracity, the illustrations certainly do no less. Mr. Fuertes has caught the characteristic attitude, the poise of the body, the intelligence of the eye, and the gently modeled surfaces, with great skill and insight, he has made his birds live upon the page instead of presenting them with hopelessly stuffed and distorted bodies, after the manner of the average illustrator of bird books.'

Louis left Dublin about the first of September, called to New York by news of his father's illness. The Thayer children wrote after him, Miss Audubon wrote after him, Coues couldn't locate him, Gerald wrote to his father in Ithaca to find him. On October 2 Mrs. Thayer wrote asking him to come to Dublin for a week before the twentieth; whether he did or not, early in November he called upon Miss Audubon in Salem, and he was soon settled near the Thayers in Scarborough for a stay of six or seven weeks. Gerald, called Gra, wrote him September 2, 25, October 9, 18, letters full of exclamation points, underlinings, the 'who-oo-hoo-hoo-hoo-hoos' of great horned owls, and excited accounts of ornithological prowess. A polite letter to Louis' father is subdued in comparison.

GERALD THAYER TO E. A. FUERTES

Dublin, N. H., Oct. 14, 1897.

I think from what I know of Louis that he hasn't got a bit too much of the 'wild cub' in him for us, and it would be hard to imagine anybody less conventional than we are. I guess our friendship with Louis is built of pretty good tough wood, so to speak, and longer acquaintance will not tend to shake it; in fact, I have an idea that we know him pretty well through and through already, and—you know what we think of him. Also, I think we are fully as bad as he is about answering letters.

We hope more than I can tell that we can have him near us this winter.

This year the A.O.U. met in New York, November 8-11. Mr. Coues showed more of Louis' pictures, and Mr. Thayer gave another demonstration of concealing coloration. After the meetings Mr. Coues took Louis' paintings to an agent for the Macmillan Company in an attempt to arrange for their publication. The publisher was not willing to risk the cost of good colored plates, however, and the whole plan, so glowingly suggested in Coues' letter of July 22, had to be abandoned. Louis returned to the Thayers' neighborhood.

L.A.F. TO JOHN PAUL YOUNG

Sing Sing, N. Y., Dec. 11, 1897.

You may wonder at my address—nothing confining; I am still undiscovered. I'm simply living here because it is near Mr. Abbott Thayer's house (one mile) and it's with him that I am working. I'm merely studying, and not producing anything. . . . I paint every a.m. and go out into the country with Mr. Thayer and his boy every p.m., and stay up there to supper, and then generally read Stevenson aloud till about 9, when all hands go to bed, and I take my moonlight, pitch dark, or sloppy, but always solitary walk down the Croton aqueduct to my joint here in Sing Sing. I enjoy life tremendously, in spite of the quiet, finding immense pleasure and profit in the company and conversation of Mr. T. and his boy . . . Last Monday, to try my nerve, I accepted an invitation to address the girls of the Brooklyn Girls' High School—2,000 of them—on the subject of birds!!!! I talked twenty minutes, gave a few pointers on Hat trimming, [this was the era when plumes, wings, even entire birds appeared on ladies' hats] ended up with a few silver-toned though unrecognizable imitations, which went, and was warmly applauded, upon which I shut one eye, to myself, and 'considered I'd done excellent and quit.' Wouldn't it frost ye? . . . I'm going down the Florida coast in a sharpy with Mr. Thayer and Gerald after the north-bound birds of the spring migration, to be gone a month or six weeks. Isn't that a cinch for me?

$$4$$

To Florida with the Thayers

O N THE TRIP to Florida Mr. Thayer's party consisted of two young men, Louis Fuertes and Charles R. Knight, his son Gerald Thayer (aged fourteen), and himself. They sailed from New York on March 15, arrived in Jacksonville, Florida, on the eighteenth, and presently went for a few days' collecting to Lake Charm, near Oviedo, where they were the guests of Louis' Alpha Delt friend Teddy Meade. They proceeded to Titusville and Merritt's Island, which they left on March 29 for Grant on the Indian River. Louis kept a journal for these first two weeks of the trip; it records birds seen and hints at adventures, ('Mr. T. had a rather amusing experience with another man's whiskey bottle'), but when the collecting really got under way, writing stopped. If he wrote letters home, they were not saved, and this first experience of camping and collecting with the Thayers in a strange country teeming with birds would have been lost to us entirely but for a stroke of luck that blew a boat ashore near where they were. With permission I here include substantial portions of Alden H. Hadley's story of this chance meeting as he wrote it for American Forests, February, 1931, under the title: 'With Fuertes in Florida.'

It was literally an ill and tempestuous wind that, many years ago, blew me into my first meeting with Louis Agassiz Fuertes—a meeting out of which was to come one of the most delightful experiences of my life. . . .

One morning, under favoring winds, we headed our schooner up the Indian River for Melbourne. The steady breeze of early morning continued to freshen, and some wisps of flying white scud came driving ominously across the sky out of the south-west. Sail was shortened, for we knew we were in for what the natives called a 'howling southwester.' The gale continued to increase in violence, and we were soon plowing along at a great rate, leaving in our wake a seethe of boiling, churning foam. Driving thus along, we had expected to reach Melbourne before night, when all of a sudden, our schooner, perhaps driven a little off her course by the boisterous wind, stuck hard and fast on a mud flat north of Pelican Island and near Oak Lodge, the famous rendezvous for naturalists which Mrs. F. E. Latham had maintained for many years. The more we tried to get the schooner afloat, the harder aground she was driven by the violent wind. All efforts were of no avail, and it was finally decided that further attempts were useless until the wind abated.

In the meantime two rowboats were manned, and we headed for Oak Lodge, and were soon pulling through the sheltered mangrove 'creeks' that led to Mrs. Latham's resort. As we neared the house, I noticed on the porch a bronzed, heavily bearded young man whose garb of brown duck well accorded with his beard and general complexion. Under most surroundings, I believe, he would have been a fine example of concealing coloration. He was squatted on a somewhat sheltered portion of the veranda, and seemed to be engaged in skinning a bird which was half-buried in a generous quantity of corn meal . . . As I walked up the steps, he looked up from his work, arose, gave me his name, and, at the same time, a hearty handclasp. Naturally, it was with a thrill of delight that I met, for the first time, this gracious and gifted young artist-naturalist, about whom I had already heard. . . .

He ended by asking if I would not conduct him and his companions to my favorite collecting-ground. My delight, of course, was unbounded at the thought of the privilege of such companionship, and I hastened to tell him that I would be more than glad to go.

Fuertes now turned to his companions, whom I had already noticed under a clump of cabbage-palms about a stone's throw from the house. Mr. Thayer and his son, Gerald, who at that time was about fourteen years of age, were busily engaged skinning birds, while Charles R. Knight, whose most striking external characteristic at that time was a luxuriant shock of wavy hair which fell almost halfway to his shoulders, stood idly looking on. . . . Thayer and Knight immediately gave hearty approval of Fuertes' suggestion of a trip to the headwaters of the St. John's, and it was agreed that they should meet me in Melbourne early the following week. . . .

A trip by wagon to North Indian Field at that time consumed the greater portion of a day. . . . By late afternoon we had reached North Indian Field. In those days this was a lovely spot, unspoiled by the destructive hand of man. In my limited wanderings I do not recall ever having seen a place possessing more romantic beauty and charm.

It consisted of a narrow grove, eight or ten acres in extent, of unusually stately cabbage palms. Rising a few feet in general elevation above the bordering marshes and savannas, it often became an island in time of high water, and always constituted a most conspicuous feature of the landscape in this entire region. On the savannas bordering the grove, at the time of our visit, were luxuriant acres of sweet flags in full bloom. This only served to give added charm to a picture which has long lived in my memory. In the midst of the grove was a prehistoric burial mound, crowned with lofty palms, perhaps more than a hundred feet across and rising thirty feet above the surrounding level. Near the base of this we pitched our tent. Distant not more than a stone's throw began the marsh—a strange jumble of luxuriant aquatic vegetation, which stretched away for miles until lost in the haze of distance.

Immediately in front of our camp the marsh consisted of a thick massing of lily bonnets and 'lettuce rafts' which in turn gave way to extensive reaches of maiden cane, the whole being interspersed with saw grass tussocks, and floating and willow islands. Through this the narrow, tortuous, hyacinth-choked channel of the St. John's wound its sluggish way.

To Fuertes this was a new bird world. He reveled in it with a sort of wild, half-restrained, ecstatic joy. It was a veritable bird-lovers' paradise, and a paradise for birds. Purple and Florida gallinules daintily strutted over the lily pads and 'lettuce rafts.' Florida dusky ducks were constantly rising as we quietly pushed our boat through the fascinating intricacies of this great marsh world. On a willow island, near our camp, many anhingas were nesting, while farther out in the marsh, on other willow islands, were rookeries of the yellow-crowned, Louisiana, and little blue herons. . . .

At that time, I was wholly unfamiliar with the estimate which Coues had placed on the work of Fuertes, and the prophecy which he had made concerning his future attainments. I, however, quite vividly recall, as I watched him . . . that I had an instinctive feeling . . . that here was a man whose unusual talents, combined with an infinite capacity for hard work, would one day take him very far.

[Earlier, in a paragraph omitted, Hadley described their fore-noons 'invariably spent wandering about the marsh.']

Our noons and afternoons . . . were spent under our deep canopy of cabbage palms. The specimens taken during the morning were carefully skinned and prepared, and Fuertes made many studies and sketches. No moment was devoid of interest; something was always transpiring. Great 'leather-backed' turtles crawled up out of the steaming marsh to deposit their eggs in the loose white sand of the ancient burial mound—as it were life coming out of death. Now and then, an Audubon's caracara went hurtling by; and, ever and anon, there came from across the savannas the trumpet calls of sandhill cranes. Often, during the heat of noonday, looking up through a rift in the palm tufts, we would see numbers of vultures, anhingas and wood ibises soaring far overhead in the blue empyrean.

Among my happiest recollections of those days at North Indian Field are memories of the evenings spent about the campfire. Here Fuertes' versatility and geniality were displayed to marvelous advantage. He was past master in the art of story-telling, and the embers of many a campfire faded to a dull glow ere we turned in for the night, so intrigued were we by his entertaining talk and delightful companionship. He was a really wonderful whistler, and could, with apparent ease, produce rich, mellow, flutelike notes. I have heard him, for an hour at a time, whistle the difficult parts from grand opera, or innumerable snatches from popular Broadway hits . . .

I cannot conclude this sketch without a word concerning the relationship between Fuertes and Abbott Thayer. The affectionate regard of the younger man for his teacher, as I sensed it in those days, was splendid to behold. Their affinity was much like that of a father and favorite son between whom had grown some special bond of sympathy and mutual interest; or, perhaps, even more like that between master and disciple, only there was perfect freedom combined with gentle deference and due restraint on the part of the younger man. The source of Fuertes' affection, and even reverence, for Abbott Thayer, whom he always addressed as 'Uncle Abbott,' lay deeper than in the mere bond of their mutual interest in art and natural history. It had its roots far deeper than that, for it was essentially mystic and spiritual.

The Florida trip lasted about six weeks and was followed almost immediately by the departure of the entire Thayer family for Europe. They went to England, Norway, Holland, France; Mr. Thayer went alone to the picture galleries of Italy, and they were all back at Scarborough by December 17. The following letter was written just before they sailed, and Louis' summer, which seems to have been spent at home, was colored by an abundance of letters from abroad.

ABBOTT THAYER TO L.A.F.

Berkshire, Mass., May 3, 1898.

I keenly realize that I was just simply a spoil-sport down there in Florida even for Gerald. I suppose I fretted at wishing to hear you tell people of Gerald's wonderful gifts in painting, and grew a little sour while I wholly knew that you are *purely kind*, and that the reason you don't tell these things is because you don't see them. . . . I have always said to myself: 'When Louis gets further on, and sees the notes of nature more purely in his own work, he will be amazed to see what he doesn't yet, in these things of Gra's. . . .

You are all right—and very gifted too, wholly so—yet you are coming into bird-art through the bird end, *like* a bird, in fact, while Gerald approaches them through Art itself.

You are extraordinary in the intimate way you represent them, and manage with impure values and color values nevertheless to unite in each picture so much revelation of the secrets of each bird's personal appearance as to mark *genius* on it.

Well, good-bye, don't love me less. We shall never go apart from our most solid relation I am sure.

Abbott Thayer to L.A.F.

[From Europe, fall, 1898.]
[This letter is also on a torn-off scrap of brown wrapping-paper.]

Day after day I am getting scareder and scareder for fear I have lost, by delay, the chance to have you and your wonderful painting going on at Scarborough this winter. It seems as if it had happened that it was only since I saw your pictures that I had noticed live birds. You know how I at the first was struck by your things and truly I have gone on admiring more and more, and every aviary I see amuses me about the tremendous truth and life charm of your things, and if I see that you often overlay them as it were with some degree of cheap values as to relation of black in light and black in shadow, etc., or degree of gray light on a hot color, it is because I have an absolute passion, more than most people could understand, for what you already do, that I long to be at your elbow and see you through into a still more exquisite justice-doing to their wonderful surfaces.

And if you will try me again you will find me still more deferential to your own inclinations, as to getting you to draw from cast, etc.

Only do come and let us have dear last winter over again, or better. Your dear father and mother would spare you and Kippie would too, if they fully (as perhaps they do) understood how

: 38 :

peculiarly I can help you. And believe me it is only because I find a real diamond that I positively *yearn* to see it polished. . . .

Abbott Thayer to L.A.F.

Florence, Italy, Nov. 21, 1898.

My dear fellow, we are to sail for home Dec. 1! Your good parents are to see the fitness in sparing you for one more winter under the circumstances and you are to do us a colossal benefit by being, if not Gerald's tutor, still of the young tutor age in the house, and are to live with us in the little smoky room (no longer so). The terms are that you allow us to feel your young man life and influence in the house in pay for my attacking your beautiful bird portraits.

This is cheap for us since we would *hire* such a person as yourself this year if we couldn't get him this way.

Our birds will get there somewhere near the same time as we, Dec. 12-15 about, and you must be there.

The custom-house may be pokey of course.

How we wish Kippy would be there too; can't she? I always feel conscious of cheek in proposing so much for another family, but we wish it. We will have Hazen [Mr. John D. Hazen who played for them as part of the children's education.] at the little piano soon, soon.

I now believe in your doing just birds. You are too *peculiar* to need or profit by academic training. The rest are in Paris. I join them and we sail from London—*Don't* disappoint us.

Observe what Mr. Thayer says in this letter about Louis: 'You are too peculiar to need or profit by academic training,' and compare it with Coues' remark to Louis' mother in the letter of March 29, 1897: 'With Louis it is different.' His experienced practical advisor felt that Louis did not need to become self-supporting in some trade or business before he could indulge himself in his interest in birds, as he advised other young men to do. His teacher of painting felt that Louis did not need the academic training he advised other young men to undergo. As President Farrand of

Cornell said long afterward, there was no precedent for Fuertes, and the special nature of his gifts was apparent to the two wise men who had him in their charge at the beginning of his career.

Louis did spend the remainder of that winter with the Thayers. Gladys Thayer Reasoner, in a letter already quoted above, wrote:

Louis introduced us to skis. . . . He really started the rage for them in that entire neighborhood I think. . . . It was he who used to mark out with thrillingly professional style our shuffle-board game, which, he and Gerald against me and our dad, played assiduously on our long covered piazza, through the winter. (They 'licked' us, of course.) Beneath the old student lamp Louis read us many delightful books and magazine stories. And we loved his 'weeps' over the moving parts.

ELLIOTT COUES TO L.A.F.

Washington, D. C., Jan. 31, 1899.

I have two important matters to lay before you: kindly give them careful attention.

1. In regard to the beautiful plates you have been generous to let me have for the *Osprey*. I think in justice to yourself you should refuse to give the *Osprey* any more. I should like to use the hairy woodpecker and perhaps the Cooper's hawk, but after that do not think I can conscientiously accept any more from you, for the simple reason that Dr. Gill declines to copyright the *Osprey*, and thus throws wide the door for anybody to steal and appropriate your beautiful work. . . .

2. Now I have something *pleasant* for you. I am authorized by the publisher of the new *Key to North American Birds*, which will soon go to press, to offer you $20 apiece for a large series of your pictures,—'spot cash' for every one, as soon as it is finished and approved by me—the subjects to be selected by myself. I don't yet know how many I shall want—probably at least 50. Now here is an opportunity for you, quite equal to that which I failed in effecting with Macmillan, and I am delighted to be able to make you the offer. Besides the cash payments, I shall of course be glad to give you all possible credit in the preface of the book,—or even, if you

make pictures enough to warrant it, I may be able to place your name on the title page of the *Key* with my own. We are going to bring out the work in two styles,—an *edition de luxe*, with plates *colored by hand* from your paintings, and a standard edition with the same plates black. Also, if we come to terms about the plates, I shall probably want a lot of pen-and-ink pictures of bills, feet, etc., to make small cuts in the text. But of this more hereafter, when we come to final details.

If you are at home, show this letter to your parents and consult with them; if at Scarborough, take Mr. Thayer into your counsel, and let me have your reply at early convenience. Sleep over the proposition, and see how it strikes you on mature deliberation. I myself think it is *almost* as good as anything I ever dreamed of for you, and far better than anything that has hitherto fallen to your lot.

Louis consulted with his father by mail and was advised to accept Dr. Coues' offer. Professor Fuertes wrote: 'I do not think that at present price should be as much of an object to you as to have your work known. As in tuning a fiddle, you may screw up the keys later on when the string can stand it.' Louis never did learn to screw the keys very tight, and he could not have hesitated long over this offer to place his drawings in a book that would be in the hands of every serious student of birds, young or old, amateur or professional, in America. He completed an order already begun (five illustrations for a U.S.D.A. Bulletin by C. Hart Merriam, North American Fauna 16) and then set to work on the drawings for the new edition of the Key. Many were small profile heads in black and white wash, but these he drew and painted with a simplicity and delicacy that makes them as delightful as any of his later work. He was busy at this work and living happily in the Thayer household when his next invitation and opportunity arrived.

5

The Harriman Alaska Expedition

I N THE EARLY SPRING of 1899, Mr. Edward H. Harriman planned an expedition to Alaska as a pleasure trip for his family and a few friends. He found that the comfort and safety of his party made necessary a large vessel and crew and preparations on a scale disproportionate to the number of persons. He decided, therefore, to include some more guests, and after conference with Dr. C. Hart Merriam, Chief of the Biological Survey, added a group of scientists, who should gather material of many kinds and increase the store of knowledge about Alaska. Specimens of birds, animals, plants, rocks, marine life were to be gathered, and the Indians and the glaciers studied and reported upon. Dr. Merriam suggested the names of three artists and twenty-five men of science, representing various branches of research, 'and at least one dreamer,' as John Burroughs, the official narrator of the expedition, put it. The scientific party consisted of William H. Brewer, Wesley R. Coe, Frederick V. Coville, William H. Dall, W. B. Devereux, Daniel G. Elliot, Benjamin K. Emerson, B. E. Fernow, A. K. Fisher, Henry Gannett, G. K. Gilbert, George Bird Grinnell, Thomas H. Kearney, Charles A. Keeler, Trevor Kincaid, C. Hart Merriam, John Muir, Charles Palache, Robert Ridgway, William E. Ritter, De Alton Saunders, and William Trelease. The taxidermists and preparators were Leon J. Cole and Edwin C. Starks; the artists were Fred S. Dellenbaugh, R. Swain Gifford, and Louis A. Fuertes. It is a distinguished list; the name of almost every man upon it is famous to the present generation of workers in his field.

Mr. Harriman was lavish with funds for the expedition, providing a special train to take the party across the continent and every luxury on board ship. On May 30 the party sailed from Seattle. They went north by the inside passage to Sitka, there entered the ocean in view of the spectacular mountains and glaciers, turned southwest along the Aleutian Islands, north again to touch at Siberia and glimpse the Bering Sea, and then doubled back. Frequent landings were made for collecting, and Dr. Fisher saw to it that Louis had many opportunities to go ashore as his assistant.

John Burroughs' narrative was included in the expedition report and printed separately in 1904 under the title Far and Near. It is delightful and should be read with Louis' letters. As he was an author of long experience, and as his account was 'official' and prepared for publication, it is more self-conscious and more polished than Louis' letters home, but throughout the journey these two, the oldest and the youngest members of the party, seemed to enjoy the same things and react in very much the same way.

Mr. Coues sent Louis off with fatherly advice.

ELLIOTT COUES TO L.A.F.

Washington, D. C., May 16, 1899.

Now you are about to start on a grand trip, which you will enjoy, and pleasantly remember all your life. You already have good friends in the party, as Elliot and Merriam, and doubtless will make others. Of course you will use your time to the best possible purpose in your art, and I need say nothing about that; but I want to impress upon you the necessity of taking the best possible care of your health. You will have plenty of beastly weather, and often be much exposed to the wet. Look out for that—you cannot go too well provided with clothing—both underclothes for a dry change, and waterproof outside. Also look out for accidents, in the small boat business on a bad coast, and come back with very full port folios of all sorts of interesting things, as well as in perfect health, ready to resume and push to completion the important business you have on hand with my publisher and myself. The new *Key* must not be delayed a day longer than is necessary.

L.A.F. TO HIS FAMILY.

Near Granger, Wyo., May [18?], 1899.

John Burroughs says (he and I are like two kids in our enjoyment of the country's novelty) that the old Rockies have a broader back than he had supposed. . . .

As I sit here in the car window, writing, the yellow warblers and western robins sing exactly as they do in the trees by our house— and Bullock's oriole, the Arkansas flycatcher and crimson-fronted finches recall eastern relatives, but have a decidedly foreign accent. The meadowlarks you would never know, as they sound like a mixture of bobolink and wood-thrush, with the accent on the latter, done in a clear flutey starling quality.

[*After the first trip ashore, on the way north from Seattle.*]

I struck right into the forest along the left shore, and found it next to impenetrable. It had been raining and the brush was wet, and the logs, which were almost the only highway, very slippery. I had one quite bad tumble, but it didn't do any damage beyond a red pancake mark on the slats—and a jolt in the wind. I heard a pileolated warbler, and after an hour's search within a few yards of it, through the deep brush, and all within a radius of 100 feet, I finally got a glance at it, as it disappeared over a mossy boulder into the ferns beyond. Saw a creeper go into its nest on the side of a dead spruce tree, thus (sketch) and saw some more rufous hummers—the strangest thing to see a bright fox-colored humming-bird s-s-sing like a creeper, with a big bumble-bee buzz—curve up into a giant forest, where everything in view is vast; poise with its tail, pendulum-like, swinging under it, look around, and brooooooom off again, all before you quite notice it! Or to hear a little undertone hum, look up, and see through the leaves of a red-flowered black-berry bush a tiny white-throated female looking at you solicitously for a scared second, and quietly fade away.

I had been hearing the most curious and loud noises up in the forest, and started toward them, when they got so queer and human sounding that I thought that Dr. Fisher, who is summat of a jollier, was doing it to get a rise out of me. So I got proud, and turned off. When we got back to the ship, after hearing a shot or two, Dr. Fisher appeared with a great big northern raven, which I have made some right careful drawings of. . . . I seem to find ravens and rufous hummingbirds always together. The latter were so common that almost every proper 'spitz' had its little red ball on top, and the ravens were astonishingly common and allowed one to get very near—within 40 or 50 feet. They are great devilish jokers who give you a jolly and then chuckle, peep, whistle, grunt, croak, bark, cackle, gobble, and everything else, about it. . . .

No one here has ever seen such vegetation as fills the woods—one can go all around in them without setting his foot on the ground once in ten steps, by walking the fallen logs—from no distance at all to ten or fifteen feet above the ground. The sphagnum and other mosses are feet thick, and a rich green underglow suffuses everything—and the great majestic spruce columns—often eight or even more feet in diameter, and as much as 200 feet high, gray where not clothed in some bright green or yellow moss—and the immense stillness broken only by a hummer's squeak or a raven's great raucous yells, make a combination which it is a little beyond my power to describe. . . .

June 7. 10 p.m.

This has been about the most curious and delightful day we've had yet. Early we had breakfast and got things together to take the narrow gauge train up to White Pass. The town has long log-cabin suburbs, and the line passes through this settlement and follows the Skagway river up to the summit, nearly 3000 feet up. The day was drizzly, and we were in clouds most of the way—20 miles of climb. We got out and looked around every little while, and when nearly up to the big curve, two-thirds of the way up, Dr. M. suddenly jumped up, saying, 'Well, there are some of my boys!' And the train stopped, and backed a little distance, and sure enough, there was a little outfit, with three men, one of whom was Osgood, a young fellow I knew in Washington very well, collecting mammals and birds. It was a joy to see him, and he seemed glad to see me, even with all the others he knew of the party. [This was Wilfred H. Osgood, later curator of zoology at the Field Museum in Chicago, and leader of the expedition to Abyssinia on which Louis went in 1926.] He came with us to the summit. This is the line of the old trail to the Klondike, and the old trail is visible for most of its distance. It is known as 'Dead Horse Trail,' and gets its name from the fact that year before last, over 3000 horses and 26 men died in going over it. . . .

As soon as we stopped, everyone started right off on his stunt without waiting a minute. I struck up the side of the hill, in the snow and scrubby fir. The ground is all granite rock and boulders, dense and deep in mosses and lichens, with thick, tough, flatly-growing spruces, as high, in some places, as three feet, generally one half of that. Snow fills all the hollows, and the air is chilly and damp. Ridgway was also near me, and soon I heard a sweet clear sparrow song, which I guessed to be that of the lovely golden-crowned sparrow, a bird like our eastern white-crown . . . with a golden yellow crown. Pop! went Ridgway's auxiliary, and the bird came my way, and lit above me over a ledge. I climbed excitedly up to it, and it looked up, nearer than I thought, for when I shot it with a pinch I ruined it. I was very sick, but got another, a beauty, in a few more minutes. . . .

While I was at work in my studio over the engines, I heard the old glacier booming and roaring and tore out in time to see the most majestic of sights. Great combers and promontories of ice were falling off, and the deep rumbling thunder of its parting, the seething roar of the water, and the sight of the great pieces, some of them 300 feet long, tottering forward, and sending first a towering fountain of snowy foam and spray clear over the glacier top, then an immense, dark wave that would set all the bergs moving, go crashing to shore where it would pile and tower between the

Northern Raven
Corvus corax principalis
♂
Lowe Inlet, Al.
June 1, 1899.

NORTHERN RAVEN. Lowe Inlet, Alaska, June 1, 1899

Red Tailed Ha
Buteo borealis ♂ ad
♀ Ithaca, Sep. 10, 99.

RED-TAILED HAWK. Ithaca, Sept. 10, 1899

stranded ice boulders, and roll in roaring surf along the shore, and finally reach us and give us a long deep roll [were majestic] but the most majestic thing of all was the rising of the fallen mass. After the big 20 or 30 foot wave, the water would seem to be quiet, then dome up close to the glacier face a clear light blue vault, which would rise—rise—and finally break to let out the great ice mass, and recede from its apex in seething streams. The great thing would lift, rocking from side to side, until it was as high as the glacier top, and then slowly subside, and float silently away from its bed for the past thousands or so of years. All this evening the 'Old Man' has been booming and reverberating, and all through John Muir's lecture after dinner, the boat would suddenly begin to pitch or roll, according to which side of the glacier the ice mass fell from.

One of the boys borrowed my gun and went ashore, and came back with two noble gulls, and I have been at work on their bills and feet, with a lot up my sleeve for tomorrow. These days are busy ones already. Palache found a white-tailed ptarmigan on her nest, and got her and six fresh eggs, which he gave to Merriam. No telling what's on for tomorrow, but it's sure to be busy. The music and amusements haven't been touched for the last day or two. . . .

June 10, night.

Dr. Fernow, Dr. Fisher, Robert Ridgway, Kearny and I and Cole are in camp, at last, on Gustavus point. We got in about noon, made camp, got lunch and went out. It is a most ideal spot, the woods are most beautiful, deep in soft moss, so that one makes no sound in going through them, and the trunks are covered with light blue-gray mosses and lichens, so that the colors are soft and harmonious. I got a number of birds, and did a good bit of collecting in the nest, eggs, and parent birds of the lovely lutescent warbler. Indians came in this evening, sold us some salt, and taught us some Indian names for things we had shot. The dwarf hermit thrushes are making most lovely harmony in the woods on all sides of this clearing, and the crackling campfire and Dr. Fernow's Franco-Prussian war stories make it very nice to be here. But though I'm writing in broad daylight, and have made two drawings since supper, it is after 10, and we want to make an early start, so I'm going to bed—adios.

Sunday, June 11.

It is about 5 p.m., and Cole and I are writing up, out on the beach where mosquitos are less bad than elsewhere. This a.m. we awoke to find yesterday's rain and mist had given place to a regular June day, one of the 'rare' kind, in which we could see the horizon clear to Mt. Fairweather, a 15,000 footer between 75 and 100 miles away. It has been so all day, and the only clouds to be seen are little fleeces hanging off the south sides of the high snow peaks, with which the seaward horizon is lined. We are in a cove between two rocky and sandy points, with fine spruce forests behind us, the long blue bay in front; we can't see out to sea on any side, but the deep blue is cut by white or light blue ice cakes floating on the tide, some near enough to show their queer fantastic shapes. Three or four whales are sporting around in the bay, snorting, lunging out of the water and landing with a big splash, or just curving up and under, giving a final swash with their tail— they look like this, reading from l. to r. (Sketch)

There has been a bird note which has mystified us all. We all heard it yesterday, and determined to ferret it out this morning, and I was the lucky man. The note came from deep in the woods, was very loud, pure, and beautiful, the quality of a veery's call note, only intensely pure and loud. It was absolutely a monotone, as true as a flute, beginning *piano* and going through a fine *crescendo*, and dying out again at the end. First it would be given in a fine soprano, and after a few seconds it would come in a deep contralto; the third would perhaps be between the two in pitch, and so on. The range was about through five or six tones, and no two seemed ever to follow less than two full tones apart. The high ones seemed, when heard well and near, to have a slight tremolo. It seemed like some Grimm's fairy-tale bird, never seen, but heard, and luring the child on and on, and the woods are of a character quite in keeping with the illusion, so that one expects to see a witch's hut any minute.

I was going through the woods early in the p.m., and the idea came into my head to try and imitate the note, as I could remember it. I had hardly done so, when a beautiful reply came 'a touzen times louder,' from nearly over head. It was easy to make it continue singing, and the whole set of notes came, and mixed in was some chuckling and twittering which sounded natural, and finally I saw the bird through the twigs and cold-bloodedly pulled on it, and the mystery was solved, for it turned out to be a fine male varied thrush, a bird about the size and general build of a robin, but deep slate blue on the back and chestnut on the under side, with a black ring around its breast. I have one for the Thayers, too. (Sketch)

When we first saw the mountains this a.m. the far ones looked like icebergs, the distance-blue of the rocky parts was so light. The blowing and snorting of the whales, the screaming, way out on the bay, of gulls and loons, and an occasional goose, and, near by, the licking of the little waves in the pebbles and hum of a big bee, with just a thin 'ray' of the hermit's song way over across the bay in the spruces, make the part of the picture that you see with your ears. The other part goes beyond my vocabulary, which has gradually become dwindled down to Wow and Gee.

Tonight we are to dine on grouse, and tomorrow goose it is. We have a bully little camp, and are enjoying it to the top notch. We shall probably be here a day or two more—I'd like to make it a week or ten days, as I'm soft from much food and sleep and little exercise on board the good ship *Geo. W. Elder*, which feeds us too well.

Monday, June 12, 5 p.m.

This is probably our last afternoon in camp, as the G.W.E. is expected to pick us up this evening. Cole and I went out at about 7:30, after an early breakfast, and were in the canoe until 1:00 after sea birds. I don't think I ever had so many 'moments' in one morning before. The mosquitos had simply changed the whole topography of our faces during the night, and I had to lift one eyelid with my thumb for about an hour after I got up. The first bird I shot was a pigeon guillemot, which was the only one we got. Marbled murrelets came along with a delegation of five, and we got seven violet-green cormorants, five of which were males. I saved the two finest for me and the Thayers, and gave Fisher and Ridgway the rest. We have made a full study, comparatively, of the fauna and flora of this place, and have pretty full collections of the interesting forms.

The whales are continually in the bay, and make a noise like the Frontenac [a steamer on Cayuga Lake] blowing off steam, when they blow, and we were near enough to them this a.m. to be uncomfortable, though nothing happened.

June 22.

The only thing, about, that has happened to me to-day that is worth writing down is the remark made by the poet-stenographer of the expedition, in response to a small rave I made about a magnificent Arctic tern I was just working on. 'Yes,' he said reflectively, 'that's a very pretty bird; built on the lines of the swallow; one of the most artistic color-effects there is, too.' [This kind of absurdity always amused Louis. Many years later he relished the remark of P. G. Wodehouse's character in *Leave it to Psmith* who spoke of how beautiful the stars were, and, 'if I may say so, how artistically arranged.']

Monday, July 10.

At Unalaska, a most interesting place, we lay to to water and coal, and Fisher and I piled right ashore to hunt, and were filled with new sensations right away. Some of the loveliest birds, whose names had become familiar, but which had in themselves become myths, were found to be very common, and easily obtainable, and their singing brought one back to the bobolink-filled meadows of the east. The Lapland longspurs were the finest singers, and among the most beautiful. The beautiful rosy finches, or *leucostictes*, were also quite common, but shy after the first shot, so that I didn't get many, though I'd like to have gotten them for the Thayers. I got an owl, new to me, the short-ear, and the type song-sparrow. Late the next afternoon a small party went ashore for an hour at a great sea-lion rookery, and came back very glowing with the wonder of it. I didn't get in on that trip, which included a look at one of the most wonderful colonies of sea-birds on this coast.

The Bering Sea is just like any other, strange to say, except that it is colder than outside the Aleutians.

Back at Popoff I., July 18.
I begin to feel as if my face were turned homeward, and it's not a bad feeling, though I've had good luck and a bully time. I've got ninety-five skins put up, and a portfolio full of studies, and suppose that a dozen more of each will about conclude this trip's work. . . . Making studies in colors of all the sea-birds, whether of my own or somebody else's collections, takes so much time that notes, letters, and everything has to go by till it's done, and lately things have bunched so that this is the first time I've sat down to write without 'oughting' to do something else.

Fernow is playing Lohengrin, and the baby Harriman is laughing and playing with a cloth ball and things are generally cozy and pleasant. Everybody seemed to 'get through' about the same time, so that we had a sing after lunch.

When we were up at St. Lawrence I. . . . some of us went ashore in a ship's boat against a hard wind and had a good hunt. Dr. Merriam got after a couple of polar bears, which, when he was near them, took wing, and flew away—swans! and the laugh was onto him. We got some good birds there, too, but by far and away the most interesting place we have seen at all was our next stop, at Hall I. We got there at about 7, and having had dinner early, a lot of us went ashore at once. We had seen many sea birds around the island and found that the cliffs were densely populated with nine or ten species of sea birds: one of those wonderful sights that I had heard and read so much about. But all descriptions failed utterly to make the impression that the thing warranted, as it is truly the most wonderful sight I've ever seen. Thousands and thousands of birds—tame to stupidity, seated on every little ledge or projection—from the size of sandpipers up to a great white gull that spreads five feet—all the time coming and going, screaming, croaking, peeping, chuckling, with constant moving of countless heads—all where you can reach over the cliff and catch the birds from the top in your hands—makes a wonderful sight, and one not soon to be forgotten. Beautiful pure white snow-buntings, an island race peculiar to these two islands in the Bering Sea, were found to be very common in the tundra, and their sweet prismatic song was always to be heard. A pair of snowy owls had a nest right near where we landed, and the male and young ones became government property before they knew it. I spent a long time, all my patience, and a good deal of hard brain work and energy trying to outwit an old owl—probably the female of this pair—but she was too foxy, and I couldn't get anywhere near her, however I'd try, even by crawling through the wet sphagnum moss on my stomach for a quarter of a mile—but no go—I think foxes had tried every trick I had thought of long ago, and the old bird was up to her game in every detail. We went back to the boat at about 11:30 (I had shot my last bird by daylight at 10:30!) and at 4 next a.m. Fisher and I and Ned Trudeau went ashore on Matthew I., to get F's traps he'd set out the night before while we others were on Hall. I was in the bow of the boat, on watch, and saw near shore a small dark-headed gull, like that splendid Bonaparte's gull I got just before I left home, and said, 'There's a Bonaparte.' F. said, without looking around, (he was rowing) 'Pot that, it's a Sabine' and I did, and sure enough, it was one. He got another in a minute, and we had the finest bird the trip has yet produced. They look like Bonapartes, something, but are rosier in the breast, and more delicate and tern-like all through, and have a black ring separating the slate-blue head from the snowy neck. (Sketch) . . .

The last letter Louis wrote from this expedition was dated Seattle-Portland, July 31, and said, 'there is little use in writing this, as you will get me almost as soon as you will it,' so he must have gone east directly. The party broke up in friendly spirits, promising to meet together at least once a year. Louis had acquired, besides his bird skins and his portfolio of sketches, a good many permanent friends;

after this he addressed Dr. Fisher as 'Pop' and signed himself 'Sonny' and referred to Mr. Burroughs as 'Uncle John.'

Louis, back at home, reported ready for duty to Mr. Coues.

Elliott Coues to L.A.F.

Santa Fe, N. M., Sept. 1, 1899.

On returning from a long tour among the Indian pueblos of this territory, I find your good letter of Aug. 10 awaiting me, and am delighted to hear of your success in procuring and being able to study so many rare birds, new to you—and particularly, that you have got back safe from such an inhospitable region. No doubt you have had a pleasant as well as profitable excursion, and did not mind the personal discomforts in your enthusiasm for your studies. I hope you are now ready to go to work, and we may soon have some beautiful specimens of your art. You may take the Pribyloff sandpipers, McKay's snowflake, and Siberian yellow wagtail as subjects for colored plates. I want a lot of characteristic heads of auks and other sea birds, for black washes, to go in text. I have received no proofs as yet, as probably Mr. Estes has been awaiting your return, but see no reason why the work should not now start up and be vigorously pushed, if you are ready to come to terms with your share of it. I think you had better advise Mr. Estes of your return, and of about how fast you now propose to go ahead. I shall be at home about Oct. 1, and hope the publication of the new *Key*, with all your fine work, may not be much longer delayed.

Last May, my patience being utterly exhausted . . . I withdrew from the *Osprey*, taking you and Johnson off also. I do not know whether there has been a June number, but learn indirectly that G. intends to start up a new series of the magazine this month. I shall always be sorry I had anything to do with it, and would not touch it again under any circumstances.

It is unlikely that readers of this book will search the stacks of a library to look at copies of the old Osprey, although there is a good deal of interest to an ornithologist therein. A respectable small magazine, it appeared first in September, 1896, under the editorship of Walter A. Johnson and Dr. A. C. Murchison. It was illustrated with photographs; the first and third numbers contained articles by Otto Widmann; Dr. Shufeldt contributed to the third. No. 7, March, 1897, contained four black and white reproductions of paintings by Louis A. Fuertes, together with a photograph of him and a laudatory article by Elliott Coues. Dr. Coues took over a column in the next issue, and his name appeared with Johnson's through October, 1898, when Theodore Gill and Louis Fuertes were added to the staff. In December of the same year there was a new department of book reviews entitled 'In the Osprey's Claws.' The next number continued it under a large cut of an Osprey's claws, done in pen and ink by Fuertes (for Citizen Bird). It makes one wince to look at it, and a book reviewed by Coues was in the Osprey's claws indeed. He dug them into Frank Chapman's newly issued Bird-Lore, into J. A. Allen's review of a work on color change in feathers by Keeler, and into everything that added sentimentality to bird study. Reading these reviews, one learns a new aspect of this vigorous and brilliant man and appreciates what he could have done to destroy the opportunities of a youngster, if he had thought it was what the young man deserved.

During the period of Coues' editorship the magazine expanded, increased its illustrations, using many by Louis Fuertes, and was very lively. All names went off the masthead in September, 1899, and no new Fuertes drawings appeared thereafter, though the screech owl of March, 1897 was reprinted in February, 1900. 'In the Osprey's Claws' was dropped for a section called simply 'Literature,' but the drawing of the claws was used once more in an article about the bird itself. After six months of a new series, much reduced in size, the final issue of the magazine appeared in June, 1902.

Louis got to work at once, in the fall of 1899, on the illustrations for Coues' Key. Mr. Coues was not well during the fall and was unable to attend the meetings of the A.O.U. He wrote to Louis in November that he was 'still in bed, with great suffering,' and wanted Louis to come to him at his house. After two surgical operations he died, on Christmas day, 1899.

His part of the work for the new Key to North American Birds was done, however, and the publication plans went forward. *Perhaps Louis was relieved of some immediate pressure, as the Key was not finally published until 1903; at all events he made plans to be with the Thayers again that winter.*

L.A.F. TO A. K. FISHER

Scarborough, N. Y., Mar. 26, 1900.

It is extremely backward here as to spring birds—cowbirds and redwings hardly here yet, only very few straggling ones, and redpolls still hang on. We have recently had a cold snap which brought a great flock of redpolls, and they stayed here in mass for a week, and have been seen off and on ever since. They were wonderfully tame, and in fact didn't mind our proximity or approach in the least, exactly like the Kadiak siskins, and we had the exquisite pleasure of lying on the crust in the stable yard and having a flock of 30 or more feeding, actually on our sleeves and between our arms as we lay. . . .

I'm settling into the work for the H [arriman] A [laska] E [xpedition] report, and trying to do a bit too much, I am afraid, but haven't a fear in the world that I actually will.

The published report appeared in 1901. It is in two handsome volumes illustrated with photographs, black and white drawings, and colored reproductions of paintings made on purpose for this publication. Fourteen of these colored plates are landscapes by Dellenbaugh or Gifford, seven are flower paintings by Frederick A. Walpole, two are animal paintings by Charles R. Knight (the two artists just mentioned were not on the expedition), and sixteen are pictures of birds by Louis A. Fuertes, who also contributed three black and white drawings and the photograph of Mr. Harriman's bear. Though he was the youngest member of the party, his work received the lion's share of expensive reproduction.

GERALD THAYER TO L.A.F.

Scarborough, N. Y.,
[after Christmas] 1899.

You mustn't think, because I haven't answered your letter before, that I am not duly excited over the good news—I think you understand what this kind of laziness is. Who should know better than me, that your thinking of coming to us generally means that you are coming! It changes the whole aspect of the winter, to know that you are coming toward the end of it.

[Written upside down between the lines.] So Dr. Coues is dead! Surely our greatest ornithologist—and most devilishly brilliant man —is gone? What effect will this have on the work you are at?

It left him with a contract to finish and deprived him of a kind and wise advisor in the business of his career. But Louis was ripe now and henceforth never lacked opportunity to earn a living with bird pictures. And although he spent another winter with the Thayers, he was in no danger of being flown away with.

L.A.F. TO A. K. FISHER

Ithaca, N.Y., Jan.27, 1900.

My work has been going on right steadily, and I am getting quite a bunch of pictures done—and, incidentally, quite rich—so when this job is done, just let me know your plans, if it is convenient, and perhaps we can do up the Rio Grande, or the Bahamas, or Yucatán, or the Philippines, or some place.

6

To Texas with Vernon Bailey

. . . .

IN THE SPRING of 1901 Louis went on an expedition sponsored by the Biological Survey for the purpose of collecting birds and animals in certain southwestern areas of Texas. The experience could hardly have been more different from that of 1899 with the Harriman Alaska Expedition. Then the company was large, all luxuries were supplied, the travel was in northern foggy waters, among damp forests, or near chilling glaciers. In Texas Louis was alone at first, then with H. C. Oberholser until they joined the 'outfit' of Vernon Bailey, which consisted of a few horses and mules, a chuck wagon, and one man to cook and do camp chores. Mr. Bailey, Chief Field Naturalist of the Biological Survey, liked to travel light and live hard; their rations were as simple as they could well be—and all the coffee was burnt the first day out. On the two-day trip up the Chisos Mountains described below they had almost no food and only such water as they could catch by holding their mouths open under a dripping cliff, or find in hollows of the rocks. When they got back to camp it was not mealtime, but Louis couldn't wait. He ducked into the bushes after a bacon rind he had tossed there a few days before, found it covered with red ants, brushed them off, and ravenously gnawed upon what they had left.

At another time the temperature was 108°, the water bad, their horses gone, their shoes worn through, their food supply down to jerked venison, corn meal, and one cup of lard. Mr. Bailey mounted a mule to go after the horses and narrowly escaped serious injury when it bucked and threw him over its head to a bank of stones.

Before the summer was over Louis had made a new life-long friend in Mr. Bailey. The first letter to be given is actually the ninth he had written.

L.A.F. TO MRS. E. A. FUERTES

Tornillo Creek, Texas, May 29, 1901.

Your letter of the 21st came over with Bailey from Boquillas last night, and as we are going to send a lot of stuff over this evening I will just send along a little note to tell you that we are all right, in good health and happiness, having replenished our larder which for the last day or two has been without coffee, baking-powder, or condensed milk.

Well, I got the hawk, and had an adventure in the bargain by virtue of which I spent a delightful hour in a hole 400 feet up a 600 foot cliff till Oberholser could get to camp and back with a rope, on which to continue my journey. The bird [a zone-tailed hawk] is a Texas record, and one of the very few U.S. records, so that when I had at last shot him, after three straight days of hunting him, it would never have done to let the splendid thing rot just because he fell over a cliff down into the cañon. I don't think I was in any danger any of the time, for when I found myself unable to go any further because of a boulder that was lodged in the fissure above me, and also at least unwilling to go down, I got O. to go for a rope. Then I sat in my comfortable hole, sang to a superb echo for a while, watched lizards and ravens and got rested for an hour, and came out all right, and the bird had by that time earned his record. I painted him fresh that afternoon, and am mighty glad of it, for all his lovely plum bloom has gone, in the skin, and he is still splendid, but nearly dead black, instead of like a rich ripe black plum.

Chisos Mts., Texas, June 9, 1901.

There is a big flat-topped mountain about six miles back of our ridge, with a lot of splendid timber on it, and B. was very anxious to explore it to see if it had any chipmunks in it—for it would nach'ely haf' to be a new form. So we got aboard our ships of the desert at about 10:30—a pretty late start, to go around the range of the big mountain. It is also one of the highest points in the range, going up about 8,600 feet, and a pretty stiff one to go up. We expected to get back for late supper, so only took a couple of biscuits with bacon and peach stew in them, and my little quart canteen of H$_2$O. After a long hot ride up and down over stony hills and ridges, and a good part of the way leading the horses to save them, we got to the mouth of the gulch leading from the great basin of the mountain, which reared its forested sides up a good 5,500 feet above where we entered. We found a good little open place with grass, picketed our horses, ate our grub and started up. It was just 1:30 then, and soon after we had entered the great boulder-jammed forest B. stopped short on a fresh trail, which I could also plainly see, of a big bear and one or two little ones. So we shut up and went as still as possible to get a clip at her if we could. We continued the silent habit all the rest of the way, which, though adding to the great impressiveness of the mountain, grew very tiresome—especially as we got up into the thinner air where we got tired and stumbly quicker. It was a very steep climb; the first half was up a boulder-clogged wash or stream bed, with a good many stiff climbs to get up. It was as dry as a bone, except for a little stained pool in a rock bed at the very foot, and as the sun was cooking hot we soon got pretty dry as we left our canteen half full at the horse camp against our dry return. But at its hottest, when we were nearly up the stream bed, it headed up rapidly and began to hail, thunder and rain. We went into a cave, rested on an old bear's bed, and pretty soon each found a nice little trickle that we could sit under—thus (sketch) and we got a nice cold clean drink just at the moment we wanted it most. After that we struck splendid spring pools all along, and every concave rock held a nice little drink whenever we wanted one. Pretty soon it began to clear again, and it was fine and cool, the hail having worked wonders, and we continued our silent climb, ever on the look-out for bear or deer. Bailey wants specimens very much, and the one he got the other day gave us plenty of delicious fresh venison for a week—which was a true godsend, after our supply of bum Texas bacon had been a week 'all.' Well, to get back to the trail: we kep' a-gettin' upper and upper, into the junipers and pines, and even spruces—(the same noble Douglas spruce that comes in Alaska!) and finally, at 7,000 feet, left the bed and took to the hillsides and made for the 'high grass'—through half a mile or more of 45° smooth grass slope, sprinkled with tall-stalked agaves here and there, and all sheltered under a lovely orchard-like growth of gnarled old live-oaks and nut-pines, as still as a church on week-days. At the foot of the comb-ridge, which all these mountains have, B. and I parted to work both sides, and met again in the stunted growth on top—8,600 feet above sea level, the highest I have ever been on my own pins. After quietly enjoying the wonderful view we got, for a few minutes, B. looked at his watch, and to our complete dumbfoundation it was 7:15!! and the sun was about to set. So, though we had left our coats below with the horses, and our clothes were still a little damp from the soaking we had gotten (for we had decided to disregard the storm and push up and on) there was nothing for it but to camp, as it was a good three or four hours' climb down to the horses in the daytime, and probably six or eight very dangerous hours' work at night, and then we would have had to wait for the moon before the horses could start out, and it would be daylight before we got to camp. So we found a little cave under the comb-rock, and while B. rustled branches and grass for a bed I humped fire-wood, and by dark we had as nice a lair as ever bear or panther stretched out on. We built a little fire under a live oak log which we placed across the open side of our hole, and by moving up the sticks about once an hour (which I got so I could do without waking up) we kept our little cushion of air so warm that we both got a very refreshing night's rest, as we were both pretty weary. We

Cooper Hawk

Tex
y 8 1901

COOPER'S HAWK. Alpine, Texas, May 8, 1901

Swainson's Hawk. 15 miles south of Marathon, Texas, May 18, 1901

tried hard to find a rabbit, pigeon, or something, but the biggest bird we could get was a chewink, and the biggest mammal nothing at all, though deer were all about us and we even heard one old buck stamp as he got up and out. But the brush was so thick that we couldn't see to shoot anything more than a rod or two away. So we went to bed hungry. We got up at daylight and separated to hunt again, with no better result, so, at 8 o'clock this a.m. we sucked the water out of the little dips in the rock near 'camp' and started down. It took us until 11:30 to get to the horses, which were still there, plus a fine old hound dog which we 'allowed' to follow us back to camp, where we arrived at about 2 this p.m. about as hungry and weary as they grow, I should say. We lapped up a few mouthfuls of food, to get in trim for 'chuck' tonight [the few mouthfuls refers to the ant-eaten rind of bum Texas bacon] which is just now ready, so 'YOU MUST EXCUSE ME, MAGGIE'— I eat.

* biscuits—*—* bacon—*—* biscuits—*—* applesauce etc., repeat *ad lib.*

There, I feel better. We are truly lucky in our camp man, who replaces Kelly who broke his foot. He can cook to beat the band, and when the baking-powder gave out he quietly set to work and made up some sour dough, and we have those now, just as good as his b.p. ones.

I think the hound-dog is an old camper, for in the few hours he has been with us he has gone systematically all over the camp— beginning at the camp-tree and spiralling, cleaning up all the burned crusts, bones, etc., till it is really quite a model camp. And he doesn't come to the 'table' (i.e. that part of the ground on which our 'chuck' is spread on its yard of oil-cloth) but lies patiently about six feet off and waits till we throw him potato peelings or other delicate morsels.

We are still at the same camp we came to that first day—June 1 —and will probably stay here for several days yet. We have got representatives of nearly all the birds, though there are two or three bully good ones that are yet to grace my little tray-full of Chisos birds. I have written my two hundred and seventh label, and while we have been here we have added about six species to the Texas list and two to the U.S. Yesterday I made a lay for hummers at a big agave flower-stalk and got a male and female of one of the most beautiful of all the N. American hummers, the 'lucifer.' The male is small, (also the femelle) and on the back like a ruby-throat, but the throat, including the ear feathers, is the most resplendent amethyst purple, showing green and rich blue in other lights than the light, and the whole patch is spread out like a great star, that covers his whole breast, comme ça. (Sketch)

Another hummer, much like our ruby-throat, but belonging to the little Alaskan 'rufous' group, and the curiously painted Massena quail remain to be got by me, though the others have shot them. I guess I'll make a special try for them tomorrow, as I *must* get them. There is a fine large hummer with a sky-blue throat gorget that lives in the big forest of the gulch above camp. I have three of him, one a beauty. He sits on his perch and peeps like a little sparrow or warbler, and to-day coming down the big mountain I found a little green and yellow flycatcher with almost the identical note, so that I didn't bother with it until I happened to see it.

The other day I was coming out of the gulch after an unsuccessful day, when I saw what seemed at first to be a dry oak leaf, walking down a little leafy place between some loose stones, and it proved, on being l-l-l-l-looked at under the k-k-k-kitchen l-l-lamp to be the biggest tarantula that any of us ever saw. I don't honestly think he would go on my extended hand, all stretched out—I chucked him in formalin and will send him on as a token of my slight esteem some day.

It is just getting to the time of year when the gnats and mos-quitos are getting in their fine work. Especially in the afternoons when our hands are deep in tender birds and arsenic, they delight to crawl way into our ears and buzzzzz, or get far up into the interesting labyrinths of our noses, or perhaps fly bang into our open eyes, and it is certainly an awful exasperation to feel one's ear swell 'visibly' when he can't possibly spare a hand to stop it with, and to hear, for a whole afternoon, the social buzwuzing of the same old fly just out of focus of the flapping hand. But we have been mighty lucky so far at the hands of the bugs, and these are really no worse than those I have struck in lots of places. . . .

And here is part of Vernon Bailey's version of this summer in the Rio Grande country.

[Louis'] life in that region was one thrill after another, Bullock's and hooded orioles, blue-throated hummers, road-runners, poorwills, and Texas night hawks, and to cap them all, the vermilion flycatcher. His enthusiasm was so genuine and boundless that it was a pleasure to watch him. Long days in the saddle we had much to see and talk about.

. . . [One] camp was at the lower end of the Grand Cañon of the Rio Grande, where the river came out between 2000 foot walls of black lava rock, a cut little wider at the top than at the bottom, with many curves where the sun had never shown. [It was] the home of black phoebes and cliff swallows. The only way to get into the cañon is at the upper or lower ends, and we were camped as close to the lower end as we could get our camp wagon.

Early next morning Louis and I took our guns and traps and started up the river, which was at low water that left shores and shelves first on one side and then the other. Soon we had to cache our guns and traps and all of our clothes except shoes so we could swim from one side to the other when we came to sheer walls above and below the water, but we kept going till long after noon. Toward night we were well up to the deepest and darkest part of the cañon but we knew we could make better time on the return.

On a high bank behind a sheer point we found old drift logs of cottonwood, worn to polished skeletons of trees from long days of beating the rocks in flood times. Some were 50 feet above the water and may have been there for many years. They were light and dry and it did not take us long to get a couple just right to float us in the swift current, and, each riding our bronco log in the swirling waters, or lying flat and steering with both hands and feet like some prehistoric amphibians, we shot the rapids and dodged the rocks, paddled through the big swirls, and in little over an hour covered the return trip to our clothes and guns and traps. We guessed we had been twelve miles up the cañon in about eight hours and had come back most of the way at race-horse speed.

There was still time to set traps and collect birds and get a few pictures and again we had good appetites for a hearty camp supper.

We left the Rio Grande with regrets, as we had only skimmed the surface of the rare and interesting birds and mammals, reptiles, plants, and insects of that blazing hot and fascinating valley. We had little time to get acquainted with the Mexican people on scattered ranches who occasionally visited our camps and wondered at our collections and Louis' vivid color sketches of the birds they knew.

Our preserved specimens of reptiles and strange creatures attracted their keenest interest, and they exclaimed over the scorpions, tarantulas and vinegaroons . . .

One morning Louis found one of these long-tailed whip-scorpions in his bed when he crawled out of his sleeping bag, whereupon he promptly organized the Vinegaroon Club, which no one could join who had not slept with a vinegaroon. He remained the sole member.

At that time we were not sure how venomous the savage-looking insects might be, but later we found they were relatives of the mole crickets and perfectly harmless, in spite of their vicious looks.

On the slow trip back to the Davis Mts., and up the Pecos valley to Carlsbad and the Guadaloupe Mts., sleeping nights on the hard ground, eating at the tail of the camp wagon, collecting specimens all day and trapping obscure species at night, there were no dull or uninteresting hours. Many specimens were collected from the saddle, or on foot if need be, for our horses were well trained to shooting from the saddle, or to stay where they were left with reins dragging.

To Louis it was all new, and I could enjoy his keen interest and enthusiasm, as well as his kindly companionship and sparkling good humor. There is no place like camp to get acquainted with and appreciate the sterling qualities of a real man.

L.A.F. TO ABBOTT THAYER

(Sketched map showing Ysleta,
Texas.) July 24 [?], 1901.

It seems a year since you all showed us the last we saw of you in Berkshire last November—and I'm sure I hate the long apartness, and the way I have let being busy and scattered cut off my natural desire to tell you about the things and places that I've so much wanted you to see and enjoy with me. I've tried, in my letters home, to keep as much as possible of what has come my way before the home-folks' imagination, and I hope (though I didn't tell them to, I'm afraid) that they have sent you those letters as they did the Alaskan ones, as they have been written from time to time, mostly in the places they are about.

I am now down in the little old Mexican town of Ysleta, twelve miles east of El Paso, trying to find new western birds. I had a nasty time getting here, and it is a little *unsimpatica* now that I am here, though there are a few new birds I think, though I've seen *but* few. My train from El Paso was to have left at 7:20 p.m., but owing to a wash-out on the line somewhere west of here, which also demolished the telegraphic connections, it didn't get in till 1:45 this a.m. I got here at a little after 2, found everything in the hotel line gone out, and nothing that I could possibly do to get a night's rest, as it was raining hard. So I went into the waiting room, lit a match and found the cleanest place I could on the floor, made a pillow of my gun and coat, and slept until about 5:30 when a big rich bird-song—like Scott's oriole only much louder—began to figure in my wandering dream sensations, became more and more domi- nant, and finally woke me broadly into my day self. It was a western meadowlark, and as other things were singing too, I went out for a stroll. I shot a ♂ Bullock's oriole, which is for you if you want it, though like quite a lot of these brush birds at this season, it is pretty badly worn, and not nearly so beautiful as the spring ones. That is particularly the case with *all* my mountain bluebirds, too, though I've tried and tried to get a real beauty. Their blue is not at all like the eastern one's, but the purest deep ultramarine you can find, and the reddish is very rich and dark.

The real thing that started me writing to you finally, is the trip up into the Sacramento Mts., in New Mexico, that I have just come down from. I was up there six days, and though I didn't find Mexican crossbills, which I had hoped for and expected, I did see, hear, and get a lot of other nice things.

The place is called Cloudcroft, and is 9000 feet up. The R.R. goes up from El Paso, and rises only a few hundred feet until it reaches the foot of the range, which is a great escarpment 4,500 feet above the plain. Then it goes back into a gulch or cañon and by winding back on itself . . . and turning 30° curves on a grade of from 4 to 10 percent, it climbs up through fertile valleys and gulches, higher and higher, into trees, orchards, farms, brushy hillsides, woods, pine forests, then mixing with junipers, till finally it brings you into the most superb primitive forests of immense yellow pine, spruce and balsam. It was like Alaska, truly, and some of the spruces, (the same Douglas spruce, too) were 8 feet through, and probably 200 feet high. The ridges were all heavily forested, and between them were beautiful open glades with rich rank grass and profusely flowering pasture weeds, and on the edges of these clearings, sharply different from the solemn darkness of the spruces, were groves of birch-like aspen trees, in which I fancied, going by, were all kinds of new Canadian birds. I got up there at about 7, got a box tent, and then went to supper. (There is a big cottage and tent establishment there, full of rather cheap people, but you can always dodge them.) When I came out, my whole sense outfit was set tingling with unexpected old-new sounds, for deep in the serene darkness of the spruces Audubon's hermit was singing his marvelous song, and robins, Uncle Abbott, were caroling up in the tops. Then soon I saw a fine old red-fronted home robin running along the path, and I was so full of happiness at being in such a lovely place, and with these almost familiar sounds coming from it, that I longed for you to be there to hear it too. That made me think, though, that you were really hearing almost the same sounds and smelling the rich damp odors of the mountain woods yourself. The next morning I went out at sunrise, and it was cold and wet and delicately fragrant, and the woods were full of sounds—some I could place by analogy, like the red-shafted flicker, the slender-billed nuthatch, the red-backed junco, and the western house wren—and some were all new, and mysteries that had to be solved. I had a few splendid surprises, too, that made me gloat childishly. One of these was when, after long debating as to whether I'd shoot one or not, I at last took a wing shot at a fine white-bellied swallow that kept flying over me and up to a big dead spruce-top where there were holes. He came twirling down, and I went up and saw before my popping eyes a superb velvety violet-green swallow! You can't imagine, from knowing a skin, what a marvelously beautiful thing this creature is when he is fresh, and his feathers stand out crisply from his body. The white is like the velvety white of a calla lily, and the head is a bronzy green, different from the rich soft blue-green of the back, and it is cut off from it by a delicate little collar of deep chinese purple which just marks the pretty little line of the neck. (Sketch) I found that they were the common swallows up there and I shot three ♂ s and a ♀ , and all but one ♂ (which was shot right through the head and bled and brained himself) came out finely. Another time, I had just shot an extreme Louisiana tanager and was wondering at him, when I heard a queer 'chink,' and saw in a dead pine, about right for a full charge of 12s, a queer erect big-headed bird. He was against a bright cloud, so I couldn't see his color. So I turned the glass on him, and saw he was greenish and very big-billed—a Mexican crossbill. I shot quick, and down he came like a stone, but when I got to him, he had changed into a ♂ evening grosbeak! He was pretty badly worn, and his white was dirty, but he was well shot and not moulting badly. From the same spot I got a ♂ Harris' woodpecker and the ♀ tanager. About the most fun of any birds up there were the pygmy nuthatches. They were common, and went in little nervous flocks, suggesting, in both notes and actions, a bunch of siskins or goldfinches. Their notes don't even suggest, in the slightest, those of the brown-head we heard in Florida. I could only get one adult, but I got you a good young one, which is rather prettier than the old one, being softer. Wild turkeys live all around on the mountains, and I found a side hill where I gathered a lot of feathers, and on my last day a man shot a fine old gobbler and I got him to let me skin it. As they don't know which turkey is found there, Dr. Merriam will be mighty glad to see this one. Bailey charged me to get all the feathers I could, as evidence; he nor I ever dreamed of my getting the whole thing. . . .

I've done more painting and drawing on this trip than ever before, and have really gotten together quite a lot of useful studies. While there is almost nothing in the way of bright or changing bill colors among these land birds, there is always a great charm and beauty about any well-shot fresh bird, and I've tried to make as many such pictures as possible, just because I like to, which is, after all, as good a reason as any.

It won't be more than ten days, probably, before I start home. I'm going to stop in Washington three or four days, then, straight home. I have thought the ground all over, and looking at things the way they seem really to be, have decided to do a set of pictures —thirty full figures and about sixty heads—of western birds I've seen, for Florence Merriam Bailey's book, *Handbook of Birds of Western North America*, to supplement Chapman's *Handbook* of eastern birds. . . . After I have been at home for a little while (you know I've been away since April 9!) if I feel that I possibly can I will come up to Dublin—and if I can't you will know that I really don't feel as if I could, but will look forward all the more eagerly to the time when you come down to Scarboro', for there must be a meeting of us as soon as possible. I don't know half about your doings that I must know, though Gra and Galla have both written me splendid letters. But it seems as if I had been in this news-less, letter-less place of inevitably lonesome gloats for years, instead of months. Home sensations and surroundings have so long given place to those of railroad hotels and our outfit, that it is only when I get a longed-for letter from my home or from yours that my senses are awakened to an understanding of the real greatness of that which they are getting along without. But by the time this gets to you I hope to be on the long, hot, dusty, but welcome journey to the east, where home, water, food, and a lot of things necessary for real living are to be found. But, really, I have been surprised and rather frightened at myself for the fatal facility with which I have fitted in with things as they have come along, to the exclusion of all my mental traditions. This is, truly, a wonderful country, and every day still brings something to marvel at—but whether I am getting blasé at mere natural wonders, or whether I am just plain old-fashioned satisfied for the time, and want to go home, I am not sure. One thing I feel all the time though, and that is that the lateness of the season and consequent scarcity and poor condition of the birds hardly seem to warrant my putting in much more time out here. A week goes by, often, without a new bird being met. There are some valuable and beautiful young plumages, and I've been getting in quite a number of them. . . .

I come to the end of this aimless ramble wondering when we are really going to be talking to each other: will it be by the Dublin fireplace, with hermits squeeing in the cool damp woods, or will Hazen just have come in from Tarrytown to eat supper before an evening such as we had last winter so often at Scarboro'?

My love to every one of you—and I find it only takes a little while in this one-sided kind of conversation to awaken all the hungry longing to be back among you that I was afraid I was getting able to put away. I think that in my next letter I can tell whether I can go to Dublin or not. I don't really know which I want most— my own home or my Thayer home; in which ever one I am, I am thinking a lot about the other, and in each one I feel the same lovely feeling of being at home. And without any feeling of dis-loyalty to my real home, which nothing in the world but your lovely way of letting me be one of you when I am with you could bring about.

Uncle Abbott, you don't mind that incoherent spurt, do you? I know that often when I am in the midst of the splendid atmos-phere of your-my house I don't seem to be awake to it—but I only need about three months away from it to show me how I miss it, and when it is eight months and bids fair to be ten—I am sure enough to warrant me in indulging in a little explosion of love for you all—which doesn't lessen in the least that which is stored up for you by these years since I came to Scarboro' in the rain and began it all.

I'm writing in the dark and killing my eyes, which I know you'd have no patience with, so I'll stop and take this over to the office. I'm coming to you as soon as I can, whether it be in Dublin or Scarboro'. There hasn't a day gone by since I've been in Texas that I haven't longed for you, to hear or see some new or long-looked-forward-to bird.

7

To the Bahamas with F.M.Chapman

....

THE AMERICAN MUSEUM OF NATURAL HISTORY, *like other great museums, serves two chief purposes: to house and arrange collections of specimens for study and to display these collections, or parts of them, to the public. Dr. Chapman spent his early museum years classifying the bird-skins already owned by the museum, but in the first decade of the twentieth century his attention, his ingenuity, and much of his effort were directed toward methods of display that would at once attract and teach the public. The device that he helped to perfect was the so-called 'habitat group,' in which mounted birds are displayed in an exact replica of their surroundings in nature. For ten years all his expeditions were made for the purpose of collecting birds, nests, eggs, and characteristic plants for the twenty-seven groups that ultimately formed the Hall of North American Birds in the museum.*

The museum party traveling to a specific site to collect and photograph would sometimes include an artist who could make colored sketches for the background. If it were Louis Fuertes he would help in shooting and skinning the birds and make field studies of their characteristic looks, with accurate color notes of the parts that change color after death: the eyes, bills, feet, and exposed skin. When they returned to the city, preparators would mount the specimens, an artist (Bruce Horsfall, C. J. Hittell, Hobart

Nichols, Carl Rungius, Walter Cox, or F. L. Jacques) would paint the background, and Louis would sometimes paint birds against the sky or in the middle distance.

There had been some correspondence with Dr. Chapman about a trip to South America in the spring of 1902, but by the time the next letter was written it was decided that they would go to the Bahama Islands instead to assemble material for a museum habitat group of tropical island birds. Mrs. Chapman was to accompany them—Louis said he would gladly sleep on the boom for the sake of having her aboard—and Mr. and Mrs. J. Lewis Bonhote. Mr. Bonhote, an English ornithologist, had been secretary to the governor of the Bahamas and had had the opportunity to learn a good deal about the haunts preferred by flamingos. Although their route had to be altered and their plans changed when Dr. Chapman became ill, they were able to see and obtain for the museum specimens of the thrilling pink and scarlet birds.

Louis wrote home only on the outward voyage of the expedition, which lasted only a few weeks, so a letter to Mr. Thayer just after his return provides his record of the experience. Later he wrote an account for Outing magazine, and Dr. Chapman included an amusing chapter on his share of the adventure in Camps and Cruises of an Ornithologist.

L.A.F. TO ABBOTT THAYER

Ithaca, N.Y., June 3, 1902.

And now the Bahamas are of the past, along with Florida, Alaska, and Texas—and the books are about closed on that score, as with the others. But there is a lot to be blown about to you, and I have a few things for you, though not as much as I hoped. For we had a little bad luck on this trip, which, while it didn't result in anything serious, made us lose the trip to Inagua, and lost to us all chance of tropic-birds, parrots, spoonbills and boobies, and some other things. I think I wrote that Chapman got the measles, and that we had to put back to Nassau just as we were nearing our journey's objective point. After that we went down to South Andros and the adjacent keys, and did well with what time was left to us—and saw noddies, sooties, royal, Cabot's, bridled, gull-billed and least terns, most of them in great numbers. All but the *least* I was able to get for you, and within a short time I will send you these and a few other things, including both plumages of the reddish egret, and some of the island land birds. There's a mocker which is mighty interesting to compare with ours, and a beautiful big blue thrush (*mimocichla*) with red legs and a big scarlet eyelid skin.

The Cabot's terns still hold their pink, and I have a little hope of being able to keep it, as you have with your roseates. Nobody seemed to know about the glorious pink in breeding Cabot's terns, but it was like looking into a tea rose to look into the loose feathers of a live or fresh bird.

A pair of Audubon's shearwaters, an island form of yellow warbler, a black-whiskered vireo, and a nice little nighthawk, *C. minor*, about complete the list of skins I brought you. They are all packed up, and will get to you about as soon as this does.

My photographs came out fairly well this time, and I'm now sorry I didn't take a lot more; four dozen was all I exposed, and I got something fairly good on all but four of them.

Now I know what you saw, with your flamingo. I never supposed anything could be as glorious as they are, and with the scarlet and pink of the American one for the pink and white of the European, I believe that I have perhaps the most exciting memories. I finally succeeded in getting one—six feet from bill to feet, when held up by the head—but he was not *very* brilliant, as his back was faded nearly white and his red neck was worn very pale. But I've seen them, in bunches of from two to seven hundred at least, and seen their nests; one colony had over 1500 nests in it. But we were too early for the breeding, and could get no photographs of the birds.

ABBOTT THAYER TO L.A.F.

[Monadnock, N. H., June, 1902.]

You are a royal giver! When I think (or rather I don't have to *think*, every part of me knows,) what each well-prepared skin means especially when one has too many to attend to. Well we have had several fine gloats since yesterday p.m. What a sight the Cabot is! What a charming extension of the lovely family of terns you have given us—the mocker is a charming bird and each other one I delight to have—the mimiocichla (is that recognizably nearly spelt!) is a most new sensation and the herons; how remarkably they keep their beauty! I never saw a reddish before and had no guess of their beauty.

I dare not begin talking of you ever coming here yet, but you know.

What a trip you have had. It crazes me to think that all the thousands of pictures are in your head and can never be in ours—

L.A.F. TO ABBOTT THAYER

Ithaca, N. Y., June 14!!

[A continuation of the previous letter to Mr. Thayer, which was not mailed until this date.]

Just see how I've neglected! While I was writing I thought I'd go over my skins and get your box started, and before I knew it it was all packed. So I sent it off, as you know, and now I'm writing to tell you about it, long after the stuff is all absorbed into your own. And yesterday I was further ashamed by getting a great bundle of Thayer letters—from you and Galla and Gra—and that after a splendid long one from Gra the day before. So now I'll tell you what I have been doing to get so occupied.

I got here about the first, and of course unpacked my birds the first thing, to see how they had stood it. Tropical skins don't always come out very well, however anxious we are that they shall. But these were in good shape. And here it makes me feel pretty small to have you appreciate so hard the little I sent you. There was no reason why you shouldn't have had as good as my best in all these skins—but you haven't. I sent you 'seconds,' or thirds, except the Cabot's and the bridled terns, which all came out well. I was a ninny about sooties, for we didn't have to shoot those at all, but could easily catch them in the bushes where they bred. When we get together I've got a vast lot to blow off about those southern terns. I studied them hard, and have a pretty crisp idea of all those we saw. . . .

It has been three years since a Thayer lightened our doors, and we are all more anxious than you know to have it happen again. So, to begin by begging, we want you to let Gra and Galla come here for at least two or three weeks to play with us—they can carry on all their work but the wood-pile—and then have Kippy go back with them for a while when they can stay here no longer. Galla, you know, has never been here, and Gra hasn't seen my stuff since '99, including all my Alaskan, Texan, and Bahama birds and those I've got between trips, and one of you *must* see it, if for no other reason, to put a stop to your thinking that I've sacrificed myself the least thing for you. . . .

We are delighted that you are up on such a wave of successful painting, and long to see your pictures. Give our love to Aunt Emma, and to every one of you, and send the kids along, *please.* It will inconvenience us *badly* not to have them.

They came. Gladys recalls the visit in the letter of November 10, 1941, from which portions have already been quoted.

We spent three marvelous weeks there in the warmth of . . . [the Fuertes'] rich hospitality. They were living in that campus home, and we slept in tents, among glorious huge dahlias in the campus gardens behind the house. We had wonderful trolley rides, and canoeing. Sometimes in the evenings . . . [Louis] would sing to his mother's accompaniments, which was a joy to hear—such songs as the old English ballad *The Golden Vanity.*

The tents were those used by the engineering students in their summer surveying camps; the trolley rides were probably to take them down the hill from the campus to the boat houses on the inlet of Cayuga Lake, where the canoes would be kept. Among their companions that summer were the children of another faculty family, Margel and Clair Gluck. Miss Gluck in a letter of 1950 wrote this reminiscence:

I have a most lovely memory of that visit, because I adored Gerald Thayer, or Gra as he was called. The lake was very high that year and all the woods on the bank flooded. Louis, Gra, and I spent days paddling through those woods in a canoe, hunting for specimens of various insect life to illustrate a book Gerald was then planning: *Concealing Coloration in the Animal Kingdom*, and I was the happy finder of the insect used in Plate 15 of the published book. They had various animal models set up in the Fuertes back yard too, showing how in deer and other creatures, the light-colored belly, which reflects the ground color, makes them so much less noticeable. . . . I don't recall *Mr.* Thayer being in Ithaca but it may be that he was there and just another 'Olympian' to me. Louis was of course just the age of whoever he was with. He is one of the first people I remember in this world, and I adored him. . . .

FRANK M. CHAPMAN TO L.A.F.

New York City, Sept. 3, 1902.

Since you assume that I had no interest whatever in your safe return to the bosom of your family, we'll let it go at that and say no more about it. Let it be understood therefore that I am no more concerned about you than you are about me and in consequence we may regard this communication in a strictly official and commercial spirit. Hence to business: Colonel Fox of the Forest Commission has just called to say he would like to have me do the proposed paper on economics, to be illustrated by twelve colored plates figuring two (2) species each, the lithographer to be chosen by me. [This was the *Seventh Annual Report of the N. Y. State Forest, Fish, and Game Commission*. It led directly to Fuertes' employment by the State for the *Birds of New York*.] Can you do them? At what price? and how soon? . . . There is need for haste and the first thing for you to do is to take your pen right in hand and give the postman a note addressed to

Yours truly

F.M.C.

I got some bully pictures in the Bahamas last spring. Sample enclosed. Perhaps if you show the proper spirit I may show you the pictures.

L.A.F. TO FRANK M. CHAPMAN

Ithaca, N. Y., Oct. 3, 1902.

With a most commendable spirit, I have been working like a clock, and have got four of your pictures about done. I shall take a couple of days' rest from them, look them over in a fresh light, and then give them a final go and send them on . . .

Honest, I've worked like a pup—in fact a little too hard, and have had to give my eyes a little rest for a day or two. So I went to Elmira and married off a classmate, and came back this morning to pump out the mines again.

Just think: I've got your work almost half done. I'm anxious to hear from you about it, and see if you approve of the way they are done.

Dr. Chapman did not entirely approve; Louis patiently and good-naturedly doctored several of the pictures and painted one entirely over. The correspondence on this transaction, which displays very well Louis' amiable combination of humility and self-confidence, was published in Dr. Chapman's 'Memories of Louis Fuertes,' in Bird-Lore, January-February, 1931.

In the meantime Mrs. Bailey's Handbook of western birds had appeared, and Louis sent a copy to the Thayers, with word that he might be coming for a visit. Mr. Thayer wrote, 'God speed your coming. How your illustrations shine out in Mrs. Bailey's book.'

GERALD THAYER TO L.A.F.

Monadnock, N. H., Jan. 16, 1903.

Nothing that you could have given me for Christmas could have come more pat to my need and desire than the *Handbook* of western birds. And Louis! Your pictures, every one of them in that book, shine out in a delicious, triumphant perfection such as I'd scarcely realized your best things could bear through the ordeal of reduction and reproduction. As Papa says, the folks whose mediocre

or fairly good books you illustrate don't at all realize what they are getting from you. And even publishers, who wish to urge the utmost claims for the value of their new bird-books, illumined by you, dare not say anything stronger in your praises than that you are well known to stand in the front rank of contemporary bird artists! I would rejoice my soul, if only I commanded a magazine, to pick such timorous mediocrity of opinion into little pieces. I would challenge them to name some of your fellow-jostlers in that broad-crowded rank! If, after some head-scratching, they named that in four title 'mutabile semper' Theton Sompson, I would laugh in their teeth and give them a lesson which they should not soon forget. To think that the common herd believes Thompson's maudlin little sweetish inaccurate sketches to be nearly of a class with your real pictures! It shall come by slow degrees into the irregularly and imperfectly working and fashion-swayed mind of the populace, that you are not only the single living bird painter worthy of the name, but by long odds the greatest that has ever lived. For, unless I have been singularly misled by the few Audubon originals I have seen, that man could never approach the excellence of your pictures. This would shock many folks, no doubt, this opinion, but times shall change: (and between you and me, Louis, I know better about these things than anybody else in the country).
. . .

Heaven grant that nothing more of sickness or disaster has come to the Fuerteses since we last heard from them. They're a very scary family, and I'll be damned if I'd like to go two months without having news of them. Of course your father's delightful letter, so recently made, proves that no new catastrophe had come to you people up to a few days ago. . . .

Professor Fuertes had resigned as dean and director of the College of Civil Engineering in November, 1902, and he died on January 16, 1903. A tablet to his memory was placed in Sage Chapel, with this citation:

In Memory of Estevan Antonio Fuertes, Professor of Civil Engineering from 1873 and Director of the College of Civil Engineering from 1890 to 1902. In him were blended authority urbanity and a love of justice. He was expert in letters and science beloved of his pupils esteemed by his colleagues.

Born May 10, 1838

Died January 16, 1903

Louis did not go to the Thayers now, or later in the spring, as he was hoping to attend the A.O.U. meetings to be held in California in May.

ABBOTT THAYER TO L.A.F.

[Monadnock, N. H., Mar. 4,] 1903.

Of course I must be glad you are to go to California but the fear it lessens our chance to have you here is a cloud over me—we want you so much. How good it would be if you three could spend the summer here! And as for special reasons, Gerald has told you; we want you to come in with us on our book [*Concealing Coloration in the Animal Kingdom*], and pull us through by doing in one week, some time, three or four beautiful pictures. Gra's inimitable ones take him six months each! Three of yours with their own elements of superiority, your look of *life* and personal character that as far as I know no one has equaled, will take you about a week!

The A.O.U. met in San Francisco, California, in May of 1903, and Louis went west with Dr. Chapman on a train full of ornithologists. Following the meetings, the journey became a museum collecting trip, lasting until July 14. Some account of it is to be found in Chapman's Camps and Cruises and in 'A Note on the Prairie Falcon' by L.A.F. in The Condor for March-April, 1905. Louis' letters were not saved, and his note-books contain only dates, names of places and lists of birds.

Going west the train took the southern route, with a three-day stop at the Grand Cañon of the Colorado River. In June Louis and Dr. Chapman went to the famous bird islands, the Farallones, and they returned for longer visits to two unique collecting grounds that they had had a glimpse of in company with the larger group of ornithologists: Pacific Grove in Monterey County, and Los

Baños in the interior valley, where irrigation ditches had attracted many kinds of water birds. They spent nearly two weeks at Glen Alpine near Lake Tahoe and visited Pyramid Lake, Nevada, where pelicans were nesting, and where Louis found the prairie falcon, the subject and the setting of several of his best bird portraits.

ARROTT THAYER TO L.A.F.

[Monadnock, N. H., August, 1903.]

Just a word at the moment least suitable for me to write. What a faithful Louis you are to still for ever share so generously the booty of each trip you make!

The prairie falcon alone were enough delight—he goes so finely into our falcons—a queer half kestrel, half gyrfalcon, half peregrine! And the gull—I didn't know there was such a thing.

During part of this summer Mr. E. W. Nelson was in Ithaca writing on Mexican birds, and Louis was working with him, preparing illustrations for his text. Louis was never satisfied with the pictures, as they were made from museum skins of birds he had not seen in the field. They remain to this day part of a large collection of Fuertes originals, most of which have never been published, owned by the Fish and Wildlife Department, successor to the Biological Survey.

8

Engagement and Marriage

·······················

E‌AGLESMERE IS A *tiny lake set high in the hemlock-forested hills
of northern Pennsylvania. At the northern end of the lake is
a sandy bathing-beach, at the southern a group of comfortable summer cottages and hotels, with laurel-bordered paths going through
the woods on the east and west from one end to the other. Louis'
characteristic description of the place, from a letter of 1906, is this:*

I'm up here in the noble old woods of Sullivan County where
ravens croak and hermits sing o'evenings and fourteen (identified)
warblers breed and pileated woodpeckers and horned owls whoop
it up. Great place; winter wrens and juncos too.

*Louis was often invited to the Eaglesmere cottage of Mr. and
Mrs. John M. Young of Williamsport, Pennsylvania. Mr. and Mrs.
Young were most hospitable, and the eight children of the house—
five boys and three girls—had been friends of Louis' since college
days. Other old friends went to Eaglesmere, too; Mr. and Mrs.
Dudley Finch of Ithaca rented one of the cottages for thirteen
years during the girlhood of Mrs. Finch's daughters by her first
marriage, Harriet, Louise, and Margaret (Madge) Sumner and their
younger half-sister Katharine Finch. These young people with some
other cottagers and their own house guests formed a close and
happy fellowship.*

The summer colony enjoyed a quiet vacation. They came to settle down for the whole summer, bringing servants with them, or perhaps taking their meals at one of the hotels. Their leisure was marked only by the occupations they devised—tennis, golf, brief regular periods of swimming (it was thought dangerous to stay in for more than twenty minutes), walking in the woods, and a good deal of boating. They spent hours in canoes and row-boats tied to overhanging boughs at the edge of the lake, reading, chatting, the ladies doing embroidery. Besides being small, the lake is shallow, and often calm enough so that they could fasten groups of boats together and have their supper on the lake. When daylight was gone and the moon rose, they would sing.

Here in August, 1903, Louis and Madge announced their engagement. They had been friends for a good many years, and hoped to marry, but because of the illness and death of Professor Fuertes and the uncertainty of Louis' somewhat queer profession, they had not been able to make their plans until now.

During this fall and winter Louis seems to have stayed at home ('working hard is my present and past way of spending my time,' he wrote to Dr. Chapman). Part of his work was to keep an eye on the building of his house, which was to be ready for them by summer.

They were quietly married on the second day of June, 1904, and took ship for Jamaica, B.W.I., on a wedding journey that rapidly became an ornithological collecting trip, somewhat to the bride's dismay, although she thinks now that she should have known what to expect.

They were both good sailors, but she recalls discomfort at having to sit on the captain's right at table and watch him eat his favorite meal; a baked potato which he scooped out of its shell and covered with olive oil.

As soon as they touched land, she says, Louis was off after birds like a shot, and she hardly saw him again. He found the botanist William A. Maxon collecting plants for the National Museum (Dr. Chapman remarked that Louis everywhere found old friends), and they at once joined forces. Madge and Louis went up the mountain on mule-back to Mandeville, by a trail that overhung space, where the mules stumbled through thunder storms, and quaint wooden crosses marked the spots whence other travelers had not returned. If it had been possible she would have stayed at Mandeville for ever in order to avoid the trip back down. Mr. Maxon joined them there.

The men spent their mornings collecting and their afternoons skinning the day's bag of birds—in the hotel bedroom, the bride choosing to be absent. She thought they might emerge for tea, but they were far too busy; let the tea be sent in to them. On one occasion the bride entered to fetch the tea tray. Louis, both hands be-gooed with the insides of the little tody he was preparing, bent over to pick up with his teeth the last bit of cookie. Madge: 'Louis! What are you doing?' Mr. Maxon, enormously amused: 'Do you always eat that?' Louis, nonchalant: 'Why it's the best part of the whole bird!' After this, the tray was left in the room.

This was Mrs. Fuertes' first and last field trip. She did not enjoy camping, shooting, or skinning birds, but stronger than her distaste for this was her conviction that the presence of a woman hampered the collector's activity. She felt that she—or any woman—was a nuisance to the serious naturalist who was willing to work without the comforts a lady in those times required; she observed that some of the wives who went on expeditions were in fact their husbands' chaperones and she scorned placing herself in that position. Before many years were past she had young children to keep her at home, but she always encouraged Louis to go. She knew how he loved and needed to do it; she told commiserating friends that she was always glad to see him go and glad to see him come back.

F. M. Chapman to L.A.F.

Nassau, Bahamas, June 27, 1904.

You have been much in my mind, dear Boy, both because of the events in your life, in which, of course, we take the deepest interest, and because of the assurance that you would learn of our doings not only because we did them, but for themselves. As we sweltered in the 'swashes' of Andros we have fancied you in the delights of Jamaica's mountains. Let us hope your surroundings, wherever you and yours have been, were all you deserve to have them—little, then, would be left to fill your heart's desire.

As for us, much, much anon. In the meantime, on the eve of sailing for home I send you this line for I know that three months' dammed-up correspondence will give no opportunity for social intercourse, by mail, for weeks to come. By the same token, this is the first attempt I have made at this same kind of converse since leaving Florida—so wholly have I shaken the responsibilities of letter writing that even its pleasures have been neglected.

I've a long tale to tell of disappointments unspeakable and success undreamed of—the latter, fortunately, last. This only need I say now, that I have lived among flamingos as a flamingo, having a nest of my own amid a colony of nearly 2,000 occupied adobe cones. Over my nest, to be sure, was Chapman's patent umbrella blind concealing its occupant from my neighbors sitting patiently on their eggs, or feeding their young six feet from my lens. Such an experience as no man ever had or even imagined, so potent in its mind-disturbing possibilities, that it made sleep out of the question and brought me so near the verge of nervous exhaustion I was forced to abandon all study of the birds for two days—yea—I could not have forced myself to go near them. Sixty-three flamingo skins (sixty skinned by your aunt) from the newly hatched, exquisitely downy chicks to adults (of which two shots, at the end of our stay, killed thirteen,) a series of embryos, three nests (twice the weight, because water-soaked, of those taken before) twelve dozen photographs, and page after page of notes make the result of the week we lived with the birds. And all this at Grassy Creek—(or near it.) Which we entered from the west side of the island. We were encamped fifteen miles from our schooner, and every day and every night it rained as it loves to rain here in the summer. May 17 to June 10 gave us 20.26 inches downfall of the wettest water heaven ever dropped on earth. One afternoon yielded six inches, a gentle dew most surely.

I live now on the development of my plates and from them some landscapist as yet unknown or unchosen, and yourself will paint, I trust, a background which will do justice to the great pink bird with its background of blue water and green coppet. But I cannot go into details for once I begin where would I end. Suppose I should tell you how the 3,000 superbly dignified birds with much blowing of trumpets marched down upon me, surrounded me, *absorbed* me in color and clarionings; or how this pink and red and black-garbed army suddenly took to the air and swept overhead with a clanging of horns and rush of pinion terrifying in its effect? It would be words only, mere words, and you would have no more idea of the scene itself than my two years of dreaming gave me of the fortune which has been mine.

When you'll see these lines neither you nor I know, but at any rate I send you this Bahaman breath before another clime dispels the presence which has affected me more powerfully than any scene among the creatures we love ever has or ever will.

L.A.F. to F. M. Chapman

Ithaca, N. Y., July 19, 1904.

I was up at the Thayers' when your letter with the proof came— and I assure you I was heap thrilled. Man, what you have been doing! My poor country blood boiled with not envy exactly, but a longing to share with you the sensing of those pink and scarlet regiments of on-rushing trumpeters.

There is only one way: Madge and I must come across you some-where and have a half-a-day's talk with you.

We landed on the 11th, went to Dublin for two days, and then home, where we have been getting the house in order. It is a lovely little place, and though we are still far from settled, it is sweet beyond our imaginings to be living in our own little house, sur-rounded by our own things and the atmosphere of a little world all our own about us. You and Auntie must contrive some way to come and see us.

I can't begin to write you anything about our trip—the long-tailed emerald hummers, the solitaires and lovely mountain doves, the fine *merulae* etc. *ad lib*—your wonderful flaming experience and the Thayers' magnificent Trinidad work make my little puddle of half-done work dwindle sadly, but there are many [palliations] and the main thing now is to see you.

I must run. She's calling me and there may be one egg shy or the fire may not be drawing!!

We're as happy as a kid with a new toy: truly the fun is just commencing—and we both send you all our love and a double-ended welcome back home.

The house into which Louis and Madge were settling, and in which they lived all their married life, is a three-story shingle and clapboard building on the corner of Thurston and Wyckoff avenues, to the north of Fall Creek gorge and the Cornell campus. It is to be distinguished from countless other modest houses built in the eastern part of the United States during the first decade of the twentieth century only by the presence of a very large wild cherry tree in the front yard and by the fact that it is a double house. Louis' sister Kippy planned it so; Madge and Louis were to live in one side, she herself, with her mother, on the other. Kippy and her mother lived there only a few years, however, before moving to a farm in Orange county, leaving their half-house to be rented for the next thirty years or so.

It was a pleasant neighborhood. University people were in the few other houses that had been built on these new streets, then hardly more than roads enclosing fields. Next door lived the young professor of Latin, Charles Love Durham, with his family. After breakfast Charlie would come out onto his back steps with his cup of coffee and the cigarette that was not tolerated in the house; 'Missy' Sterett, wife of the professor of Greek, would trail over from her house in an old red dressing sacque; Nikoline Brauner, the 'little maid from Norway' of Celia Thaxter's poem (her husband was Olaf Brauner, artist and teacher) came across the field, her two braids hanging almost to the ground; Louis and Madge came out of their back door, and for a half an hour or so, before the day's work separated them, there was neighborly society of much warmth and fun.

: 86 :

Brandt's Cormorant

Rose Breasted Grosbeak

Louis Agassiz Fuertes

ROSE-BREASTED GROSBEAK. Ithaca, May 12, 1905

That first year (only) Louis had a garden of flowers and vegetables. One day Mr. Franklin C. Cornell, from whose garden Louis as a boy had regularly taken melons the night before they ripened, drove by in his smart horse-drawn trap. He pulled up on seeing Louis working in his garden, and called out, 'Planted any melons, Louis?' 'No,' Louis returned, 'they don't mature in this climate.' Mr. Cornell was laughing as he drove away.

L.A.F. TO ABBOTT THAYER

Ithaca, N. Y., Sept. 1, 1905.

My dear Uncle Abbott and all my dear Thayers, your Louis is the happiest being in this good world! Our little son came into it at a little past midnight, and my Madge is doing finely and the boy is a splendid lusty fellow, and as good and contented with his lot as if he'd picked it out for himself. I can't write more than a little note, as I have so many things to do, but I want you all to know of my great good news and rejoice with me. Kippy will tell you all about him when she comes up—in the meantime, be glad with us; for we are content beyond words.

Until the spring of 1907 Louis' new experience was that of being husband and father. He drew on the past for his painting, which included a portrait of the prairie falcon and a series of plates of North American warblers for Bird-Lore (later used in Dr. Chapman's book on the subject) and for the illustrated lectures he began about this time to undertake. He was a successful speaker, and although the lectures never added much to his income, the travel and social intercourse they entailed were sufficiently refreshing to him to make them worth his while.

L.A.F. TO VERNON BAILEY

Ithaca, N. Y., Nov. 6, 1905.

The *Fauna* [*North American Fauna* #25, *Biological Survey of Texas, U.S.D.A., 1905*] came a few days ago, and I have been enjoying it a whole lot. Every few pages I hit something that yanks back a whole horizon of unremembered familiarity: a bunch of rangers eyeing us suspiciously at our various peaceful jobs, the Ord Mts. sprinkled with black junipers as we came up to Alpine, the red dust of Terlingua and the mercury mines, the fragrant cottonwoods at the R[io] G[rande] cañon at Boquillas—and a bunch of other happy days and nights—among the best those when you scorned me for sleeping in the open in the glorious Chisos nights. . . . I'm coming to Washington for about three days to talk to you, Drs. M[erriam], F[isher] and others, and to get some slides of our Texas and Alaskan trip et al. I'm going to give some talks this winter and want to make good on my descriptions.

L.A.F. TO JOHN P. YOUNG

Ithaca, N. Y., Nov. 8, 1905.

I have about finished your picture, and I hope the subject is one that will please you. It is a prairie falcon (*Falco mexicanus*) that I got two summers ago on the concretion island in Pyramid Lake, Nevada . . . This pair of falcons had their hang-out on the peak of the main island, and brought their prey of quail, sage grouse, etc. from the mainland, from one to seven miles distant. It is in the heart of the Pahiute reservation, in western Nevada, and the Mts. in the distance are the Sierra Nevada about opposite Eldorado County, Cal., near Truckee. . . .

I want to take it with me, if you are willing, to New York, to exhibit at the Am. Ornithologists' Union Congress next week, as it is pictorially my most successful effort 'up till yet.' I have done it in a very high key, and if you can give it a place in a full strong light you will be best pleased with the result, as I have tried to give it the full clarity and brilliancy of the desert sunshine, and it needs a good light to bring this out.

Thank you, Pokoto, for this order—the first from any of my 'contemporaries.' If the picture pleases you as much as the order did me we will be well satisfied all around.

In another letter to Mr. Young, written December 4, 1905, Louis says, 'Abbott Thayer, to whom I showed the picture, said it was my top notch, which I give you, not for your money's worth, but as it may interest you as coming from a sure enough artist.'

L.A.F. to F. M. Chapman

Ithaca, N. Y., Dec. 15, 1905.

I have at last got my slides together and 'try them on the dog' at our Town and Gown Club to-night. Hope they go along all right. I have about four bird pictures to three locality slides—ranging mostly through Alaska and the S.E. It is fun coloring the slides, and I've become quite proficient.

Gerald Thayer to L.A.F.

Monadnock, N. H., Nov. 4, 1906.

About our 'book' I don't like to talk. To me it has the smell of a shameful carcass and I doubt its ultimate triumph even. No fault of Papa's, but of mine—or, in part, the work of fate. But cheer up, the worst is yet to come! Things stand so: the text, left for finished when I went south last spring, and then re-read and deeply slashed into by Papa, has now at last been smoothed out again, from end to end. Work toward this result has been intersprinkled with all sorts of trafficking for pictures, with fruits of sad smallness in proportion to the time and labor spent. . . .

New comradeship has wrapped me around here, and I do not often keenly yearn toward you and Kippy—for the heart of the beast is filled too full, and strained and scratched and buffeted too much, right here at home. . . .

Are things the same with you, Louis? Yes, they must be, or even further gone toward forgetfulness of the fine faraway days of our upbringing—mine by you and yours in some degree by me. Because to you have come far bigger, newer, and more heart-seizing changes of life-experience. But see, my Louis: all that good past time is built in adamantine bricks into our foundations: where we stand to-day and look around us, with our heads not near together, and often hidden one from another by things that stay and things that flow between, we stand by virtue of that past we lived and made together: And I believe we are well-based, don't you? Besides, man, the world is young yet, even for you and me so weather-beaten and be-mossed. . . .

All well here—Galla in high feather, and a great painter.

: 89 :

Hiram Corson [Professor of English Literature at Cornell University, 1870-1903] to L.A.F.

Ithaca, N. Y., Nov. 10, 1906.

Most hearty thanks for the bird picture, which I value highly in itself, and doubly so as a product of your sympathetic art.

I have often said that you realize what Keats says in his lines entitled 'Where's the Poet?'

'Tis the man who with a bird,
Wren or eagle, finds his way to
All its instincts.

In you the scientific and the poetical are united. The picture is a lovely birthday present to a young bird-eyed old man.

F. M. Chapman to L.A.F.

New York City, March 4, 1907.

I am planning a trip in June and part of July into Assiniboia, for the ducks and general marsh birds of that region, and to the summits of the Canadian Rockies for the ptarmigan and leucosticte and anything else I can get on my way up.

If you can arrange to accompany me on these trips, I can guarantee the payment of all your expenses, asking in return only a few water-color sketches of plants with some little study of sky effects or of the general tone of the landscape.

During these years when they were much together Dr. Chapman often signed himself 'Tudy,' derived from F. M. Chapman 2d, and addressed Louis as his 'little pet' in reference to some joke they shared.

L.A.F. to F. M. Chapman

Ithaca, N. Y., Mar. 6, 1907.

My dear Tudy, what can I tell you !!??!! Was I ever intended to deny myself such a chance? I doubt it. First of all, before I forget it, here's a good trip to Florida for you, and best remembrances to your mother, whom I suppose you will see.

Well, there are difficulties, of course, and they may be insurmountable. I can't, in any case, answer you now. But as I am not, by your confession, side-tracking anybody else by my demurrer, I will say that I will consider it. (Probably every night till I go or don't go.) I am thinking of Maine for my family this summer, and if we go it will be in early July. My wife's family are taking a house at *Christmas Cove* and I think we will join them. It resolves itself into a matter of time, principally, and hangs largely on the amount I can accomplish by June. I have done fine this winter, and my streak continues. I will say that it is strongly possible I may go with you. That's all I dare say now, but Gawd, Toody, I'd be a good boy for a while, you bet, and I *do* need a freshening trip, and this one would largely fill my gaps, too. . . .

The eagle group [at the museum] is a hypnotizing marvel. *Glorious.*

Yours, my dear Sir, by gosh.

P.S. I go to Ossining one day every month, to give a young boy [Courtenay Brandreth] a boost toward bird painting, and the next time I come (when you're in N. Y.) I'll make it a day more and see you. Mrs. is very anxious to have me go with you, and you bet I want to if I can be sure that she and the small package are well looked out for, and that I can be far enough along on my job to warrant it. I'll work for it, you can be sure, as this thing bites harder and harder as I think it over. I'm keen to get out an atlas and go over the ground with you. And I'm mighty grateful to you for thinking of me in this connection.

Louis did go with Dr. Chapman that summer to the prairies of Saskatchewan and the mountains of Alberta. There is some account of their experience in Chapman's Camps and Cruises. The next letters are chosen from those Louis wrote to his own family in Maine.

L.A.F. to Mrs. Fuertes

On the way to Winnepeg,
June, 1907.

We are spinning along over a boulder-clad country through which fires have burned, leaving the old stubs and boles of birch and pine and fir—a graveyard some 500 miles long. Passed a few towns with

Indian suburbs—about forty miles apart they average here. By early afternoon we will be along the north shore of Lake Superior (now at about Lake Suberior?) Chapman has one of his hard headaches today, and all of them are asleep but me and I most am. This writing, however, is due to neither sleep, nor heavy drink—nor yet neglected opportunities, early indiscretions, nor inability to learn—but to the seasick swinging and swaying of the twenty-car train.

We get to Winnepeg tomorrow (Sunday) a.m. about 9, leave about 10, and arrive in Maple Creek, Saskatchewan, at about 7 Monday morning.

We had a fine time in Ottawa, and spent most of the a.m. at the museum with Dr. McCown, author of *Birds of Canada and the Provinces*, best book on the north half of North America.

This country is very backward. Pussy willows just coming out, and the leaves, even on the birch and poplars are not yet started—alders just putting out catkins.

Little lakes, scrubby half-grown woods unlimited, of close-grown spruce, fir, pine, birch, and poplar, with alders in the swampy boggy hollows; no high hills. Saw one loon and a gull, and two or three ducks.

Maple Creek, Sask., June 13, 1907.

Yesterday I wrote you a hurrying scrawl while the train was being late, and now I am at a somewhat similar stunt, only with a little more time. C. and I went down to Crane Lake (20 miles east) to look up conditions there, and found them so fine that we are going back to-day for a stay of three or four days. Out twenty miles north, the other day, to Big Stick Lake; we found an island about a third of a mile out in the lake, absolutely white with pelicans, bunched closer than I've ever seen them, and nesting (eggs just hatching). Also about five-hundred ring-billed gulls (new to me) and a great number of ducks, and about thirty geese, hanging around the lake. There were a number of 'swan grebe'—as big as ducks, and the most graceful creatures I ever have seen. . . .

We are very comfortable here, and it is interesting as a place. The English 'occupation' of it makes it have quite a different character from the similar towns in the U.S., and it is generally about half full of Cree Indians, who still dress picturesquely and wear blankets. They are not on a reservation, but still live their own way, camping along the creek.

The prairie here is most beautiful, and the only unchanged prairie I have ever seen. Once away from the town (and that is only a good long spit) and you're in it: not a tree nor bush anywhere, but rolling gentle rises in the land—a bunch of horses now and then, or cattle or sheep, and right near town you can sometimes see real wild antelope. We saw three by Crane Lake as we came through on the train, and the ladies and Frank stalked a band of thirty yesterday, from town! and got up to good seeing distance—five hundred yards or so. The sandhills still have a few deer, and prairie grouse. Gophers are everywhere, and mosquitoes are worse than I have ever seen them anywhere. Right out on the prairie, a thousand miles from anywhere, you couldn't tell the color of a horse they're so thick on him. But they are not very vicious biters, though they get to you all right. We wear nets when they are real bad, and 'citronella,' a juice that C. has, will keep them at a safe humming distance.

Great black quaking thunderstorm last night, soon after we got in, of which there is an ominous hangover this a.m.

Last winter was terrible here, and everybody lost a big slice out of their cattle and sheep. Two young fellows had twenty-six hundred sheep in November, in fine shape, and one big blizzard left them with only six hundred . . . and these were cleaned up later by another; no feed, no shelter, and they just froze—cattle die in bands of fifty to two hundred, and their bones and carcasses lie everywhere in the sandhills, where the coyotes are still feasting.

The prairie birds—western meadowlarks, two new (to me) beautiful longspurs, and the pallid horned lark, are delightful and busting with music. As there are no trees they all have to do flight songs, and they are the loveliest you ever heard. The air now is constantly tinkling with frosty songs of the longspurs and lark, or the great bursting song of the western meadowlark (you'd never guess it was the same kind of a bird) and the ground is all green and sprinkled with flowers—pale yellow 'loco' (a lobelia), a buttercup-yellow

clover, like a lupin, wild cyclamen, white star flowers, and a lot I
of course don't know at all. Roses are just putting out leaves. . . .
I didn't suppose I could get to a place with so much of brand new-
ness for me.

Good-bye, let me know all the news, and be good to my wife for
me—

*There are no letters from the mountains, but the men did find
the ptarmigan they were after, birds so confident in their amazingly
protective coloration that they were easy to approach—provided they
could be seen in the first place. In August Louis joined his family
in Maine, where he was surrounded by still different kinds of bird
life.*

L.A.F. TO F. M. CHAPMAN

Maine, Aug. 17, 1907.

Fine up here. Quite a few birds I'm glad to get into, especially
H_2O sorts. Arctic terns, puffins, and several unidentifiable (from
native descriptions) ones on the out islands. We're going to take a
day in a big sloop and get busy with them. Good chance for fall
shore birds (and young).

GERALD THAYER TO L.A.F.

Monadnock, N. H., (!) Aug. 28, 1907.

Louis, you scoundrel pup, explain yourself!—I can't understand
it—though I doubt not I might do the same and worse in your
shoes ('Wa-wa,' the whopping red-and-blue macaw, won't stand
for any more writing, and I must put him to bed before I go on.
He's climbed down my arm and begun tearing up papers on the
table, and snatching at my pencil with his enormous, savage bill.—
Now he's gone back to perch on my shoulder, and behaves more
calmly—though ruffling up his head-feathers and wildly bobbing
his head, and muttering—I left him out in the too-cold evening air,
and just now found him shivering on his perch, so I thought he'd
better stay by the fireside a while before going to his cold night
quarters in the cow-shed. Now once again he's getting excitedly im-
patient at my intense preoccupation, and trying all manner of tricks

of voice and gesture in order to make me wake up and attend to him. Pretty soon, I see, he'll bite too savagely in his impatience, and then I shall have to quit—A most amazing human-like, big-natured comrade is this cuss—if one made the most of him one would learn marvels of comparative psychology.)

x x x x x x x x x x x x

Now then, to business—Wa-wa's in bed. The point is this: You've been away in the far N.W., and since then you've been at home in Ithaca, and now you're in Maine and to get to Maine you must almost have dodged around us in the dark— Furthermore, and worse, your not writing suggests that you intend to dodge around us in the dark again on your way home— That is all natural, *perhaps*, and it *may* even be excusable, and possibly even necessary, but it's nevertheless damnable and disgusting. You have pretty much lost the sense of our live, carnal, immediate existence, no doubt, as I have, except in seldom moods, of *yours*, but the unfortunate and inexorable truth is that we're *here*, warm and alive and kicking, as of old, after all this time—and I say that Maine is too near for decency—too all-fired near for you to come to us and these old stamping-grounds of yours and mine without being pulled into the vortex. Explain yourself—I've put you to the pain of cooking up some pretty husky eloquence in begging off, at the very worst. Kippy betrayed you—sent me your address, because I asked her to: and the card I sent her had to be forwarded from Ithaca to *her* Maine perch.

Look you, Papa's been in England, and is now, we suppose, on the ocean, and will be home in a few days. We have room and food here for two brace of Louis-and-families, not to mention one solitary example—room upon room, and all Monadnock to wander on, and a wonderful macaw to please the boy (and his father) and boats and folks and quietness for Madge—Over and above all things, there's us, practically the same old us, happy and busy enough, and extraordinarily eager to break the shameful crust of temporal aloofness which has formed for us around our Louis.

Come, because we've nothing to talk about that can't be kind of squinted into a blink of manful mutual understanding among blueberries in the early autumn sunlight, or lengthened out into sweet, casual, fragmentary narrative and questioning when uncalled impulse and occasion prompt. Come, because we've nothing much to show you, and love you very much— Nothing has changed for me in the heart's desire matter about which I once wrote you such a sorry outburst—but if you expect to find me a solemn and cadaverous lover you are savagely mistook.

This is my name, cojoined with my address:

Gerald H. Thayer,

Monadnock, N. H.

'Monadnock' is the name of a mountain which stands very near us. The town we live in is called Dublin, 'Monadnock' being the name also of a small post-office barely a mile from us. My father, Abbott H. Thayer, is an artist, and has also devoted his attention to the study of protective coloration among birds and other animals. I want you and him to meet—I think you would find you had much in common.

This message crossed one from Louis. announcing his plan to visit the Thayers.

GERALD THAYER TO L.A.F.

Monadnock, N. H., Aug. 31, 1907.

Aha Louis, you wrote too, after all. So you are coming, alone, leaving Madge and the boy in Maine! I wish we could see them too, but it makes a great halleluja to hear that you are coming.

9

To the Magdalen Islands with L. C. Sanford

N A LETTER dated February 10, 1908, Louis wrote to Vernon Bailey: 'My calendar stole all my fall and winter up to just now. I lost nothing but my time, as I had no money in it, but I also took out nothing.' This was a calendar of Game Birds, composed of thirteen large paintings by L.A.F., handsomely reproduced in color by the Beck Engraving Company of Philadelphia. On the cover was a ruffed grouse in snow, and each month had its picture. Because of the color reproduction the calendars had to sell for a high price. Louis was no merchandiser and did not make money on them in 1907 or the following year when they were re-issued. He was able to sell most of the originals from which the calendar was printed, however, so the time spent was not all lost to him.

The spring of 1908 brought an opportunity to go to the Cape Sable region of southern Florida with Dr. Chapman to collect materials for a habitat group of Cuthbert Rookery birds, including the beautiful and already rare roseate spoonbills. On the trip they did see and photograph, but they did not shoot any specimens of spoonbills in this location where the species was nearing extinction. It was not until 1910 in Mexico that Louis was able to add to his own collection a series of these birds.

He was at home and at work during the summer and fall; his second child, a daughter, Mary, was born on November 28.

It was during this year that Dr. Chapman's Camps and Cruises of an Ornithologist appeared, illustrated with a profusion of photographs. Louis was present in several of the pictures and most of the experiences, and he responded to Dr. Chapman's gift copy of the book with a hope for more camps and cruises expressed in a burst of the foolish doggerel he was fond of composing. They did have more, indeed the best were still ahead. In the years between, when they stayed at home, the expeditions were never far out of mind. Sometimes Louis wrote of the joys of their travels when there were no definite plans a-foot ('Any time the raving bug of fancy tickles your wander-ganglion, put the resulting effervescence in an envelope, that I may co-froth') or sometimes plans were made for trips that did not materialize, as in this letter from the spring of 1909 about a suggestion that they go to North Carolina.

L.A.F. TO F. M. CHAPMAN

Ithaca, N. Y., May 18, 1909.

You beast, when do you go? How long? How much? What for?

I'm frightfully busy, with *piles* of important work, no money, and a flatly demoralized off-streak when a warbler song makes me squirm, and the woods alive and crawling with warblers. That's *some* squirmin'!

If you really want me to go, why didn't you let me know soon enough? It takes some time to desert one's family and duty and feloniously leave home behind for purely hoggish glutting of bird joys before. I'd naturally shed my few lingering hairs to do it, but I don't see how I can get ready on this short notice. Vol. I [*Birds of New York*] about to be pulled off the presses, all but six plates . . . late June is set to mark appearance of Vol. I.

I have three large pictures: gulls and big wave, imperial woodpecker and golden eagle, to do right soon, besides about a dozen Biol[ogical] Survey pictures of sorts, and God knows when I'll get decently in shape to pull them off.

Your warbler book is better every time I look something up in it.

Often a letter would end with a sketch depicting some of the pain, much of the joy of their collecting trips, as here, from a letter of the same spring.

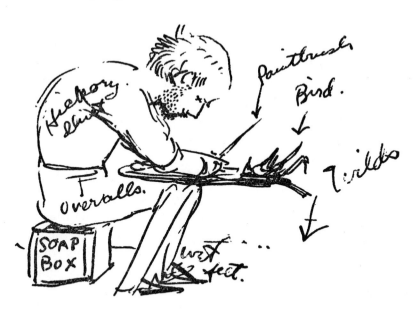

Louis' trips to enlarge his own experience and complete the collection of bird skins and field studies necessary to his profession were not always taken in company with Dr. Chapman or under the auspices of the American Museum. One of the ornithological sights Louis had not yet seen was that of the colonies of sea birds on the Magdalen and other islands in the gulf of the St. Lawrence River, though the museum already had a 'Bird Rock' group from this locale prepared in 1899. Fortunately for Louis, Dr. and Mrs. Leonard C. Sanford of New Haven invited him to visit the Magdalenes with them in August, 1909. Dr. Sanford, a physician and collector of birds, had met Dr. Chapman and become interested in the museum earlier in the year and as all ornithologists know, came to be (in R. C. Murphy's phrase) a patron of ornithology in the grand sense. He persuaded Frederick F. Brewster of New Haven to finance the South American circumnavigation of Rollo H. Beck and to order for the study in his mansion then being built twenty-four oil paintings by L. A. Fuertes; he persuaded Harry Payne Whitney to give the Whitney Memorial Wing of the American Museum and to finance the Whitney South Sea expedition. At his suggestion Mrs. Whitney and her children purchased for the museum the Rothschild collection of 280,000 skins of birds of the world. . . .

Beginning now, Louis was for the rest of his life one of Dr. Sanford's dearest friends. Their companion on this trip, William Spencer Murray, was an electrical engineer for the New York, New Haven and Hartford Railroad, and in Dr. Sanford's words a very jolly man.

L.A.F. TO MRS. FUERTES

The Magdalen Islands, Aug. 17, 1909.

It seems a week, although it is only about three days, since I wrote you. For we have been to the Bird Rocks, and returned, and had a glorious time. I should have felt that I had missed the whole point of the trip—as I should have—if I hadn't had this trip, and now that it is over I feel as if I'd done a big week's work, and well repaid for it. For, though only there two days, we made up some twenty-five birdskins, nearly all of large sea birds, including every species on the rocks, and I also painted studies of every one that showed anything strange or interesting.

We left on the schooner *Amazon*, and as soon as we were all aboard and the anchor up she got becalmed, and it took from 10 a.m. to about 5 p.m. to go four miles (or less) to House Harbor after the lightkeeper. We slept (?) that night on deck, and toward midnight a fair breeze came up and landed us at Bird Rock at 9 of the next a.m. I can't describe the rocks to you, but the excitement of seeing thousands of great gannets nesting on the ledges, and hearing their croaking and the screaming of the myriad Kittiwake gulls was exhausting, and I found it very bewildering to know where to commence. But we did commence, and I soon had my day's work staked out. I painted all morning and skinned all afternoon and evening. Same the next day, and yesterday at 10 a.m. we were ready to take the schooner back to Grindstone, and did so. Same performance as going—no sooner had we boarded than the wind died, and we lazily rolled on the swell in the sun—all day long, and had

Great Blue Heron. Ithaca, N.Y. Oct 30, 1908.
(Geo Foote)

GREAT BLUE HERON. Ithaca, Oct. 30, 1908

YOUNG HORNED GREBE. Magdalen Islands, Aug. 31, 1909

to spend the night aboard again. As she is just a common dirty old freight schooner, full of bugs, we all stayed on deck, and slept more or less. I think I have the best, by long odds, of the sleeping proposition, and tried hard to make Mrs. Sanford take the mattress, but she wouldn't, spending the night in her clothes in a deck chair.

The crowd wears awfully well: Sanford's a corker, quiet and very self-contained, and the essence of unostentatious generosity, insisting on either Murray or me taking the best blinds, giving me his best birds, and evidently enjoying it. Mrs. S. is a real sport, refusing to take any 'special treatment,' and taking everything as it comes without a murmur, and behaving quite like a man—which makes it bully to have her around. Murray is six feet six inches of good nature and optimism; there's never any friction, everybody does as he likes without apology or explanations and the busy days go by only too fast. Just now I feel a little the worse for wear, for I've had several days of unremitting work, and nights of only half comfort.

Grindstone, the Magdalenes,
Sept. 7, 1909.

We drove, Sunday afternoon, with one tent and an outfit for just the three men for one night and day, across the island and along the north beach—about six miles—and got there about 7 p.m. Wind blowing great guns. Sent Isadore back, with instructions to return at 11 next day. This was so that we could catch the early shooting Monday a.m., as the tide was figured to be high in the lagoon at about 5:30, and then the birds fly. Well, we finally got the tent up, and the beds down and a fire going, and had some birds from yesterday's kill for late supper, when the lantern melted apart and left us in the black dark about thirty minutes after we lit her, and I sat down in the frying pan full of warm grease while Murray was driving tent pegs with a can of peaches—nothing else being findable. Finally we got turned in, and all were resting as well as the flapping, tugging tent would allow, when, 'long about 1 o'clock, it began to rain, and it *poured*, almost horizontally and drove Sanford out of bed to a place on the ground between Murray and me. Then we stuck around and talked until it was getting light; of course the fire was out and all the wood soaked. So we ate a couple of biscuits and though the rain had stopped the wind had increased, and everything was drifted full of sand. We went out and built our blinds, and found to our disgust that the wind had buffaloed the tide in the lagoon so that it was already about two hours fallen, and the flight was over for the day. We got about five stray shots between us; enough for breakfast, and came back to camp about 9:30 or 10, and sat around in the cold wind waiting for Isadore. I got wet in my blind, and was shivery and not too strong in my stomach, so I thought I'd put on some extra underclothes I'd providently brought along, so I went in the tent, telling Murray as I stepped inside the flap that the durn thing would probably go down on me, to cap the climax. I had not more than got on one leg, inside, when whing! crack, swag, and I was being yanked endways, my shins soaked with tent pegs, and me a little captive, wrapped around with ropes and canvas. When I finally swore my way out I found six feet and a half of Murray prostrate in a cranberry bog, laughing his head off. So I withdrew to the privacy of a lea sand dune, and made the additions I needed.

Pretty soon Sanford, who had been off on a small hunt along the beach, came in, and we held a consultation, the result of which was that we packed up the outfit, hid it behind a dune where Isadore could find it when he came, and we started out to walk the six miles home, expecting to meet Isadore, send him in for the stuff, hunt the 'Hospital Hill' for curlew on the way, and maybe ride part of the way with Isadore when he came along, if 'me mare, May' (sketch) could stand it. So we hit out, but no sooner had we got over the dunes to the open beach than we were buffeted with a gale of wind, and the sand was drifting just like snow, only it cut like fury. When we got into it, on the long strip of flat sand between the tide and the lagoon, it was a constant fight to stand up against it. I was walking alongside of Murray, a few feet behind, and crossed back of him, and when I got in his 'wake' where the wind was not blowing, I not only yielded to it, but actually fell right over on him, forward, from the let-up. (The below is a correct portrait of my running-mate, Murray, who's a BIRD [sketch.] Well, to return to the trip: we fought our way against the gale, the roaring, snatching wind and the searching sand, from which there was not a second's let up, for about a mile and a half, when Isadore hove in sight, and we made him drive us over the rest of the way to the 'main,' and then go back after the stuff. We then hunted curlew till I. returned, two hours later, but we were so tired and storm beaten, and it was still so wild and windy that we couldn't hit much and were only able to get one curlew (Sanford)! I missed four shots clean at curlew and two at a black duck that came up and lit in a pool only about thirty-five yards away.

Pictou, N. S., Sept. 12, 1909.

Sunday in Pictou is an experience. We saw an owl and a gull in the hotel lobby, and found out they were stuffed by one Scott Dawson, who lives out about a mile. So we took a walk, all four, and finally found him. Sanford opened on him, saying: 'We are strangers, passing through Pictou.' 'Eh? I'm a little deaf.' S.: 'We are strangers, PASSING THROUGH PICTOU.' 'Eh? Oh, raccoons?' 'No, STRANGERS!' and then it all got too much, and we spluttered, and I took another tack and yelled: 'You stuff birds?' 'Oh, yes, come in' and all was merry. It's a pretty old maritime town, on a wonderful lovely harbor, but deader than Etna on a summer Sunday. It died when the sail shipping passed into the hands of steamers, and is now decadent and in a dream.

I shall be home now the first minute I can get there, and I am more than ready, you bet. . . . I've saved one of the little tents we had, and am going to put it up for the boy to play in. They are bully little tents, and I think he'll have fun in it. Tell him about it.

WILLIAM S. MURRAY TO L.A.F.

New Haven, Conn., Sept. 27, 1909.

Just how delighted and how much I appreciated your letter, the bird plates and the pictures, all of which reached me upon my return from New York Saturday . . . I am sure I will be unable to language. However, you know, or ought to by this time, what I think of your work, and I shall treasure these, and any more that may come, good and properly. As usual, what I see upon those plates represents in faithfulness what I saw in the Magdalenes. I have many times taken the stand that perfection cannot exist . . . but by thunder Mr. Fuertes—asking your pardon for my language—you are the one exception and I mean it. They say a man is never satisfied with his own work (this is as it should be and I agree to that) but I am satisfied with yours.

Although at the time of his death in 1927 (before Dr. Chapman advised her to save everything) Mrs. Fuertes destroyed a great many of the letters that Louis had received, those that remain fill to overflowing three filing-case drawers twenty-six inches deep. In this large collection there is to be noted following each trip afield a spate of letters from new friends made on that trip, new persons who wanted to thank him for sketches, pictures, prints, who wanted to keep in touch with him, and particularly who wanted to do something for him. Such letters might naturally be expected from the personnel of the expedition, from Charles Knight and Alden Hadley after the Florida trip with the Thayers in 1898, from Dr. Fisher and other 'Harrimen' after Alaska in 1899, from Vernon Bailey, Dr. Chapman, or Dr. Sanford and Mr. Murray, his companions among the Magdalen Islands. More touching and possibly more eloquent, however, are those from Peter Bannister, the Negro guide to flamingos in the Bahamas; Mrs. Mary Scott, hostess to the expedition at her husband's sheep ranch near Crane Lake, Saskatchewan; Fr. Alejandro M. de Valencia who shared the voyage down the Magdalena River in 1911; numerous Boy Scouts who knew him one summer at Camp Otter in Ontario, Canada; collectors and taxidermists everywhere. Among this last group were Ashley Hine of Edmonton, Fred Simpson of Banff, Fred Barker of Parkers' Prairie, Minnesota, and Hermano Apolinar Maria of Bogotá.

He received a letter written after the visit in 1909 by a French-Canadian taxidermist at House Harbor, Magdalen Islands, who says in part:

The pictures are beautiful, also the glass eyes will be very handy to me. The paint box and brushes has not yet reach me, I fear they might be astray, but do not mind it I thank you same. . . . If you desire anything that I can do for you I will always do my possible.

10

Yucatán, Mexico

E VEN BEFORE IT opened, the new year was brightly colored by
anticipation of a collecting trip to Mexico. During a visit in
1897 to Central America Dr. Chapman had been impressed with
the supreme suitability of the slopes of Mt. Orizaba for the purposes
of a museum group. In his autobiography he writes (pp. 153-4):
'Never have I seen a more impressive illustration of the effects of
altitude on the distribution of life. From the luxuriant, liane-draped
forest with their parrots, toucans, and trogons, I could look upward
to pine and spruce-covered slopes with their permanently resident
crossbills, juncos, and evening grosbeaks.' Therefore he proposed to
build for the entrance to the Hall of North American Birds a group
that should show 'this great mountain with its lesson in distribution.' He asked Louis to go along and received enthusiastic letters in
reply.

It should be noted that Louis' 'spigotty' Spanish, which he played
by ear, had no basis in book study. His father's speech always retained a strong Spanish flavor; Louis' ear was excellent, and his
Spanish sounded right, whether in English ('Yais, Ai go') or imitation español.

L.A.F. TO F. M. CHAPMAN

Ithaca, N. Y., Dec. 29, 1909.
La communication de U. qui apertiene ala familia de los Gullos
me gusto mucho. Carramba! Mas el parte que apertiene ala espedi-

tione para Mexico y Yucatan me fecha dir *Grrrande goddam!!*
Perche no puede contemplar esta espedition con una consciencia
clara, y dir verrawel, yais, Ai go, tambien mucho con gusto!

All of which, in purest Castilian, the handsome rascal purred in
his velvety voice, as his helpless toy repined in sad suspense. But
wait! A ray of hope steals up over the purple evening horizon, while
nought but the contralto quaver of a belated mole-cricket disturbs
the sad serene quietude of the tropic crepuscule.

It were well to understand that the above was meant to subtilely
convey the idea that, other things being equal, (and they usually
are, whatever that means) the proud blood of old Castile quickens
in his high-strung arteries, and the thrill of pre-experience vibrates
through his faultless frame at the idea—already sub-sensed—of roam-
ing, trusty brush in hand, through the vasty glooms of lower
Orizaba, the tick-tormented tortilla belt of Mexico real, the bird-
beridden barrancas of Bajo Mexico, the wondrous wanderings on
Ornate Orizaba, the very crux of Vera Cruz, the platitudinous
platalean swashes of tidal Tampico (I laugh heartily—Ha-ha-aja--
jajaja.)

O Hell, Frank, I'd better be working than thus—however ably—
immortalizing this opportunity. For things, I find, like mere men,
aren't immortalized till they're dead, and I don't want this to die
till I've had my whirl out of it . . .

I have before me the thirty remaining State plates, which shall
come P.D.Q. Then the Brewster panels [oil paintings of game birds
to be used as a frieze in the new study of Mr. F. F. Brewster in New
Haven]. The pheasants [for Wm. Beebe's *Monograph of the Pheasants*] are in abeyance just now.

Well, deah, I must away to my chahming wark. Remember me
sweetly to Miss Cook when you see her, and tell her it was a cow-
bird. [In place of signature there is a sketch of L.A.F. painting a
spoonbill that is posing on a sawhorse.]

L.A.F. to F. M. Chapman

Ithaca, N. Y., Jan. 7, 1910.
Hooray for Boreas! he's boreated us borey-eyed. Yards upon ver-

tical yards of snow, icicles hanging like Spanish moss from every-thing, trees looking like Orizabae, and now a dazzling blue sky over all; really, Grace, it's more than swell, it's ellagant.

I've been planning Brewster's work—done. Now I'll push the State job to the end of my time, and turn all else loose. Then, ten minutes before leaving home, I'll pack, and join yez in your hazy dream.

L.A.F. TO COURTENAY BRANDRETH

Ithaca, N. Y., Jan. 16, 1910.

Many thanks for the duck! He is a most interesting beast. . . .

Since I saw you I've hatched a grand plan with Chapman, and on Feb. 18 we sail from N. Y. for Progreso, Yucatán, go into the interior to Chichén-Itzá, the famous and gorgeous old Mayan ruins, where that marvelous ocellated turkey lives, among other things of interest, then back to the coast and over to Vera Cruz by steamer, and in to Córdoba, a small town at the base of the great 18,000 foot volcano of Orizaba. Here we make a base, and run surveys (biological) at different altitudes, for Orizaba begins in the dry tropical, and ascends, furnishing its own refrigerating plant, through wet temperate up to perpetual arctic. Some interest at-taches to that proposition. Then, leaving O., we head for Mexico City and then up the coast to Tampico, where we do our main work: a careful and zealous lot of study and collecting on and around the great lagoon running from Tampico a hundred miles or so down to Tuxpan. Here are spoonbills in swarms, ibis, herons of all sorts and conditions, jaçanas, rails and gallinules of many kinds, jays of sorts, jacamars—all the typically 'tierra caliente' birds. We'll be gone till nearly the first of May.

L.A.F. TO MRS. FUERTES

Mérida, Yucatán, March [2?], 1910.

I have been in a strange world. We got here last Tuesday and went by sail through mile on mile of henequin (yucca-hemp) plantations, to Citas, and there Mr. Thompson met us with three volans—three mules per volan—and over eighteen miles we bumped, tossed, lurched, and pitched at breakneck (literally) pace, and landed at Chichén—which I must tell you about later. Most wonderful ruins—so impressive that I all but forgot that the woods were ringing with cries and screams of parrots, motmots, and all sorts of new tropical birds. I stayed there four days, but the others only two, visiting other ruins. I collected about fifty birds, but lost out on the turkey, though I had about six Indians on the trail for all the time. We've seen Maya dances, social and ceremonial, and all sorts of strange and weird things. The Mayas are the most perfect people you ever saw: good-looking, strong, but above all gracious, courteous, simple, and *honest*! . . .

Here it's tropics, rain one minute in torrents, sunshine the next, but always hot daytimes, and cool and lovely at night. The whole surroundings and atmosphere are very Spanish—I can get along pretty well with it. . . .

Just landing Friday p.m. at Vera Cruz. A bully trip from Progreso; Orizaba was in plain sight thirty miles at sea, ninety miles away!

Córdoba, Mar. 6, 1910.

You can't imagine what a sublime mountain old Orizaba is. It is only visible till about 11 a.m., when the haze and clouds always conceal the cone. But between 6 a.m. and 10 it is a great distant opal—pink-lavender with a moon-cold snow-cap extending far down the north side, its feet in velvet forest, and a foreground of tropical forest and light green sugar fields, with lovely warm old red-tiled white-walled Córdoba with its stately ancient cathedral (and *such* bells) I could hardly get my breath when I first went out, yesterday morning, to see it.

Just now there's a very good band playing delightful music in the square out of the open door-windows. Oh how I wish you could be sharing this wonderful experience with me: you'd be perfectly carried away with the strangeness of everything. We shall be here, as a base, probably till April first. Anyway write me once more here. And send me a list, if you can take time, of the people you think it would be nice for me to bring some little dinky thing to when

I come out. And tell me something about Sonny and Sister. You see I want to know if she's walking yet, how Sonny is coming on— what's doing, in short, on the Fuertes plantation.

I suppose I shall paint Orizaba from up the line, where it is a little nearer and we get a more tropical foreground. Here the country is very old, and all the big stuff is long since cut off. . . . The ticks are pretty bad here, they have two sizes, so * and so • and the little ones are hard to see. . . .

It is cold here nights and till about 8:30 a.m., but through the day it is roasting. I spent all this a.m. in a big ravine, with tree-ferns and great hanging vines and orchids and lovely butterflies. I saw one of those immense ones with a pale turquoise blue shine all over his wings; and some brown and pale green ones that sink out of sight when they light in the grass or ferns. Shot a big gray and red squirrel, and a gorgeous purple hummer and two tiny green kingfishers and an enormous brown jay, most as big as a crow. . . .

Córdoba, Mexico, Mar. 9, 1910.

The painting is exceedingly interesting, and every day the same thing happens to the mountain. At sunrise it is crystal clear, and though it is about thirty or thirty-five miles away, every detail can be seen, with a glass, and it is a lovely pearly pink cone, white-crowned, rising majestically up and up into a wonderful clear blue sky. Its whole upper cone is bare of trees, and is very full of opalescent color, but the tree-line is sharp, and makes it look pale blue or lavender, in a straight line. Then come the still blue, but darker, foothills, very sharp and abrupt, forest-clad from top to bottom, and then the flat plain—like Africa, with open parks and pastures and occasional flat-topped trees, with a nice varied foreground. My kit is very compact and light, and easily portable. I've found a comfortable root under a big tree high above the road—made for me—with a most incomparable arrangement of picture.

St. Pat.'s day, Mar. 17, 1910.

. . . We've had eight days of either rain or dull weather, during which the mountain has been visible just thirty-eight minutes all told. I beat it out, one and a half miles, to where I've been painting, and had ten minutes in which I could correct my picture before the clouds shut it out. Some lucky, as it was enough. It was between seven and eight a.m. I am in bully shape, physically, and have nothing worse than a number of large and small bites of sorts, and the nettle stings. These tropical nettles beat anything I ever heard of: if they get you when you're hot there seems to be no limit to what they do to you. I got stung the first day or so of my stay here, and though I've nearly nailed them by killing the skin with formaldehyde, they are still doing business. . . .

Sunday I was four miles south, with the Chapmans, and had only my little pistol, and I got into a flock of nearly two hundred parrots, and couldn't get any. They were making a fruiting tree grass green—*thick*, and yawping their bills loose, and after I got two futile pop shots into them they flew screeching away, and in ten minutes came low over me again in a tight flock. I could hear them a mile before and after they passed.

Córdoba, Mexico, Mar. 21, 1910.

We have been making the best of the bad weather by side trips to various points along the down-end of the line. Motzorongo twice, where a regular hot-house condition of life exists: perfectly gigantic forests of silk-cotton and wild fig, with curious small palms and tremendous ferns, climbing vines like a ship's rigging every-where, from wire size to the thickness of your body—reeking, steam-ing, moist, and where live trogons, toucans, parrots, all sorts of tanagers and hummers, queer new and unimagined birds, jaguars and even monkeys, and orchids of all sorts and colors, air plants un-nameable, odorous of queer flowers and reeking with strange and very impressive smells, silent except for unguessable bird-notes. If it weren't for an old trail that follows the stream, it would be impenetrable: as it is it is a perfectly ideal collecting ground (except for the sweltering dampness and the mosquitoes) and more than anything else like a limitless hothouse of wildly strange exotic plants. Trees start out of the ground that make me think of St. John's Church, and you come face to face with them so big that you have to stop and plan your way around them. I shot four times at a little falcon from the base of one, and never touched it with my shot—or if I did, it was so spent that it didn't hurt him. I also saw, out over the open valley, a pair of hawks. No mistaking them, for they were as big as a red-tail, and absolutely gleaming snow-white!! Fourteen years ago Chapman saw one in this very place, and if he hadn't told me of it I'd have thought I was dreaming. They looked wonderful and beautiful circling in the thin air against the great foliage-banked mountain side, and I watched them with my glass a long time. How I wish you could be enjoying some of these wonderful days with me. When I left I had no idea of the marvel of true tropics; and yet I've hardly seen a taste of it, for Córdoba is so high as to be strongly tinged with upland vegetation and birds— also so much cut out and so long inhabited that it is more like a farm country, only the barrancas being truly tropical. I am perfectly well, and capable of a hard day's work every day. In fact, I'm the only one who hasn't had any setbacks. . . . I suppose that at Tampico we will be largely out of the world, as few have gone where we're going. It's the only corner of Mexico where Nelson and Goldman never went, and we may get some new things there, though it's not likely.

Córdoba, Mexico, Mar. 28, 1910.

We got so sick of lounging around the hotel or collecting locally in the rain, and time went on so, that finally last Tuesday (Mar. 22) we packed our outfit, Chapman, Patterson and I, and took the 7 a.m. train in an overcast and threatening day for Coscomatepec, and got there at 10, being on time. There, after some slight palaver, we got our two men and seven horses, two of which were pack animals, and after a lunch at the village tavern we started, about noon, on our twenty-one mile ride up to snow. It was still cloudy, and before we'd been out an hour it rained. Well, we went on, and at about 5 p.m. came to a camping place on the 7,000 foot level. Here we made camp, and Patterson got our first meal, with wet wood—in an Indian's back yard. We were objects of keen interest, not to say open amusement, to all the Indians—the youngsters could not control their smiles, the men stood quietly around till dark, and every woman in the *jacal* was peeking over or between something. However, we had a good camp and a good meal, and broke at 6 next a.m. and pushed up out of the corn belt up into the zone of pines. The trail, by the way, runs the entire distance along the top of a knife-like ridge, or hog-back, twenty-one miles long, with deep *barrancas* on each side; so that as we were in the clouds all the time, and could frequently look from our horses down into eternity on both sides, the sensation was much as I should suppose ballooning would be. Well, anyway, we went till about 1 p.m. and then found at 9,500 feet a perfectly ideal place, in the superb forest of long leaf pine and oak. Here, under an oak 120 feet high (guessed at) and ten feet around, shoulder high, we made our camp. In the afternoon we hunted, and I got a magnificent crested jay, of the Steller's type, the gorgeous little red warbler—cardinal red with square silky white cheek patches—and a lot of other things. It was still in the clouds, and I shall never forget the beauty of the noble pines, as they faded into the mist or became distinct as the clouds rose through the *barrancas*. We collected again at camp till about six, when it gets suddenly dark, and also cold. After supper, when we were all sitting around our fire, Frank looked around, let out a yell, and there gleaming between the pines in full moonlight, was the glorious crown of Orizaba, visible for the first time in two weeks!

I can't describe the wonder of it to you. It is the most marvelous thing of beauty I've ever seen, and when, next morning (after gazing at it for an hour or more and photographing it by moonlight) we got up in the dark and went out into the deep frost-silvered forest and watched it come into being, get distinct, and finally, while the deep valley was still black in shadow, catch the first gleaming ray of the sun, and finally get creamy, then rosy pink in a bluebird's-egg sky, our senses kind of left us, and we could understand why the Mexicans worship their snow mountains. From that moment, the peak was never long out of sight, though occasionally in the afternoon the clouds would drift up and hide it at times for a few minutes. Of the thousand varying appearances—

never, indeed, twice alike—that were given us while we were there I can't tell you. It was my most marvelous mountain experience, and I shall never, I hope, forget any of it.

Well, after a glorious morning of admiring and photographing we broke this camp with a feeling we'd like to live there, and went higher. Passing through about 1,000 feet of cleared land, we at last entered the upper zone of trees (short-leaved pines) and got up to the high level of 12,000 for our camp. This was too high, for at night, when the sun set, the thermometer dropped in fifteen minutes from 57° to 12°, and we suffered (and the horses most died) from cold. Before noon next day, the mercury in the sun was 112. 100 degrees' change in twelve hours! I think that's a record, and incidentally a hard thing to cope with. But we were all right, and in the morning we took the riding horses, and went up to the head of the trail, at an even 13,000 feet. Here, I forgot to say, the Indians come all the way from Coscomatepec to cut ice, which they carry down in big squares, on burros and on their backs, to sell in the cities. Think of the strength and hardihood of these nearly naked Indians, to do this at this altitude. We couldn't climb thirty feet of hill without losing our breath and having our heart make a noise like a dog barking, and having to rest.

Chapman got a fine series of pictures of the Indians getting ice out and down, then later as they passed camp he got them on the trail, with Orizaba for a background, and to-day, when we got off the train here at Córdoba, the first thing we heard was, 'Nieve,' (snow), and when we'd cleaned up, and went out on the street to the P.O., it was ten minutes early so we sat down, and for the first time in Mexico, ordered ices on the sidewalk before the hotel. When we asked the boy where the ice came from, he said, 'El pico, señor, del volcán'—the peak of the volcano! So we saw the whole thing, from start to finish. One of the most picturesque industries, I think, in the world, and very old and very romantic.

L.A.F. TO MRS. FUERTES

Tampico, Mexico, April 9, 1910.
Our trip up river . . . was wonderful, and each day brought new

Motmot. Chichén Itzá, Yucatán, Mexico, 1910

Trogon

Trogon melanocephalus
(# 2283)
Tampico, Mex.

TROGON. Tampico, Mexico, 1910

wonders. Three pairs of parrots, some parrakeets (four species in all), big wild pigeons, great red-capped woodpeckers like pileateds all had nests right in the yard, and up the trail a way was an immense fig tree fruiting, where there were always at least fifty, and sometimes a hundred and fifty or more parrots feeding. They are almost impossible to see in the trees, and the excitement of looking for them, without seeing one, and then having the tree suddenly explode into a screaming swarm of red and green birds is great. There were also great numbers of red-billed pigeons feeding there. The parrots are of two kinds, the big 'yellow-head,' the common big cage parrot that talks and whistles—all green with a yellow head and red in the wings—and one a size smaller, with the same body and wing coloring, but a red crown, and blue streak on the side of the head. The parrakeets are (two species) all green, with almost no color variation. There are big sloughs on both sides of the river where water birds—(snakebirds, white herons of all kinds, cormorants, etc.) were common, but inaccessible, as the lakes were full up of a kind of acacia, with pink spicy flowers and devilish hooks. Ticks were pretty bad, and in spite of daily swims in the river, and daily co-operative hunts, we got pretty well chewed up with them. We were a week at the ranch, and I put up about ten birds a day. . . . I found a parrot's nest, which F. took and is going to make a small group of for the museum. I also thought I'd discovered a new bird, a tiny oriole, but F. afterward got others in later plumage, which prove mine to be only the tropical form of orchard oriole—a good bird nevertheless. [It was a new bird, subsequently named *Icterus fuertesi* and described in *The Auk* by Chapman, Jan. 1911.]

Pájaro I., Tamiahua Lagoon
Mexico, April 17, 1910.

This is the real thing. We left Tampico a week ago with a launch and two small boats, loaded with gasoline and food and camp stuff, and the first night camped on the little canal that leads from Tampico into this big lake. I shot a lot of ducks (a pot-shot) and we had a good enough camp, though mosquitoes were very bad. Next a.m. we got a fairly early start, and expected to make Toro I., the first bird island, by 3 p.m., but as it got on toward 5, and the wind got up, and we weren't there yet, we decided to camp on the shore (east) and go over in the a.m. At about 5:30 we were ashore and had a camp going. There was a hut near—two, in fact, and one of them turned out to be the home of one Maclodio, a hunter with whom Sheldon and Sanford stayed while they were here. There we learned through Mrs. Maclodio that Toro had no birds, Frijole some, and Pájaro most of all. So after two days of hunting and photographing on shore, where there is a noble forest and some good swamp holes—and myriads of ticks and mosquitoes—we broke camp and came over here. There was a new (to us) parrot over at Maclodio's woods—a big blue-headed one. Well, when we got over here, all was glum and not a sign of birds, though we'd seen some pelicans and cormorants on the way over. So, Frank came ashore to reconnoitre, and pretty soon came back and said, 'All right, we'll camp here.' So we all came in, and just inside the fringe of man- groves near shore was a rookery of about 200 pairs of spoonbills, with big young, with a few big white egrets, a thousand Louisiana herons, a few reddish egrets mixed in. We hadn't been ashore five minutes when Piu, our boy, came in with a big pink and black iguana, three feet long, and in a minute Julian, the other, had one four and a half feet long. They are great lizards, with a row of long spines down their back, that look like this. (Sketch) They are absolutely harmless, and as quiet as a lamb, and can be handled like kittens, never showing any spunk, but they look as if they'd eat off a leg if they had a chance; great jaws and fierce little eyes, and some of them lovely colors. We have one now that is mostly coral pink, with a strong black pattern, and another that is the most beautiful rich grass green, but when they get big, they weigh from five to eight pounds and generally look as if they were made of cast iron, rusting in places. They grow spines three and four inches long, the whole length of their backs, and old ones have five or six on the nose, and great wattles of skin under their throats. There are lots of them on the island, and they go thrashing out under foot like a frightened steer. . . .

I got tired of seeing spoonbills on every side and above and below me, so day before yesterday I went out to the end of a long sand point at the far end of the island where the spoonbills go in ones and twos to feed (among cormorants, pelicans, skimmers, coots, ducks, plover, stilts and ibis) and dug a little trench in the shell sand and lay down in it. I hadn't been there three minutes when— whish—whish—whish—whish— and bing came a rosy old cock spoonbill and sat down in the shallow water. So I shot three—all I can use—and brought them home, all beauties, and I spent yesterday painting their heads and feet, and skinning them.

And so the expedition returned to New York with paintings and photos of Mt. Orizaba and a good collection of bird-skins including the much desired spoonbills and a series of the newly discovered Icterus fuertesi.

II

Concealing Coloration

T HE THAYERS' GREAT book, Concealing Coloration in the Animal Kingdom, had at last appeared late in the autumn of 1909. Published by the Macmillan Company, it was a large volume, well printed and profusely illustrated with photographs, diagrams, and sixteen colored plates engraved by Hoen and Company of Baltimore. The text was written by Gerald, who painted two of the four full-page illustrations, the cotton-tail and the ruffed grouse. His father wrote the introduction and painted the frontispiece of a peacock amid foliage and the smaller pictures of wood-ducks, blue-jays, spoonbills, and flamingos. Various persons, among them Richard Meryman, Rockwell Kent, Mrs. A. H. Thayer, and L. A. Fuertes, worked on the other illustrations.

In the introduction Abbott Thayer states at once that the matter of protective coloration has been in the hands of the wrong custodians. Appertaining to animals, it has been considered part of the zooligists' province, but it properly belongs to the realm of pictorial art and can be interpreted only by painters. 'For it deals wholly in optical illusion, and this is the very gist of a painter's life.' The critical moments for an animal are the moments of catching food and being caught as food, and in these moments sight is the indispensable sense. This book demonstrates, he continues, placing the statement in italics, that 'the colors, patterns, and appendages of animals are the most perfect imaginable effacers under the very circumstances wherein such effacement would most serve the wearer.'

Concealing coloration means coloration that matches the background. Since animals move about, they are seen against countless backgrounds; the most brilliantly colored and boldly marked are the species that move most freely, against the greatest variety of background in sun and shade. Patterns on animals' coats represent the utmost that nature can do to overcome 'the vicissitudes of silhouetting.'

In the first three chapters the subject is explained and the terms defined. There follow sixteen chapters on birds, three on mammals, one on fishes, one on reptiles and amphibians, and three on caterpillars, insects, butterflies, and moths.

Gerald concludes, where his father began, with insistence that it takes the eye of the artist to recognize the truthfulness of the pictures nature paints, that the patterns of animals 'are, in the best sense of the word, triumphs of art. . . . He who would learn the surely typical color- and pattern-scheme of a particular kind or detail of natural landscape . . . has only to look at the disguising-costume of the moth or snake or bird or butterfly which habitually has such a background.'

In the amassing and arrangement of an enormous amount of detail there is some repetition where species of different kinds accumulate to illustrate the same principles, but the truths displayed are subtle and exquisite, described in language that is at once precise and graceful. The whole work is weakened only by its tone—not arrogant, certainly, but admitting of no doubt as to the correctness of the views held—and by the ambiguity of some, and prominence of others, of the illustrations. For example, in the photographs of models used to display the effect of countershading (facing p. 30) the shaded model disappears so completely that you cannot believe it was ever there in the first place; an altered or falsified picture would have been more persuasive. The paintings of spoonbills and flamingos against sunset clouds (facing pp. 147, 156) seem to show only that it is possible to paint these birds in such a way that they become *invisible*, and the *illustrations* offer a ready target for *ridicule*.

It is a handsome book. The pictures are so striking that one tends to go through them, read the captions, form an opinion, and then feel that he has read the book, without studying the careful, thoughtful, provocative words of the text.

Louis Fuertes saw this danger at once and feared for the reputation of the book and the truths it was revealing. He wrote Dr. Chapman right away, assuming correctly that he would be one of the first and the most influential of the reviewers, and he sent Gerald a whole-hearted appreciation to which the answer is given below. Unfortunately not one of Louis' letters to Gerald is known to have been saved.

L.A.F. TO F. M. CHAPMAN

Ithaca, N. Y., Dec. 29, 1909.

The *Concealing Colors* is out; doubtless you've seen or soon shall see it. I think it's a beautiful book, and Gerald has done, to my mind, an entirely unique and utterly admirable piece of work, which must make a deep dent on the field it covers. I hope it will meet the serious consideration of reviewers, and not be glanced at and condemned. Certainly some features will be criticized adversely —not to say roasted—by reason of preconceptions and prejudices, and doubtless some conceptions are doubtful (paradox) but the whole great and loving piece of work is, to my mind, a greatest contribution and merits the most serious thought and study. A few of the ideas, [as] the spoonbill and flamingo pictures suggest, are, from the very fact of the presence of plates, given so much importance that I fear they will bring down a burden of criticism on the work as a whole which it far from deserves. These are errors in proportion, rather than in anything more serious, and I have not yet had time to read what is said about them. And that's what I fear will happen in the reviews: that the reviewer will look at the color plates and judge from his previous personal ideas and knock the work.

I'm aware, on reading this over, that it sounds like a warning! You surely know better than that and that I am talking from the heart out, about the rank and file of critics who like to hear themselves talk, and criticize for the purpose of airing their own views . . . and certainly not with any idea of influencing you one way or another. Whether or not you review it, you know what the work means and stand in no need of suggestions from such advanced thinkers as *I* am!!

GERALD THAYER TO L.A.F.

Monadnock, N. H., Jan. 10, 1910.

Not twice in a fellow's life-time will he get a letter such as you have sent me. It is the high-water mark, up to now, in some ways, of our fine friendship. Sometimes, in semi-inspired moods, I could have said as much on my side, but always with a dread that I was, or rather, would seem to you to be, over-reaching through a sort of one-horse fervor of imagination. Now you have outdone me, once and for all.

It *is* an event, for me to sail clear at long last of that incubus of a wholly undertaken but only half-loved and only half manageable book on Protective Coloration; and this letter of yours signalizes and illumines the event as nothing else has or could. The book has value and beauty, that is true: I realize it now better than before; and its excellence, such as it has, is the peculiar product of the union of three temperaments, Papa's, mine, and Addie's. [Addie was Mrs. Thayer.] If you could know what *Addie* has done in the making-up (into an actual *book*) and *holding* up and seeing through! (To say nothing of the money she has put into it.) The book is more believed-in and more loved by her than by any one else, I believe— though Papa too seems quite satisfied and immensely elated.

As for me, I know of miserable meagernesses and even errors in it. Never mind, it is, in the main, a sound foundation, the *first* one, for this endless, difficult, and exquisite study. The chances are I shall contribute again, perhaps even with pictures, before the end of my life. *You* cannot help contributing, marvelously, sometimes, as the years go by.

Brewster has written us a wonderful letter in praise of our book.

It was not until summer, after the trip with Louis to Mexico, that Dr. Chapman set to work on his review of the book for Bird-Lore. He sent a preliminary draft to Louis, who discusses and finds some fault with it in the next letter. Dr. Chapman did alter the review as Louis suggested.

In the meantime Theodore Roosevelt had returned from hunting big game in Africa and had seen the Thayers' book. One of the parties given to honor him upon his return was a luncheon held on the roof of the Waldorf-Astoria, where the Camp-Fire Club was host to two hundred and thirty persons. The decorations were elaborate, and revolvers were fired for applause during Roosevelt's hour-long talk. A headline in The New York Times for June 23, 1910, reads: 'Roosevelt raps fakers. Tells Camp-Fire Club animals don't rely on color for concealment.' He referred to the Thayers' book and said that his experience in Africa disproved its main tenets. The account proceeds:

The color protectionist, said Col. Roosevelt, goes too far on this theory. Most of the animals he saw in Africa, he said, depended so little on color and pattern protection that it could not be noticed. The ones he came to know there tried to conceal themselves behind material objects, just like a man would do, and if that couldn't be accomplished they took to their heels when they saw or heard him coming.

The lions he encountered did not lie against a sun brown rock and expect to pass unnoticed. The dik-diks that crossed his path relied upon no resemblance of their coloring to near-by trees and shrubs to hide them. The gnus did not look for a gnu-colored tree when Col. Roosevelt approached. But all these and more depended solely upon their hoofs and legs when he and his party came along.

L.A.F. TO F. M. CHAPMAN

Ithaca, N. Y., June 26, 1910.

I am very sorry to hear that Mr. Roosevelt couldn't restrain himself about the book, for I had thought he was one of the ones who would be able to see the far-reachingness of many of Mr. Thayer's observations and ideas. You know so well how I feel about it; how much the valuable in the work overtops the shaky or even valueless. Of course your criticism of the purely speculative is eminently just —as is your evident purpose to give full credit to the great field of work done, and observation stimulated by the rest of the work, and I confess I was disappointed that Mr. R. didn't go under the shell and see all the real meat. For while many times Thayer's expression is unfortunate and his argument faulty, the book is so fundamentally earnest that it demands studious reading, and any hasty perusal is bound, like reading an algebra, to produce an indefinite and useless impression. For instance, in the lovely wood duck picture, few note the *prime* fact that the entire painting is made absolutely of colors and tones taken directly from a male wood duck, in contemplating the entirely *secondary* fact that the picture is beautifully natural and true, and that the wood duck himself is comparatively inconspicuous. Also, anent the zebra, which Dugmore, T. R., et al assail as a false theory, saying that said zebra is conspicuously visible as far as you can see anything his size,—*can it not be true*, as Thayer says, that at times of foaling or of pursuit or other critical moments, the striping must help marvelously in the reedy retreat which is sought as sanctuary? You see my point is only this: the book, being the serious work of two very serious students for a very long time, merits serious reading, and most careful study by its critics, and I thought T. R. was going to be one of the very fairest in his judgment, and uphold my solid belief that he was *not* hasty, but remarkably quick to see real values. So much for that.

I think your review is very just, and to a less earnest and perhaps empirical nature than Mr. T''s, could not fail to be received as such. If you have not already put it in type, however, and think it worth while to avoid opening a sore or two, I think I can suggest a few unimportant changes of wording which will not alter your criticisms. . . . I should also incorporate somewhere, if I were you, the very important point so insistently noted by Thayer, of the necessity for throwing over the human five-foot-high viewpoint from which man has hitherto viewed all questions and adopting the one-inch-high level from which the weasel contemplates *his* problem, the three-hundred-foot plane of the soaring red-tail, the minus elevation of the shiner, and all the other *special* problems of seeing and being seen that confront every species in its own sphere. It is only just to note this great evasion of the common stumbling-block of the ages, in contemplating protective coloration. There is no reason why you should agree with everything T. does. I'm quite sure I don't. But I think so loving and deeply-rooted a task as he has done deserves fullest consideration. It is vastly too important to just drop with a few hot words, as T. R. has done, for, true in its entirety or not, it opens to the open mind vast vistas of beautiful adaptations of nature, and is the first open door to *Imaginative* Natural History that has been swung by a naturalist and unsentimental truth lover. For without imagination we would all remain *******s, you get my point. And to my mind, this beautifully prepared exposition of what lies before the open mind—even if it slops over in its enthusiasm at times—is the most precious gift, leading away from systematic science back into the delightful paths of philosophic natural science, that the next school of naturalists will have reference to.

To tersely state my judgment of your review, as I take it from the fact you sent it to me, you wanted me to do—here it is: I think it is eminently just, perfectly honest, and a real, just appreciation. I think you would save yourself from contra-criticism without weakening your argument by making the one change suggested, and that you would do your subject better justice by including the point I note concerning the viewpoint matter. The remainder of my letter is simply a private exposition, to you, of the way I feel toward the work, without reference to my well-known love for the workers. I consider it an enlightening guide to the greater seeing, applicable to the contemplation of all problems of the animal kingdom—with faults, doubtless—but nevertheless, a real eye-opener and mind-opener—and, as such, bound, for the present at least, to excite much condemnatory criticism which it will eventually live down, and come into its own proper position. I wish fervently that all the criticisms may be as fair and as open-minded as yours: if so, no injustice will be done, and the world will get the full benefit of a really great piece of work.

F. M. CHAPMAN TO L.A.F.

New York City, June 27, 1910.

Thank you cordially for your letter of the 26th. I wish that somewhere you could review Thayer's book yourself, for it seems to me you put the case admirably. As for your comments on my review, I already had in mind the desirability of emphasizing Thayer's insistence on viewing an animal's colors from a proper point of view.

L.A.F. TO F. M. CHAPMAN

Ithaca, N. Y., June 29, 1910.

I was much pleased to get your good letter yesterday, for after I had sent my last to you, I thought that perhaps I had said a little too much, though I really feel all I said, particularly as concerns the royal dictum from the camp-fire side. I do wish, myself, that there were some way in which I might comment on the book, rather than review it, for it seems to me with my experience, knowledge of the work and its authors, and my rather particular occupation, which demands a lot of objective study, revealing many of the adaptations cited, which to the hunter alone remain unrevealed, my say might have some weight, and bear upon a side of the subject that will probably have few champions.

F. M. CHAPMAN TO L.A.F.

New York City, July 22, 1910.

You will be interested to know of a very satisfactory conversation I had with Mr. Roosevelt concerning Thayer's book. As I supposed, his remarks before the Camp-Fire Club had been interpreted as a general condemnation of the affair, whereas, in fact, he regards his work very much as we do ourselves. He says that like Agassiz, with his glacial theory, Thayer would apply his theory in regard to 'protective coloration' to every living creature. Agassiz, you remember, thought he found erratics [boulders believed to have been deposited by glaciers] in the valley of the Amazon, just as Thayer believes that flamingos are sunset streaks. With much of Thayer's work Mr. Roosevelt is in hearty accord, but he believes as we do, that many animals have other means of escaping from their prey than by mere hiding alone. Roosevelt, you know, had prolonged experience with the antelope in the west, and he totally disagrees with Thayer's explanation of the white rump patch, and can give you no end of what seem to me to be excellent reasons, all based on personal observation, for his own beliefs. For example, when he tells you that this patch is conspicuous in the night against a black sky background, it is rather difficult to harmonize this fact with Thayer's theory, and when you further know that Thayer himself, so far as I am aware, has never seen the antelope in nature, or at least studied it there, one must defer to that opinion which is based on original observation.

Dr. Chapman was over-confident in Roosevelt's sympathy. Appendix E (Protective Coloration) to Roosevelt's volume African Game Trails, published in August, 1910, contains little 'hearty accord' with the Thayers' ideas. He does admit that 'the night-hawk, certain partridges and grouse, and numerous other birds which seek to escape observation by squatting motionless, do unquestionably owe an immense amount to the way in which their colors harmonize with surrounding colors,' but he discounts entirely the concealing effect of counter-shading. He states from personal observation that the white rump-patches of hares and prong-bucks, instead of obliterating their silhouettes against the sky when looked up at from the ground, are often the only cause of the animals' being seen at all. He devotes several pages to a denial that the zebra's coloration is ever of help to him in escaping observation at a drinking place and says that to maintain that the black-and-white colobus monkey is protectively colored is as preposterous as to say that a soldier in a black frock coat and top-hat with white duck trousers is protectively colored. Each might conceivably find himself in a situation where his coloring concealed him, the soldier for example compelled to fight in a coal-cellar with a white-washed floor. But there are dun-colored monkeys with the same habits as the black-and-white ones, (he had previously pointed out the fact that dun-colored wild asses live in the same environment as zebras), and 'it is quite impossible that both forms can be protectively colored, and, as a matter of fact, neither is.' Of the Thayers' suggestion that the war-paints, tatooings, head decorations worn by North American Indians tend to obliterate them, he says, (p. 519), 'This simply is not so.'

The great disagreement, of which a good deal gets into these letters, sprang from a basic difference in point of view between Mr. Thayer and Mr. Roosevelt and was never resolved. Roosevelt looked at the matter as would a human hunter, often on horseback; Thayer as a hunted animal, or an animal hunting. Roosevelt saw a zebra driven across grassy plains by his beaters and found it conspicuous. Thayer, in imagination crouching at a water-hole among reeds and bushes, waiting for his zebra to get thirsty, saw only stems against the sky. Roosevelt knew he was right because he had seen the animals himself, and he did not take into consideration the ones he did not see. Mr. Thayer knew he was right because he had an artist's trained eye and a naturalist's sympathetic imagination.

In the meantime Louis did have his chance to review the book, for the magazine Science. In the review he, too, emphasizes the idea, not welcomed by indoor scientists or hunting sportsmen, that in the study of appearances in nature the artist is the specialist. The artist, trained in optics, knows the colors you must use to paint a white garment—a technique, incidentally, of which Mr. Thayer was perfect master. The artist knows how to paint out a shadow, making a solid body look flat, and knows what patterns and colors epitomize a forest floor, or sunlit tops of trees, or reeds and branches with sky between. The Thayers, trained artists both, rejoiced to discover that nature, by means of natural selection, had been the supreme artist, painting upon the grouse, the parrot, the zebra, pictures typical of backgrounds against which the creature would be seen at moments of its greatest need, when it was being hunted, or was itself hunting. Louis ends his review with this sentence:

The greatest value of this unusual book lies not, therefore, in the array of specific fact it contains, vast though this be, but rather in its wholly enlightening effect upon the search for biologic truths, and for this alone it is worthy of deep study and a lasting place in literature.

Abbott Thayer to L.A.F.

Monadnock, N. H., [Nov., 1910.]

One of us sh'd have written days ago to say, what you know, that your *Science* notice is all *heart-warming*.

Say, can you get to the A.O.U. for a day ahead of the meeting and help me look up places (so difficult at that late season) for my out-door show? and let me have your help at the show? My only hope is the class of garden vegetation, shrubs etc. that live on so late in a Botanic garden or any shut-in *grounds*.

Even you will really be bowled over at the endless chain of perfectly inchworm and bark moth and whippoorwill adaptations I now *show* macaws, hummers, quetzal, flamingos, peacocks, to be.

Your only slip was in saying the book's photos rested on the blue sky's taking white in a photo. All those illustrations were pure matches as well to the naked eye—either by virtue of the day being cloudy or the fact (a main one) that the low sky (the one concerned) averages very near *white* not blue.

But as you say most of all the premium is on *brightness* of whatever tint.

Mr. Thayer wanted people to see for themselves what he had discovered—one recalls his demonstration with sweet potatoes in 1896. He was constantly devising new means of persuasion: placing woodpecker skins upon photos of trees against sky, hanging papier-mâché models of patterned oryx heads in trees, taking people into the woods to look for themselves at a mounted peacock concealed in bright sunlight. In the fall of 1911 he wrote Louis that he had learned a lot about demonstration since the A.O.U. meeting of the year before, and continued:

For instance, to show dullards that a white sheet's or snow's shadow is of the aggregate overhead sky color of the moment, I put the sheet in a tree shadow and let them hold a big square pasteboard with a small hole in it so that *full sun* strikes on this card, while through the hole they see the sheet-in-shadow. Then I give them pastels with which to tone the card till it matches the hole! Then I bring them a blue-jay to compare with what they have done! Would I could see old Theodore I at work once on such a card.

Have you seen his museum bulletin 110 pages?

Louis had seen it, and mentions it in a letter to Dr. Chapman by saying: 'Got T. R.'s brochure—Bing! like that.' Called Revealing and Concealing Coloration in Birds and Mammals, *its burden was: It is not so. Mr. Roosevelt had warmed to his subject, and in this article, really a book, he is unable even to state the Thayers' theories (in a section following the introduction, called 'The Doctrine of Concealing Coloration as Stated and Applied by G. H. and Abbott H. Thayer in their* Concealing Coloration in the Animal Kingdom') *without using the expression 'wild absurdities' in the second sentence. His third heading is 'Misstatements of Facts as Set Forth by Them Pictorially and in Their Text,' then comes 'The Role of Countershading' ('Mr. Thayer's theory is absolutely false') and twenty-one headings for particular subjects, eight of which contain the word* not *(i.e. 'Coloration of Woodpeckers Not Obliterative'). Over and over again he says of a species, 'it is conspicuous' without mentioning to whom or in what circumstances. 'I carefully studied the blue-jays in my neighborhood,' he writes. 'The enormous majority of the shadows, in fact all that I saw during the winter, were not blue shadows the color of a blue-jay's plumage.' Some years later, when Mr. Thayer had succeeded in showing him the hole-in-card demonstration, he still would not admit that the shadows were blue and dismissed it all as an artist's trick.*

The condemnatory paper was published in the Bulletin of the American Museum of Natural History of August, 1911. Chapman the naturalist might have championed Thayer, but Chapman the museum curator took sides with former President Roosevelt. Gerald Thayer thought Chapman a trimmer, knowing that he really under-

stood a good deal about the coloration of birds. We do not know what Louis thought, but from this time forward the subject is not discussed in the letters between him and Dr. Chapman.

Another ornithologist and author, Francis H. Allen, in an invitation to Louis to lecture in Boston, however, expressed himself on the subject of Roosevelt's paper and was answered by Louis as follows:

L.A.F. to Francis H. Allen

Ithaca, N. Y., Jan. 31, 1912.

I agree quite fully with you concerning Roosevelt's review. To use his own pet word, it is truculent, in my opinion, and . . . I have talked quite at length with him about it, and endeavored my best to find out how much—even of the more obvious facts of Mr. Thayer's work (such as sky reflections on snow, etc.) have operated on his perceptions. I found him quite adamantine—not to say rhinocerine—to them in toto. So I desisted, in the (perhaps vain) hope that he would either blow himself out or become absorbed in some other matter and at least lie fallow for a time. That sometimes relieves an acid condition.

L.A.F. to Francis H. Allen

Ithaca, N. Y., Feb. 10, 1912.

I can't tell you how the undercurrent of credence in Thayer's work expressed in your letter warms me. I find that, in common with most things hotly discussed, one cannot sympathize with one plank in a platform without being, willy nilly, arrayed against the whole of the opposite party's beliefs. So I can't start a harmless exposition of some simple fact—like the changeableness of blues in different angles of light, etc.,—simple and well-known as the facts may be, without being swarmed on. I really feel, as you suggest you do, that sooner or later the world will begin to see a few things with their eyes instead of their intellects—in other words, objectively. We don't realize how subjectively we view the world, I suppose, because what we see purely objectively makes no impression, comparatively, and might as well be, (if indeed it is not) unseen. I should be awfully glad, if it could be arranged, to bring along a little extra material and have a discussion with the Nuttall Club on this subject, if only to start some *looking* instead of cerebrating at common things. That is doubtless what foxes and flycatchers do, and what we must do if we are to come to an understanding of whether or not things are protected from their fates by their exteriors.

I could spiel along for hours, of course, but will spare you. Nothing works so deeply into my interest as this wonderful subject, and I, for one, do not fear any disruption of the universe to result from greater knowledge of the *superficial facts.* I'm indeed content to leave to a succeeding generation the causes for these facts, but as an observer of the common appearance of animals and birds in their common and normal surroundings I simply can't help being astonished, momently, at the marvel of ingenuity that some of the commonest things show in their surface painting.

Enough! I can never seem to stand up under argument, whether from natural unforcefulness or from faulty and seamy foundations I do not know. But much less can I be persuaded by 'common sense' like that of T. R., which denies *the fact* of blue snow shadows regardless of their purpose, here not important. So I might be worse than useless at a N. C. meeting. But I'd like to try.

Following the publication of a good deal of snappish correspondence on the subject in the columns of various ornithological magazines, there appeared in The Auk *for October, 1912, an article entitled 'Remarks on the Case of Roosevelt vs. Thayer,' written by Mr. Francis Allen himself. On the Roosevelt side he admits that the Thayers have not proven all coloration to be concealing. He suggests that the Thayers should have distinguished between those propositions susceptible of proof and those that must remain, at least until more evidence accrued, just theories. On the Thayer side he emphasizes that the Thayers are experts in color, that they have actually experimented where Roosevelt has only observed. He says further that Roosevelt is not a safe guide; Mr. Allen detected upward of fifty instances of his misquotations, misrepresentations, and perversions of the Thayers' statements. We should all experiment* more, we should guard against the tendency to say we see what we know to be there—the white underside of a bird, for example. We must not assume that a bird bright in the hand is conspicuous in the bush and that the only creatures around us are the ones we see.

L.A.F. to Francis H. Allen

Ithaca, N. Y., Oct. 12, 1912.

Bully for you! Your straightforward and reasonably seasoned contribution goes far toward re-establishing the equilibrium of the much-battered target known as concealing coloration.

Dropping the metaphor, and saying the thing quite straight, your article is a splendid, fair, thoughtful discussion; so frank and so fearless, and at the same time so self-respecting and fair-minded that it must make a good step forward. If you have any separates, I pray you send me one, for I am trying to gather all the 'evidence,' and keep abreast of the whole discussion. Your paper is the only one that hasn't descended to the cheap weapon of ridicule, and is essential to my 'coloratiana.' I thank you warmly for such a great help to the minds of the struggling as you have given. I cannot help feeling that it will be a long, long time—probably a generation or two—before the fascinating beauty and truth of Thayer's enlightenment on even the most evident phenomena of ensconced and circumstanced out-door colors (as against in-the-house-contemplated specimens) will be understood by non-experimenting naturalists. As a fact, they are the theorists, which they accuse the honestly experimenting Thayers of being. They stand in their own light, instead of standing aside and letting the light flood in on them.

But if anything in the way of discussion can break away the prejudices of pure objective and superficial impressions, your sober and logical and well-tempered paper is the one to do it. Personally, I am very grateful for so good an expression of what is almost exactly my own view of the general subject and the proportions and merits of the discussions of it. And I certainly congratulate you on your temperate but frank and courageous arraignment of such blundering complacency as our friend T. R. feels called upon to confess. He has apparently been unable to grasp even the most rudimentary parts of the thought, and has simply repudiated all the negative evidence, which is in the nature of the case (and as proof of it) in preponderance. You cannot know what balm it is to hear some one else bring forward these points.

By negative evidence Louis meant, you don't count the ones you don't see. Everyone who has walked in the country has been startled by a pheasant or grouse flushing almost at his feet, or by gulls rising in flight from a pebbly beach where they had stood invisible. An instance of the difficulty of seeing a hundred to a hundred and fifty parrots feeding in one fig tree is noted in the letter from Tampico. From his last expedition, that to Abyssinia in 1926, he wrote of 'open areas where spicy little sandgrouse jumped from complete invisibility into sudden existence as they burst into rapid dovelike flight.' Of the brilliant black-and-white guereza (colobus) monkeys, more boldly patterned even that the skunks or zebras, he remarked: 'It is astonishing . . . how entirely baffling their long, white, drooping hair makes their appearance when seen in thick places against the sky.' Thanks in large part to the Thayers, Louis' eyes were opened, and all his life he gathered evidence that was a confirmation of their theories. His pictures did more and more to suggest the principle, so dear to Abbott Thayer, that a bird's own colors dictated the only correct ones for the landscape he was in, although as an ornithological illustrator Louis had to make the birds stand out in contrast to their background and show off their characteristic marks of identification.

Louis also did his best to help other people to see. One of his favorite demonstrations, always, for visitors to his studio was to hold between them and the north light a little bird (one of the South American callistes, with black wings and tail) so that as they looked toward the light the feathers on its back appeared to be pale blue. He would then place the bird beyond the observers, whose backs were now to the window. As they looked away from the source of light at the bird, its back appeared to be deep aquamarine in color. Another specimen he used was golden-bronze when looked at into the light, and clear emerald-green when looked at away from it. People sometimes misunderstood the burden of this demonstration, taking it to indicate simply the changeableness of feathers, not the optical principle that color is relative to source and direction of light. But there could have been no misunderstanding of the demonstrations he used in his lectures. When he was lecturing at Cornell, in the years 1923 to 1926, four of the ten talks he gave each year were devoted to the subject of the coloration of animals. To illustrate he used lantern slides, models similar to the Thayers' sweet potatoes, and two ingenious devices of his own invention. These were racks which he placed in strong light on the window-sill of the classroom. Two uprights supported cross wires on which cards were fastened so they could be turned to any angle. On one of these racks there were cards that were black and cards that were white; by turning the black card so that it received full light it would appear to be lighter than the white card strung beneath it and in its shadow. The other rack held cards that were uniformly white on top, but tinted, each a different color, on the under side. The reflection of the colored underside would be cast upon the white top of the card next beneath it, so that each card except the top one seemed to be brightly colored. These demonstrations were completely persuasive of the fact that what you see is not what you know to be there.

Louis' clearest statements of these and other problems of coloration are found in the remarkable series of letters to his pupil, George M. Sutton, given in Chapter 15. For, problems they remain; although color photography has shown snow-shadows to be beyond a doubt blue, each generation must learn to see for itself and to interpret anew. Naturalists continue to gather evidence from the field and to interpret it—too often in the light of preconceived ideas, too often without the artist's imagination, eye, or training. The Thayers' book remains a classic, a thing of beauty in the text and in the illustrations, and during the fifty years since they were first set forth their theories have gained ground, although they still must share that ground with the notion that some animals' patterns serve for warning, some for display.

The subject cannot be pushed out of the foreground of Louis Fuertes' life and correspondence. No one who has learned to observe as Louis and the Thayers did, can put an end to discoveries of the evidence of animals' concealing coloration. Like Louis, the amateur naturalist of to-day may well be content to defer the question why and simply enjoy the new marvels of adaptation he he has been shown how to see.

12

Colombia, 1911

THE AUK FOR January, 1911, with its description of Fuertes'
oriole reached Louis at the same time as Dr. Chapman's annual
invitation—or temptation—to accompany him south. In 1911,
Colombia, South America, was the destination, and Louis felt
more than ever ready to succumb as he had been working hard and
successfully on the pictures for Mr. Brewster's study. In these
twenty-four large panels in oils 'the birds, chiefly water-fowl and
shore birds, take their proper place in a series of strongly handled
landscapes which reveal Fuertes' art in a new aspect. With no
sacrifice of his skill and insight as a painter of bird portraits, he has
here placed his subjects in a setting which adds immeasurably to
their beauty and to the appeal they make to the imagination. These
pictures, in the writer's opinion, are Fuertes' greatest achievement.'
The writer was Frank Chapman (in The American Museum
Journal for May, 1915) who was not alone in considering these
among Louis' best work. For once he had satisfied the generally
irreconcilable tastes of the scientific ornithologist, the wealthy
sportsman who placed the order, and his teacher.

L.A.F. TO F. M. CHAPMAN

Ithaca, N. Y., Jan. 7, 1911.

I am much touched by your wholly delightful references to me
in the context of the description of Icterus f. He makes a good

: 136 :

case, and I feel I am truly to be congratulated on him. And here's to you, trusty, with many thanks.

Now, not that the above covers the ground, but because there are other matters—and time comes so high and is so short when it comes—let us turn to this other proposition.

Your letters received, also Proc[eedings of the] Geog[raphic] Soc[iety] and contents noted. That's the trouble!

My job is going strong, and I may indeed be ready to stretch my legs and face by March 1. I am naturally much perturbed by these things you send me. You know that I was born with the itching foot, and the sight of a map—or even a time-table—is enough to stir me all up inside. If I finish I can afford to go, as I shall have earned a good rest, for my production has been even higher than that of the proverbial business hen—though I've laid 'em all in one basket [the Brewster pictures]. . . . I shall take all the pictures that are in any sort of condition and box them and send them to New Haven before I go west, and then run up Monday 22, and put them up and judge them. I may be going all wrong in my treatment. God permit that I am not (said fervently, with bowed head). I've been having a grand time with them, and have been in a high state of excited exaltation at the way they have slid onto the canvases. I imagine therefore, that by the same token I shall have an equally grand mental slump if I find them chalky or dull or over-bright or any of the dozen other things that can well and easily ail them. In my studio they look slick, though I says it as shouldn't: heaven only knows what another setting'll do to them. . . .

Abbott Thayer to L.A.F.

Monadnock, N. H., Jan. 25, 1911.

You should have got our thanks and enthusiasm for your photos [of the Brewster pictures] at once, but what a rush I have been in.

These paintings are your very best, and this is saying mighty much. The scaups are, sea and all, a wonder of snap and reality and wild scaup life, and the geese a *perfect* picture and the ptarmigan wonderful and in fact *no* weakling in the lot. The blue-wings are delightfully true and beautiful. I saw several flocks of I forget which river ducks at the Bronx Zoo last fall coming down out of the evening sky, back into the pond there with just that charming action and strongly rigid pose. . . . I hate to stop writing about those pictures.

L.A.F. TO ABBOTT THAYER

Ithaca, N. Y., Feb. 2, 1911.

I can't tell you how I was encouraged and set up by your too-kind letter. Those pictures were just four I had: since then I have had the rest (so far as done) photographed, and when the prints come, in a day or two, I want to send you the rest to complete the set. I think some are better than the ones I sent, but I am not sure!

I took nineteen down to New Haven and put them up, and was tremendously impressed! They really looked fine, and I think I should have liked them as much if somebody else had done them. That is a test I tried to give them. I have them all back for signing and varnishing, and hope to have the set ready to install by March. Most of it will be, surely. . . .

I hope the prints will give you pleasure: don't bother to write (though God knows that gave me a pang). Your praise, which I know you wouldn't give Japanesely merely to please, is meat and drink and opera to my spirit, and cherished and learned by heart in one reading.

The expedition bound for Colombia sailed March 13. With Dr. Chapman and Louis went Leo Miller, a young man without previous experience in the field who became one of the most valuable of the museum's collectors. William Richardson of the American Museum came from Nicaragua to join the others at Buenaventura on the Pacific side of the Panama Canal. From there they went to Cali by rail and mule, using this isolated town as headquarters for their collecting in the Cauca valley. Their first regular work was done at San Antonio, at an elevation of 6,500 feet.

L.A.F. TO MRS. FUERTES

Cali, Colombia, Mar. 28, 1911.

We are here. And in an extremely record-breaking space of time:

just two weeks from the day we left N. Y. The mail that came with us as far as Buenaventura will probably take a week more to get here. . . .

B. is a beautifully situated place as seen from the sea, ten miles up a mangrove-lined river, but once there, you see a filthy, wet, bug-infested, fever-ridden collection of shacks and 'dobes, which we were only too glad to get right out of. The tri-weekly train was there, and we left on time at 7 a.m. and got as far as Cisneros, after following the Dagua thirty-five miles through the most marvelous tropical mountain scenery imaginable. Saw where the monkeys cross, but didn't see them crossing. The forest only enters the Dagua Valley for the first 1,800 feet, but clothes the tops of the ridges over 4,000 feet entirely, leaving a great arid, desert-like (and furiously hot) basin that looks like Arizona mountain country. We passed one night at Caldas, at about 2,500 feet, and left at noon next day with all our outfit but my saddle, which didn't show up. We had the customary wrangles with the mule men, etc. etc., but finally Richardson, who speaks [like] a native and understands them in great shape, got all in motion and we were off. We climbed up and on and up and on until about four p.m., when we reached El Carmén, a little village near the upper timber line, where we had lunch, and saw a fight, and a real professional cock-fight, as it was Sunday. Then we pushed on, and by dark reached the first settle-ment at the edge of the upper forest, 'El Tigre' where we spent the night at the *hacienda*. Then we left early next a.m. after a comfort-able night on a hardwood bench and nothing but a sweat-and-rain-soaked horseblanket for both mattress and cover, and my pants for a pillow. I could have drawn the grain of the entire bench without looking at it for you, I was so familiar with it by morning. Our cargo had not caught up to us, so we couldn't get any clothes or bedding. We had a look around in the morning, as the rain had stopped and we could see down the valley. We rode about two hours, into the noble high forest, and into the rain. For the clouds hang just level with the forest line. Where the forest dips down into a valley the clouds follow it, and when a bare hill goes up above the general level, the clouds rise and leave it clear. This happens not once in a while, but day after day; all the time. Of course it sometimes rains in the open valley, and sometimes clears in the mountain forest, but these times are the exception, and the conditions as I described them the regular daily ones.

I was pretty wet when we reached the summit, 6,500 feet, at San Antonio, so I thought I'd take a look at the forest. It was sodgey-sopping wet, rain pouring with a loud shush on the drooping forest. The path was a soup of dead leaves, mud, moss, etc., from three inches to knee deep. Every tree and vine was inches deep with spongey moss, wonderful flowers, deep blue, white, yellow and red, and ferns growing out of every fork, and orchid plants in every bunch of moss. I spent an hour in this wonderful country, and shot some ten wondrous birds. I only had my pistol, so I couldn't get the big things, like trogons and toucans. We left San Antonio (which is only a road house, kept by an Indian woman, whose three-year-old girl was sitting in the door as we came up, *smoking a big black cigar!!!*) at about 2 o'clock, after our mules came up, and my clothes had dried a little. After the first half mile or less the forest stopped as abruptly as it had begun, on the other side of the ridge, and a long, hot, dry ride of several hours lay ahead of us, though we could see the sun shining on the Cauca valley, and the city of Cali, before we got out of the rain. Cali itself is the most individual and unspoiled place I ever saw. There is not a thing in it that has come less than two (and from there up to twenty) days on mule-back, and the people in it look on all the world as outlandish, and tolerate us as being harmlessly imbecile and good pay. The first sentinel to the town is an enormous palm tree: twice as big as I ever saw elsewhere. This you pass, skirt the river Cali for another half-mile, and enter the city through a lovely grove, made entirely by four trees, two on each side of the road. They are enormous ceibas, or silk-cotton trees, like [those] we saw in Jamaica, only not so high but much broader. They are set some fifty feet from the road, and a hundred feet apart on each side of it, and their shade is continuous. Just through them is the bridge, a most picturesque yellowish brick one, with a long rising arch over which you have to ride to enter Cali. It is a town of some thirty or forty thousand inhabitants, theater, etc., etc., but not a carriage or wagon, though a street railway runs some four or five miles down to the Cauca, where you can take a steamer down to Esmiralda.

We got in late yesterday afternoon, in time for a good dinner: our first square meal that day, though Apolonia, the Indian woman at the ridge, roasted us each a plantain, and opened some sardines! The combination of dinner, bed the night before, and two day's riding were too much for me, and when I flopped down, right after dinner, on my half-inflated bed, I passed away immediately, and when C. woke me up at 10:30, I only lasted long enough to finish blowing up the bed and get back on it. I slept then solid till 6 this a.m., when I got up and skinned my yesterday's birds. R. has about a thousand birds here from the mountain region about San Antonio, and I have been much interested to look them over.

We have decided to take nobody's word as to wet and dry seasons, as nobody agrees with anybody else. So we have spent the day to-day rearranging the outfit, have leased a villa near San Antonio for at least a week, and leave tomorrow for a return over our yesterday's trail, and will be *haciendados* of 'La Henriquita' for a while, where I can get a good view of the *cordillera central*, with the Cauca valley for middle ground, and the near forest for local foreground. There I will paint such moments as are propitious, and hunt and collect and help with the group materials and accessories the rest of the time. It is *marvelous* country up there; awfully wet, but cool, and *free from insects*, with an abundance of good water.

I will write whenever I get a chance, and send the letters in, and they'll go out as soon as the people here have decided they might as well go as lie around. You can put a brick on the table here and it will be there when you come back, in fifteen years!

San Antonio, Colombia, Mar. 31, 1911.
This is the biggest stroke of luck you ever saw. We took any house we could get (there are only four in San Antonio, summer houses of Cali people) and it is a peach: lots of room, beds, chairs

and tables, washing and cooking things *ad lib*. It is cool, almost cold, at night, and for two days it has been clear and without rain. The group is to be made from here, and I am waiting for a view of the central chain to begin the painting. The range is forty miles or more away, so it is not often that we can see it. I have put in the last two days in the forest, and have made up about twenty skins from this region. Our house is about three-fourths of a mile from the ridge, and near (though not in) the big forests. This afternoon I got a great black bird, as large as a crow, with a chestnut belly and a big orange ruff on the throat. Trogons and toucans are quite common, though not easy to get. The difficulty lies in finding what we have shot after it is down, as unless you mark it exactly as it falls there is no hope, the undergrowth is so thick, and there is so much trash on the ground: dead leaves as big as our dining table; moss, soft and soaking, a foot deep; and sticks and dead wood and leaf mold to any depth. Hummers are lost four to one found. I have done very well in quality, having landed some fine birds—some of which Richardson has only taken once, in sixteen weeks' work here, and I've only a small proportion of lost birds so far.

You would think our house a dirty shack, and us pigs, probably, but we think we are fine, and *know* that the house is a godsend. We get up at 5:30 (daylight) and in a few minutes an Indian woman Rich. found living nearby has our coffee ready, and we drink it and start for our day's work in the forest. It is always wet there, but warm to excess in the daytime. *No insects*, except wondrous moths and butterflies which are a never-ceasing cause of excitement. But the freedom from mosquitoes and ticks etc. is a mercy, and is appreciated as such.

We hunt the woods till about 10:15, when we turn back, reaching here about 10:45 or 11. At 11, we have our real breakfast, which is a corker: a great big plate *full* of soup, made of meat bones, rice, plantain, and vegetables, all we can eat of beans, and such birds of the day's bag as are big enough. After breakfast, in dry clothes and well fed, we sit down at the long table on the east porch and skin our birds, which we can generally clean up by about 4:30 or 5. By that time dinner is ready, and is much the same kind of a meal as the 11 o'clock breakfast; a good solid square meal of soup, beans, and stew, with bully coffee.

Our day's work ends with dinner and we generally go to bed by 7:30 or 8. That gives us all the rest we need, and we are all in bully shape. This is a cool, lovely climate, with a good deal of rain, but no such excess as there is down at Buenaventura. The views from this place are surpassingly wonderful. In the afternoon it is positively too immense and impressive and we feel afraid that some day we might get used to it, as these natives are! This is the way it piles down from our very door. (Sketch) The Cauca valley is a flat floor forty-five miles or so wide, and Cali is really in it, but at the *base* of the western range. We have once (this a.m. for ten minutes) seen enough of the central range to know of its general height and contours, but it was just a few places that showed above the clouds. Last night, at sunset, there was a double rainbow of greatest brilliance that stretched from end to end of our valley view . . . enclosing the most glorious blue and gold and rose sunset reflections you can imagine. We just stood and gugged at it like a bunch of dips.

Speaking of dips, I'm writing by one now, and as it's about out I'll knock off for now, and finish another time. Good night.

Sat. night

As there are reasons why one cannot spend his Saturday nights in the good old traditional way on this ridge, I take my pen in hand once more. There isn't much to say: I could describe scenery, or tell you how many and what kinds of birds I got, or how long my beard is, but statistics are dull. I went down the side of the mountain to-day, and got into a tangle that made me so mad I nearly cried. It is exhausting to the very limit, and when you are all soaked, and hot and sticky, and every one of ten million vines has hooks or brittle thorns that break off their points in you, and all conspire to baffle you in every tiny movement, it gets so wearisome that at times you want to yell, and hit back. If you do, however, you get all the skin scratched off your hands, and probably your face too. So just smile and be gentle—relax, in other words, and all they will do is to take off your hat as you turn to look for a way out. Never mind, put it on again—off it comes again, then, while thinking what good control you have, *bing* out goes the root you were standing on from under you, and you slide fifteen feet down a clay bank covered with climbing bamboo. Lest you think, however, that I am complaining, I will say that this place is free from all kinds of bothersome bugs, and the forests are gloriously rank and riotous: leaves as big as our dining table hang from the moss-embedded tree trunks; masses of scarlet flowers tip the ends of vines that fall from the treetops; queer human whistles mingle with whoops and hermit-thrush songs, and owl-like hoots with the thrilling buzz of a gorgeous hummer as he shoots past, or hangs with waving tail too close to shoot at. That was just an incident, we get so tired at the end of the morning that little things seem big, and everything for the time goes wrong, or seems to.

Wednesday, April 5.

I've let several days go by, as they are much alike, and we are so busy that it is awfully easy to go to bed after supper, and there's no such thing as writing at any other time, especially for me, as I have to do the best I can with collecting and skinning, to say nothing of painting every old bird that comes in with a blue face, green bill, or purple feet, besides detail of flowers, leaves, and the big drawings and paintings for the group. As that is what I'm here for, I feel that here, at least, I ought to hold myself ready to do anything that is suggested. I'm now about through with my part of the group work: I have painted and checked up the study for the background, and made notes of forest-colors for Horsfall to use, and done a lot of flowers, etc., and have also, in the week we've been here, put up about fifty-five or sixty birds, including several doves and trogons, which are possessed of tissue-paper skins in which the feathers just stick by special favor of heaven. Yesterday I shot *and lost* a beautiful small trogon which I called for half an hour. Killed him dead, went right to the spot, hunted over *an hour*, and couldn't find him. Later I got a perfectly magnificent big trogon, as big as a big pigeon, with long bronzy-green feathers that fall over the tail and wings—so (sketch) and a beautiful nasal crest and a *rose red* eye! All his plumage above and on the breast the most gorgeous metallic emerald green, with gold and blue reflection in different lights, wings black, tail black with big white side feathers, and entire under parts blood-red. Next to the Guatemalan quetzal, he's the finest of all these beautiful birds.

To-day I went back, and *found* my lost trogon. A big spider had eaten part of his head, otherwise he was perfect. I also to-day got the best bird of the expedition so far; a big shy tinamou, or forest grouse, weighing about five pounds—a queer, elusive thing that may be new. F.M.C. has never seen anything like it. It is ashy gray, beautifully pencilled with darker, and really belongs with the ostrich family. (Sketch) We had him for dinner to-night, and his meat was as white, and as sweet and tender as a partridge, and enough for four hungry tramps to get a square feed off of.

We are going to try to get away from here by Saturday noon, spend Sunday in Cali, and then go up to Eder's ranch above Palmira. Next week is Holy Week, and in this country they won't do anything but fight roosters on church holidays, so we must get out Monday or else lose the whole week in Cali, which would be a catastrophe.

Sunday noon.

Strange as it seems to do things on time here in Colombia, we actually got our horses up from Cali yesterday . . . by noon, had them packed by one, and started down the twelve mile trail for Cali, bag and baggage, by 3:30 p.m. It poured nearly every step of the way, and at times the trail was like a roaring river. From the ridge we could look a couple of thousand feet down into one valley where the sun was shining and the stream a tiny sighing thread of white, on the other side a deep purple shadow of thunder-clouds, long slanting ribbons of rain drenching everything, every gulley the bed of a roaring stream of clay-stained water, and a regular river at the bottom. To-day we are in Cali, repacking, drying our birds (all of which we got down in fine shape: about sixty for me and some hundred and fifty for F.M.C., R., and M.) and tomorrow at

8 a.m. the four pack mules start for Palmira, across the river, where Eder lives.

'La Manuelita,' which is the Eder sugar ranch at Palmira, Colombia. Good Friday, 1911.

As per schedule, we left Cali last Monday at noon, and crossed the Cauca, river and valley, and landed on our feet at this lovely place at dark. We were met a few miles out by a Mr. Macy, who is Eder's Sup't. here, I judge—a nice young fellow from Minnesota and Harvard. We found Eder getting well from a broken collarbone, from being run away with in a wagon. Nearly well now.

The ride across the valley was hot, but the most thrillingly interesting day's ride I think I ever took, what with the green valley, bamboo forests, strange and numerous birds, *miles* of immense locusts, like the plague of Egypt, that nearly obscured the mountains behind. The ranch lies some three or four miles east and south of Palmira, and is entirely devoted to the growing and manufacturing of sugar, which is sufficient to supply the greater part of the Cauca valley, and a lot goes over the Quindío pass, in the central range, to Bogotá, and a lot goes out at Buenaventura, to Colón, Baranquilla, and in on the Atlantic side.

But the best thing that has happened yet was that yesterday a mail came in, with your first letter, written just after I left New York . . . We are going to start Sunday (Easter) and go up to the mountain ranch, where there's a good house, visible from the porch of this house, though 6,500 feet high in the mountains, and stay there for the rest of our time here—a month or six weeks, and with that as a base, work the middle range as high as we can. We have had five days here, and have the best of the valley birds, and we ought to do exceedingly well up there, as it is new ground, and much of our collection should be new.

To-day I went about a mile to some old forest, and heard the howler monkeys, big red fellows that bark like a lion—full as loud —and make a tremendous roar like the howling of a gale of wind through big trees. Macy, who had Frank's 22 rifle, shot a great big old roaring male; it is a little uncanny, as the beast is certainly a human-looking thing, with his hands and his black face and long dark red-brown beard . . . (Sketch)

'Miraflores,' 6,000 ft. up
on the central *cordillera*,
April 24, 1911.

We have been up here now for over a week, and though we are in a good house, with a family to look after us and have therefore all that we need as to food, shelter, and general care, we are as thoroughly out of the world as I have ever been. Before I forget it, I want to tell you about Rita, our cook. She came up the day after we got here, in the convoy of our 'major domo's' son, Francisco, on the deck of a black mule. As she loomed out of the valley, herself as black as night, with a long tightly-swathed black shawl, she was surely the real thing in spooks. Tall and slim, sixty plus years old, she wears for daily use, as a waist, a naïvely inadequate towel, so arranged as to be no good at all, either for purposes of warmth, concealment, or even mere decoration: when she can get one, she also wears a long black cigar between her bare gums, for she has no teeth that ever meet. Her lanky arms are welted and scarred so that they look like blacksnakes run over by a train, and her wool is cropped short. She is simple, good-natured, and kind, thoughtfully feeding the whole family out of our stores, which have consequently to be replenished every few days. . . .

The birds here are fine—many kinds—probably at least twenty— of hummers, four of parrots, at least three of beautiful trogons (sketch), four of toucans, and any number of strange small birds, with queer noises and songs. Of course the insects are wonderful; all kinds of queer, enormous beetles, gigantic spiders and tarantulas, etc., etc., and butterflies beautiful beyond description. The forests are clothed in moss, out of clumps of which grow wonderful orchids, air plants of all kinds, and all hung together by a network of vines and 'wood-ropes.' Gorgeous green and scarlet trogons glide and swoop through them, and parrots yell up in the lighted tree-tops, but on the ground it is nearly dark, and queer little birds run around among the ground plants, never taking wing, but calling, like rails, almost under foot but never visible. Some of the very most common have not yet once been seen, though the forest rings with their whistles, and we can at any time call up two or three to within a few feet of us. Curiously silent motmots glide up from near the ground and sit motionless in the vines, while way up in the distant tree-tops giant orioles, like the big one I brought from Mexico, bark, scream, and hoot, up-side-down, and crackle their bills. Dark-colored forest hummers come and swing buzzing a few inches from your face, or light close by and look you over fearlessly. Way off down the mountain a forest quail rolls out his musical whistle, curiously distinct, 'Cavalry kevelry cavalry,' the first and last syllables of succeeding phrases overlapping, as if two were doing it. But I watched one the other day (and lost him for my pains) and it is a one-bird stunt. . . .

I'm getting now, as nobody outside ourselves speaks English, so that I can get along first-rate in 'spigotty' as they call the Spanish on the isthmus. I have a boy that goes along with a machete and helps find (and generally finds) the birds, and I can talk along with him quite well, and have no trouble in finding out what I want. Of course, making motions helps, and I'm long there.

Of dangerous animals and snakes we have seen nothing, and do not expect to. There are ocelots, and probably jaguars, somewhere in the mountains, but to get them requires special effort, dogs, guides, etc., which is not worth while. You needn't worry a minute about my being in dangerous country, as this is all as safe as West Hill or Newfield, and the people as friendly and a lot more interested, as strangers are about the rarest thing in these mountains, and I've no doubt that we have been the subjects of many an interested discussion. We are generally considered doctors, collecting birds for certain rare medicinal purposes: extract of hummingbird being a cure for rheumatism, etc., etc. That they can understand, while the entire idea of science or interest in the things we collect [is] entirely beyond their comprehension. So we sit tight, and let 'em think we'll sell the juice of the birds to cure man's ills for much fine gold, and thus retain their respect!

Wed., [April] 26.

On one cup of coffee, and *nothing* else, I this day hunted the high mountain trails, above 7,000 feet, from 6:20 a.m. till 1:20 p.m. As our whole time and interest go into this bird business, there's little left to write about, as nothing else makes a dent. True, we have the same troubles here as at home: mosquitoes bite here as there, and to-day the cook said she was leaving, because she'd used up all the candles and we didn't give her more. So we said 'Adios,' and she's still here, and trying to make bread, which she fries, because the dough won't rise at this height, she says. However the woman on the other range, five hundred feet higher, made fine white-flour bread.

I went up, to-day, toward the top of this range, to a trail I discovered some days ago, where I've seen or heard some good things, and after shooting a green toucan out of a high tree, in thick fog, and spending over half an hour finding him (as you have first to cut your way through vines and nettles etc. to where you think he fell, and then lay the place bare, or open it up so you can see the ground to hunt him, when half of the times, at least, he got caught in vines way up above where you can't possibly find him). Well, this time I found him, and he was a long way, by the watch, from where I stood when I shot him, though not more than thirty yards. But most of the thirty yards was up and down, and not much on the horizontal, as it's like this here. (Sketch) Well, as I said, after getting the toucan, and losing some other things, I was at last in a very dark, deep, and damp part of the old forest, looking for a little brush-wood bird I'd shot, when I dully became aware of what I would call at home the noon whistle of some distant mill: a steady, very slowly rising note. Then I thought of a toad or frog, and then again of an insect, like a locust. I timed it, three times, from the first I could sense the sound, as it began with nothing. The watch said 54, 57, 48 seconds, the longest consecutive note I ever heard any creature make. I imitated it, whistling inward part of the time, and the third time it answered, to my amazement, it was only a few feet away—perhaps twice the length of my canoe. So I knew it must be a bird—for nothing else would come so quickly to a call, and I froze still as a stump. It was foggy—thick and dark with clouds, and almost black in the densely shaded place I was hunting, and as I searched the gloom, trying to distinguish things, a ghostly shadow of nothing glided out into a small space more open than most, and there, only about 20 feet off, stood a big-eyed spectral bird; whether tinamou, thrush, quail or what, I couldn't tell, as I could only half see in the dark. But I've had my troubles looking too long at new birds before doing anything about it, so I instantly pulled up, in great and wobbling excitement, for here was a new bird, of wonderful interest. In my haste and excitement I did what I've often done before, and probably shall to the end of my days, and pulled the wrong trigger. Instead of a clean little pop of my 'aux,' BLAM went the other barrel, and a great hole was torn in the ground some 20 feet away. Hoping against hope that I'd almost missed, though feeling sure that I'd nailed him, I ran over, only to find that I had literally annihilated a splendid, rare—possibly new—bird. There was a mess of mud, meat, feathers, dead leaves, strung along for two yards. The main remnant, however, had the bill, part of a wing, a few feathers and one entire foot still held together; enough to see that it really was—or had been—a new species to us. As we'd never before heard this note, and as this family are all great and continuous callers, the chances were that we should never get another chance at it. You can be sure I was sick, and I sat there too chagrinned to even swear, looking at my poor bunch of had-been bird. Anyway, I resolved to keep that wonderful note fresh in my mind, to make a note of at camp, so, still sitting where I'd torn open the ground, I took out my watch and practised it 'by the clock.' I had done it three times, when a sharp 'wip-wip-wip-wip,' right at hand, made me look sharp. This note I heard yesterday, up in the top forest on the ridge, and couldn't locate. So I 'wip-wip'ed cautiously, and kept still with my eyes open and gun ready. A few still, tense seconds, and, right across the little hollow went another silent little shadow, and this time I was ready and willing, and pulled the right barrel, and had the excitement of going over and picking up a beautifully shot and perfect peach of a little long-legged, big-eyed thrush-like bird, doubtless the mate of the male I had blown to pieces. It sounds very cold-blooded, and I am not gloating over the killing so much as the virtual discovering, calling and identifying of a probably new species of one of the most difficult . . . tropical forest birds. [See page 182] Well, this is getting very long, and *it* is getting very late— 8:30 in fact, and everybody else is in bed. So I must go too.

It's Friday night, and raining like the devil, as it has been since about noon. But it started in nicely, and I got off at a bit after 6:30, and beat it up the trail for a look at the forest on the top of the range, at 8,000 feet. It has been in the clouds all the last week, and so dark and wet that there was no use in going there. But luck was with me to-day, for it stayed clear nearly all the time I was on the climb, and for three-quarters of an hour after I got to the top. I got some fine birds; two kinds of pigeon—one a big tree-top pigeon and the other a quail-dove, that lives in the wet dark places, and is almost never seen, though its single note, a deep, strong 'toot,' is one of the things that gives the forest its strangely impressive, Sunday-like character. I also got some fine little forest birds, rare in collections, and had some more fun with my 'noon-whistle' bird; though it was too thick for me to find them, I had them all around me when I got about 7,500 up, and practised up on the notes. To-day they only whistled 20 to 40 seconds. I got a gorgeous little tree-top bird, like those wonderful Peruvian *callistes* that I have at home. It is a *calliste* (and I have taken seven or eight other kinds, too, but nothing like this.) He is beautiful turquoise blue with black wings and tail and stripes in his back, his belly is strong rich buff, and his head bright shiny golden yellow, set all round with black. (Sketch) But it was only partly for birds that I went up, and the rest was to see the forest itself, which Frank said was the finest he had ever seen. The trail for a mile or more goes almost straight up, zig-zagging between immense trees, and bordered close on both sides with a rank growth of vines and big lily plants . . . When it rained the other day while we were in the woods, Roso (the native boy Richardson picked up) without a word, and quite as a matter of course, cut off and handed me a giant leaf—a lily— about five feet long and three wide, another for himself, and though it poured (as you know it can in these parts) we were as dry as could be while the shower lasted! (Sketch) Although there are tree ferns all through the forest here, at all altitudes, up at about 7,000 feet they get almost the predominant tree, touching each other, and forming a filmy curtain of lace about thirty feet above the ground, and making a most lovely light. Of course there are giant trees of all species, too, that make an entirely independent forest, way above, and all manner of vines, 'wood-ropes,' and creepers, hung deep with mosses, out of which spring beautiful ferns, drooping, like the finest 'Boston' ferns, many feet. When it is clear in the woods, the mass of greenery, and the immensity of things, both in size and variety, is sort of stupefying, and you just feel damned small and insignificant and wormlike, and have a strong tendency to whisper instead of talk out loud, but when it is foggy, all the infinitely complicated background is lost in gray, and you get the most beautiful silhouettes of enormous trees, isolated more or less from the great forest mass, and see the wonderful grace and form-beauty of the host-tree and all its beautiful parisitic decoration. The whole stem of the tree becomes a great fernery, for a starter, and then wonderfully beautiful great tropical lilies send out grace-fully curved stems with 'elephant ear' leaves; pineapple-like plants grow in flowering masses from the joints of the limbs, perpendicular wood-ropes, trimmed with hanging gardens, come from the distant tree-tops, and root in the ground, and a little distance away the theme is repeated, with variations, one shade less green and one shade paler in the gray of the mist. These things make me itch to paint them, but they are in themselves unpaintable, I suppose, and must be enjoyed, like sunsets and opals, only in themselves, and cannot be perpetuated. Which may be a good thing, but it makes me feel very ungenerous to be here hogging all this beauty and excitement, without being able to save it for the rest of you.

'La Manuelita,' Tues., May 2.

I left off the other night abruptly; tired, the light went out. It was our last candle, and I went to bed in the dark, except for a light-beetle that flew on the piazza and I caught 'im. (Sketch) . . .

I only did one morning's work after the high climb, and spent Monday packing up the outfit's birds (nearly 400) and getting ready to come down. The mules came about noon, and we got them packed off by about 2, and were here at La Manuelita at about 5:30. The Nima River, which we usually ford in crossing, was so swollen by the rains that it was a raging roaring river, so we got off our mules and crossed on a foot bridge built high above flood level, and shooed the mules into the river to cross as best they could. They were up to their shoulders in frothy rapids, and swept several rods downstream; it was quite exciting to see them, and uncertain-looking. But they got over all right. The pack animals, of course, had to be all unloaded, and the packs taken over the bridge on the backs of the mule drivers, and repacked on this side. In spite of this, however, they were only one and a half hours behind us. The trip home was fine. Hundreds of parrots were going to roost along the trail at about 5.

Cali, Colombia, May 8, 1911.

After leaving La Manuelita the other day, we had a long string of experiences, bumped on muleback over some seventy-five miles of unspeakable roads, got caught twice at nightfall far from our planned destination and had to take the hospitality of men who had never heard of us, bag and baggage, at haciendas on the way, found Güengüe full of fever, the house unfinished, spent one night there in awful confusion, collected some birds, and skinned them next a.m. some 25 miles away on a stranger's piazza, after a heart-breaking ride in the mud and sun, crossed the Cauca valley and were here at the hotel, our base, at 5 p.m.

Cali, Colombia, May 10, 1911.

The end of this week or the first of next comes the little stern-wheel steamer 'El Sucre' which will take Frank and me to Cartago. So, unless you have written me at Baranquilla, I shall not get any more letters from you, as we are on our journey home. It is two days to Cartago, as the boat ties up every night, and then eight to sixteen days over the Quindío pass in the main chain of the Andes to Honda. We shall take that easy, and if we like, stop over a day here and there, at different levels, as we get to places that look promising, and collect a few birds. From Honda down the Magdalena is a five to ten day trip, depending on the speed of the river, which varies much with the rains, and then, too, the boats are a little naïve about changing their schedules without notice. So one often misses a week by getting to the port on sailing day to find the boat gone the day before. A week is nothing to a Colombiano.

There is a lively account of the trip out of Colombia in Chapman's Autobiography of a Bird-Lover, pp. 234-41. They embarked on a small flat-bottomed steamer for a two-day trip to Cartago down the Cauca, a meandering river passing the bare moulded slopes of the coast range on one side, with a view of the massive central Andes across a wide valley on the other. At Cartago they crossed the valley and climbed to 11,200 feet before starting the descent toward the Magdalena. A little inn, El Pié de San Juan, housed them at the base of the eastern slope for long enough to permit Dr. Chapman to hunt, shoot, and lose a torrent duck, one of a seldom-seen species that spends much of its time under the waters of fast flowing streams. 'The story of my failure to get a torrent duck only stimulated Fuertes,' writes Dr. Chapman. 'In due time he found one which, like mine, was on a rock in the river; and when, like mine, it fell into the water, he did not, like me, attempt to follow it along the bank, but, dropping his gun and glass, plunged in after it. Swept by the current, in danger from rolling stones, he nevertheless managed to reach the bird, threw it ashore and came out where he could, farther down the river. It was a cold, bedraggled man that finally reached the inn, but he had his bird and was aglow with an inner warmth that defied the chill of mountain streams. That afternoon he painted his prize; the only time, I believe, that the species has been drawn from life studies and a freshly captured specimen.'

The party spent sixteen days traveling down the Cauca, across the valley, and over the mountains, and seven more on the Magdalena. Among the strangely assorted company on board the river steamer were an aria-singing priest and a young virtuoso of the guitar, whom Louis, on deck of an evening, decoyed to himself with the flute-like notes of his ocarina. Soon there was trio music for the pleasure of all, as they steamed along what was then Colombia's chief highway to the Caribbean Sea. By day they could hear and see 'howling monkeys and blue and yellow macaws in the forest, capybaras on the banks, and close-massed crocodiles, lying with wide-open mouths, on the playas. Herons, ibises, screamers, and, rarely, Jabiru storks flew over the marshes.'

They arrived at Baranquilla only to find that their ship was to sail from Santa Marta, and therefore ended their South American adventures with a sixty-mile launch journey through inland bays and mangrove backwaters to La Viega, and from there they made a journey by rail to the coast. Louis reached Ithaca in June.

13

The Hard Year

THE LONG LULL between collecting trips—from the summer of 1911 to early spring, 1913—seems to have been full of difficulties for Louis. His children were little, and although his household was blessed by the kind and untiring services of Eida Andrews, who prepared the meals, cleaned the house, and then changed into a nurse's uniform and took the children out to walk, this period of early childhood with its colds and tonsilitises was exhausting for Mrs. Fuertes. No doubt her worry and fatigue had its effect on Louis. He was producing pictures at top speed and sometimes failing to please those for whom he was painting them. Furthermore he was seriously bothered by the wretched reproduction of such pictures as were accepted. There occurred a hitch in the normally smooth relations between the Thayers and himself, and for the only time in his life he had a fairly long spell of poor health.

His letters from this period show signs of strain and mild complaint against those who criticized or were responsible for the printing of his pictures, and here almost alone in his whole correspondence is some description of an illness; still he was always cheerful, and the bounce and rebounce with which he replied to the fault-finding of Dr. Chapman is nothing less than gallant.

Near the end of October, 1911, Louis went to Monadnock for the wedding of Gerald Thayer and Alma Wollerman. Their marriage was followed by a honeymoon of camping on the mountain, unfortunately curtailed by the sickness and death of the pet macaw, Wa-wa. Gerald sent the macaw's carcass to Louis, hoping that he would get some specialist at Cornell to perform an autopsy and find out what had caused its death. Louis misunderstood this; taking the receipt of Wa-wa's body as an opportunity to do something for the Thayers, to whom he felt deeply indebted, he prepared the skin and painted Wa-wa's portrait as a gift for them. They did not accept it, for reasons given in the letters below, and their rejection of his gift was a bitter blow to Louis.

GERALD THAYER TO L.A.F.

Monadnock, N. H., Feb. 4, 1912.

Louis, I was touched to hear of the big beautiful Wa-wa picture which you had painted for us! And what will you say when I confess that I, for my part, am temperamentally disinclined to live with such a picture? That man Wa-wa was too near to me: I don't want his graven image hanging round! Thus, in my foolishness, if you please, I am *declining the gift* of a big, beautiful, gorgeous, lasting Louis-picture! Confound me, but I cannot help it! I know you will forgive, even if you cannot altogether understand. Papa may perhaps answer otherwise.

No other 'brute beast,' no dog, even, has ever come as close to me as that macaw, and I should never have supposed that any could come as close as that. Newcomers saw the surface only of that gaudy, rachety cuss. For his master there was revelation within revelation. Very strange has grown to seem to me the human dogma of unquestionable, abysmal human superiority over 'lower' animals, and the absolute want, in those 'lower' animals, of all the 'higher' elements of mentality.

I could not talk myself out, about that macaw, without my best friend's suspecting me of sentimentality and ungoverned imagination. . . .

Well, good night Louis. Come again to our wedding, won't you?

ABBOTT THAYER TO L.A.F.

Monadnock, N. H., April 25, 1912.

A glimpse of some of Wa-wa's carpentry on the kitchen rafters just now brings up my chronic question, in my mind, whether I, personally, ever took my part of explaining what you said truly needed no explanation; that your offer to give us W's portrait was the only possible L.A.F. picture chance that we *could* need to lose. Wait till you have such a bird five years. We simply *could not* stand such a reminder of him. He was somehow entirely supernatural or what is an equivalent he got us superstitious in some way. Strange, but not even now can we any better stand even talking about him.

It was late in November when Louis received Wa-wa's body, and his habit was, when in possession of a fresh skin, to drop all other work and paint it at once before the colors lost their freshness. He may have done so then, and at the same time designed his Christmas card (which had red and blue macaws on it), although he had been working under almost intolerable pressure during the fall. Along with other commissions and regular work for Bird-Lore he was preparing illustrations for a new edition of Dr. Chapman's Handbook of Birds of the Eastern United States. Dr. Chapman was hard to please, and Louis often felt that his criticisms were autocratic, arbitrary, and his dead-lines set by his personal schedule —not because the publication in question was pressing, but because Dr. Chapman was about to leave town as he did every winter and wanted to have the pictures in hand before he started south. Letters from the winter of 1911-12, besides carrying forward the narrative, show the nature of Dr. Chapman's requests, as well as Louis' response.

L.A.F. to F. M. Chapman

Ithaca, N. Y., Nov. 24, 1911.

Yesterday's letter, as might be expected, shot a bolt into my insides. I must confess, myself, to liking the tanager plate the least. It hung fire a long time, and while it never quite satisfied me it was plain in showing what I conceived to be the requirements of the plate, and is in many ways the most difficult of the lot. The reds have all to be built up, at intervals of several days, of different colors: Chinese white (which is sub-deliquescent, and takes sometimes a week to dry out), then an accurate covering of yellow which must not 'pull up' the white, another settling for a day or two, then lastly a graded and modeled dressing of the final red, which may not be touched subsequently and which must not drag up the willing undercolors. That's the only way I can get even a fairly brilliant scarlet, and it's some job, especially when it's mixed and varied with dull olive and yellows, which with the slightest overlapping make a black line. Send it back, and I'll do what I can —radical changes are impossible, except doing it all over new, which I will do if you like, but you'll have to wait for it till I can give it the full process, for there's no hurrying it.

I was genuinely disappointed that you didn't like the flycatcher plate, for while you are right in saying that your letter said 'like above,' meaning the thrushes, and are so technically O.K., I thought that one of the prettiest little compositions of the lot, and as it shows all the comparable differences of color, size, and pattern, besides showing characteristic poses of the most characteristic of them (contopus and E. minimus) I thought it would really be more useful than the map idea. But you are more than right when you shrewdly guess that I want you to be ultimately satisfied with these pictures, and any changes you want, if I can make them, I will gladly. Only I doubt if you realized how overburdened with work I am, for which not only the Handbook and Bird-Lore are anxious, but as well the Biol. Survey (whose appropriations run out annually and revert to the treasury, to be had next year with increasing difficulty because unused this) which has two impending bulletins—hawks and owls, and flycatchers—the big pheasant work, on which I am the most behindhand of all, having submitted only one plate, the unfinished State book, Pearson's now almost mythical Carolina book, etc., etc. All this work should be done or well in hand now, and I must, much as I dislike to do it, plead extenuating circumstances, and as I can't, at this time of year, work after 4 in the p.m. or before 9 in the a.m. from lack of light, I feel like a hobbled horse with a nice pasture just over an otherwise jumpable wall. And you must remember, too, that this work of yours (though nothing you could forésee, of course,) came up very suddenly and landed with rather a large splash in the midst of other also pressing work—and so I have just shut my ears and my conscience and gone ahead as calmly as possible under the circumstances. But I hope some day to get a breathing spell when I can with a clear conscience throw up my arms and say *Done*, by gosh, and think over a few things that have been side-tracked in the back of my head the last few years. For I can't grind out, under such pressure, the best I could do, simply because ideas and schemes don't have time, actually, to crystallize, and have to be forced into shape, a vastly inferior process.

This letter isn't a squeal—or even a justification—just a sort of blow-out in part explanation. I think you know I'm earnest in wanting only good stuff to stand against my name, but you also know what it is to be pushed and tired at the same time in any kind of creative work, when a lapse of constructive attention results in very tangible detriment to the production.

So Adoo, kind friend, and think not harshly of your
    L.A.F.

F. M. CHAPMAN TO L.A.F.

New York City, Nov. 25, [1911.]

You're a peach all right. I knew that before, but I'm glad to have this additional evidence that none of your bloom is lost! Can't you paste a piece of paper over tanager No. 2, the moulting bird, and paint a new one right over him? As for the *empidonaces*, if you can put *minimus* in same profile as *alnorum* and feather the crest of *acadicus* a bit, why let it go at that. . . .

The collection is driving me crazy! New species every ten minutes. Spent yesterday with Saville and am wild over Ecuador! It's a fine thing to be a naturalist. The fountain of youth is a mud-puddle in comparison. You follow?

L.A.F. TO F. M. CHAPMAN

Ithaca, N. Y., Dec. 15, 1911.

I am starting to-day on the *Bird-Lore* plates, and hope to get them to you by mid-week. I fully appreciate your anxiety, and am doing my eternal darnedest to relieve same. While I have given up all hope of making this year's trip with you, I am still fully aware of its importance, and of your dependence on my output for getting away. So worry no more than you really have to on my account. These damn short black, rainy, foggy, December days are the true *bête noire* of the time-pressed painter, and I have a certain amount, too, of other work that simply *must* be done—though I am side-tracking everything but the really imperative, among which yours is first. I wish I was ambidextrous and quadrumaniac—then I could hang myself up over four drawing-boards by the waist and go to it! But I ain't.

L.A.F. TO F. M. CHAPMAN

Ithaca, N. Y., Dec. 20, 1911.

E'en true to my word! Though my letter this a.m. missed the morning mail, and probably goes with this, the plates are done, packed, and go by U.S. Ex. this evening. . . .

This cleans up our color work: go to it kid! The two remaining b[lack] and w[hites] I'll do directly, and try to send them in right after Xmas. Then A.K.F.'s belated *Birds of Prey* (and pray, too, by the yard!). Then only the N. Y. plates (4) and the pheasants (12 plus), and I'll not have nothin' to do till tomorro. Pearson, I'm sorry to say, relieved me of the Carolina work. I should have enjoyed doing it, but can't blame him—nor do I—a bit. In a way, it's a relief.

F. M. CHAPMAN TO L.A.F.

New York City, Dec. 21, 1911.

In your numerous idle moments, can't you dash off a design for the Explorers' Club menu? Assuming that you can dash, at least me, I enclose a copy of the menu which was made for a curators' dinner, held here Tuesday night, and which possibly might give you an idea; assuming that you needed one.

The speakers at the dinner [to be held Jan. 6] will be C. E. Akely, George Shiras, George Borup, Wm. Lyman Underwood, and Louis Agassiz Fuertes. Shiras will speak on big-game hunting in Alaska; Akely on zoological work in Africa; Borup on proposed Arctic exploration, Lyman Underwood on the story of a bear, and

Mr. Fuertes on *ad lib.* Now, if time hangs heavily on your hand, the first page of this programme, following the idea suggested by the one I send, could deal in the same crude and suggestive way with the general activities of explorers, while the back cover page could be used for an illustrated list of the speakers: showing a very tall Shiras, stalking mountain sheep in Alaska; Akely being charged by an elephant, Borup driving a sledge team (you see I avoid all unnecessary details), Underwood nursing his pet bear, and Fuertes, through his three initials, phonetically employed, to represent l-a-u-g-h.

New York City, Dec. 26, 1911.

Fine! Genius is yours! It will make a great hit; but after I had sent for the engraver I discovered that your elephant was not pacing! I enclose a little passage I once had with Tudor Jenks on this point. Can't you paste a piece of paper over the elephant and make one running in true elephant fashion—I feel that you will want to be right here. Birds also here. Certainly top-notchers. I'll square accounts in a day or two. Great Christmas card! You're it!

Louis prepared to alter the drawing, looked again at the elephant, and discovered that it was pacing after all. He sent it back to Dr. Chapman with amiable verses:

... on a more minute perusal
The beast hands me a flat refusal
To countenance the slightest notion
Of altering his pedal motion.
So take another look, my dear:
Perhaps your eyes were acting queer.

F. M. Chapman to L.A.F.

New York City, Dec. 28, 1911.

The two drawings came this morning. In general effect they are excellent; the pigeons strike me as being the best I have ever seen, but what is your authority for the flock formation, or rather absence of it, in the birds in the sky? So far as I can learn from people who have seen pigeon flights, and I have shown your picture to two to-day, there was more or less definiteness of formation in these flights. The birds, it is said, flew in long, drawn-out bands, with lanes between. Unless, therefore, you have authority for the manner in which you have depicted the flying birds, it seems to me it would be much better to leave them out. This can be done by silhouetting the birds, leaving only the landscape and limbs on which they are resting.

The hawks are fine, but again, have you authority for the pose in which the sharp-shinned hawks are seen flying with the song sparrow? My impression is that when a hawk flies with its prey it carries its feet drawn up in front of it, and Miller agrees with me in this belief. Before sending the plates to Appleton I will await word from you in regard to details.

L.A.F. TO F. M. CHAPMAN

Ithaca, N. Y., Dec. 29, 1911.

Send back the pigeons; I can easily make the flight have the appearance you describe; I took my hunch from the impression I gathered from such descriptions as I had read—I will consult Wilson, Audubon, and Mershon, all the authority I have, but enough, I think.

The hawk is all right. I have watched practically all genera shown, and all do as I've shown *accipiter*: carry the prey at almost leg-length, and slightly back. (Sketch) Sparrow-hawks carry mice that way. Ospreys invariably carry fish (*vide* Abbott). Roughlegs carry even small field mice that way, and peregrines, doves. This I am as sure of as that they use their wings in flying, and have repeatedly observed it. In all the cases I have ever seen of a hawk or eagle carrying prey it has always been carried well away from the body. They have no instinct to bring their feet forward in flight, as they carry them stowed under the u. tail coverts and extended. I *think* only *passeres* carry their feet forward in the belly feathers in flight.

There may be others, but not *raptores*.

It would seriously affect the tone of the pigeon plate to remove the sky tone, resulting in a flatness and dullness in the birds that would look poorly, besides leaving out a very important (I think) adjunct. Better leave it out, of course, than get it radically wrong. But let's see what we can do, and if necessary, cut out the sky afterwards.

The pictures were at length accepted, Dr. Chapman left for Peru, and Louis remained behind. 'I don't even let myself look at the map,' he wrote, 'for it starts me sweating inside, and renders me generally unfit for the purposes of a provider.'

But he survived the torture of staying home and was rewarded by being available to receive a commission from H. W. Henshaw, Chief of the Biological Survey, which led eventually to still more important work for The National Geographic Magazine. The government bulletin Mr. Henshaw wanted Louis to illustrate needed pictures of common birds; Louis painted fifty charming little portraits to be reproduced in color. Gilbert Grosvenor saw and liked the pictures, used them in The National Geographic Magazine of which he was and is editor, and subsequently placed with Louis order after order, in effect keeping him at work for the magazine as long as he could think up subjects suited to Louis' talents—indeed sometimes even when he could not.

L.A.F. to H. W. Henshaw

Ithaca, N. Y., March 11, 1912.

I am just in receipt of your letter of the ninth outlining your plan for a Farmers' Bulletin on the economics of common birds. I think the idea is a capital one, and it would give me the greatest pleasure to co-operate with you in getting it up by making the color drawings. . . .

I am quite enthusiastic over the idea; such a book must be of great service to the farmers, and cannot help stimulating the youngsters on the farm to learn (and consequently enjoy) the farm birds, while learning a lot they ought to know about their vast value. I have almost felt it was hopeless to make the old farmers change anything, habits, views, or opinions, they have been so long inrooted. But the younger generation ought to actively profit by all the B.S. is doing, economically and in other fields, for its lasting benefit.

I will be also glad to assume the labor of correcting and passing proofs, if you care to use my experince in this matter. I am doing this with the big State work, and it seems the most satisfactory way in the end, though it increases my work nearly 100%. However, I have then only myself to blame if I don't like the published results!

The list I find a very stimulating one.

L.A.F. TO H. W. HENSHAW

Ithaca, N. Y., April 4, 1912.

I wish it might be possible to get the Bureau of Eng. and Printing to try some good 'process' reproductions. It is so much simpler that the results are better, by far, than those obtained by cut-rate lithography. I don't mind going on record as saying that the recent bulletins—notably the woodpecker and grosbeak bulletins—were about as bad in their reproductions of my work as anything I have ever had done. Perhaps the best lithography is better than the best four-color work, but cheap lithography that competes with four-color work in price cannot stand by comparison with what it competes with in quality. I know it is a hard proposition to attack, but I'd like to know how to begin, for I shall have to sooner or later take a stand against the injustice done to my work in reproducing it. Another point, in passing, is the trimming so that the signature is lost, as in the horned lark frontispiece, Bulletin 23.

L.A.F. TO F. M. CHAPMAN

Ithaca, N. Y., June 29, 1912.

The *Handbook* came yesterday just as I was handing your stuff to the postman, and I made him wait while I scribbled on the envelope!

I spent the latter part of the afternoon and the early evening looking it through, and after thanking you very prettily for the encomia you smear me with in your introductory chapter I proceed at once to retaliate, as I can in all honesty and frankness, by saying the new book has it over the old one like an umbrella blind without a ventilation hole in the top! There's no comparison, except where the new matter is reprinted from the old. I think the plan of the work is beyond criticism, and you have certainly rendered a service to the whole world of amateurs by stooping to tell them plainly what the philosophic basis of the science is, as well as the natural sympathetic side called 'bird-study' by the amateur who has no scientific fertilizer in his brain. . . .

If I were to speak of the bibliographies (and here comes my only criticism) I should regret that no metion is made of Mrs. Bailey's Western Handbook. . . .

Heartiest congratulations, old party, to you. You've done a grand job, and deserve all possible applause and a good rest. May you have both.

L.A.F. to F. M. Chapman

Sycamore Point, Cayuga Lake,
July 6, 1912.

We are now settled, by the grace of God, in a rather primitive cottage on the lake shore, where I am really losing my cough and picking up 'pep.' I have appropriated a vacant neighboring porch for a studio, and am working a pleasant amount each day, with satisfactory results, cleaning up the work for the Biol. Survey . . . I've set for myself a steady, even if not arduous, on-the-jobness till I've cleaned up B.S. and N.Y. Birds. Then I shan't do much painting for a while, but make a business of re-huskening myself.

This point has breeding within 50 yards of the house the following (probably more, as yet unmarked by me): robin, Wilson thrush, wood thrush, songsparrow, redstarts (one *in the house* this a.m.) chickadee, nuthatch, parula, pine warbler, La. water thrush, ovenbird, red-eye, yellow-throat and warbling vireos, rough-winged swallow (nest in the docking, 20 feet from my canoe-landing), wood pewee, crow, crested flycatcher, scarlet tanager (♂ still in full song), B. oriole, phoebe; on the gravel shore run tipups, and occasionally we may see the old Taughannock pirate [the duck hawk] clipping high by over the lake. So you see it is not birdless. All these small fry are still in full song, and the water thrushes in particular shout their wild song from the trees just over the house, or fly darting up the little ravine with their crescendo-diminuendo tep-tep-tép-*tep*-tep-tep-tep-tep. They are to me the most unspoiled

: 166 :

by civilization of all our birds, and seem to typify the primitive conditions of these richly-watered forest-hills more perfectly than any other bird. I like them much; so much, indeed, that I have never brought myself to shoot one, and have yet to hold the first one (in the flesh) in my hand. I can't say the same, I fear, of any of our eastern birds, at least from the same motives.

ABBOTT THAYER TO L.A.F.

Monadnock, N. H., July 15, 1912.

Now see here my nephew Louis.

There is science enough in Ithaca to-day to tell you, like a Dutch Uncle, whether or no you need to mount straight into a a perfect complete lung-curing régime of all out-doors (to begin with). You'll go far toward being the end of me, if you shilly-shally about this and yield to that fatal laziness that gets in the way of such athletic measures and dooms coughing people, by their lack of energy to embrace the rigors that are almost *guarantee* of cure if one will do them.

Forgive Uncle Abbott if he *ought* to have been reassured by your letter—He wasn't.

That was a fine shore-bird migration. Unless you *know* it is not tuberculosis, you ought to be out-doors exactly twenty-four hours a day till you can laugh at it.

Under perfect circumstances, *perfect*, it is now ranked as a 'favorable' diagnosis.

Your old Uncle Abbott.

Mr. Thayer, often overwhelmed by what he called 'oceans of hypochondria,' had long lived under the shadow of tuberculosis. It had been a contributing cause of the death of his first wife, the mother of his children, and in fear for their health he had mounted his entire family into that 'perfect complete lung-curing regime of all out-doors,' twenty-four hours a day summer and winter. They did not contract the disease; from the other threatening shadow, a seemingly inheritable melancholia, he was less able to protect them.

Louis recovered rapidly, and we hear little more about his health, which was excellent to the end of his life. By fall he was ready for strenuous work at his drawing-board and was looking forward to a a vacation of violent exertion in the rigors of another expedition to Colombia.

14

Colombia, 1913

THE 1913 COLOMBIAN *expedition of the American Museum included, besides Dr. Chapman and Louis Fuertes, the veteran collector, George K. Cherrie, and three untried young men, Paul G. Howes, Thomas Ring, and Geoffrey O'Connell. They sailed for Baranquilla on the Atlantic side of South America and went up the Magdalena River to La Dorada, to Honda, and finally to Bogotá on the plateau. The painting of the background for the Museum habitat group was made at Buena Vista, a stopping-place on the trail east and down from Bogotá to Villavicencio at the border of the great plains in the Meta River drainage, part of the Orinoco system.*

L.A.F. TO MRS. FUERTES

Colombia, Jan. 26, 1913.

It is just three weeks to-day since we left Ithaca, and it seems three months. We are still only a little more than half way up the Magdalena!

Since we hit the river we have been having a bully time, though it is pretty hot, and we get mighty sleepy at mid-day. For the first three or four days we ran day and night, though not very fast, as we have two big barges of freight, besides a hold full. But now the moon has failed us, and we tie up at night. At first we always landed at about dawn for a couple of hours for wood to burn in the engine, and that gave us a . . . chance to collect while things were active and it was still cool. We got between us about 200 birds, and skinned them at our leisure during the day, an ideal scheme. But now we wood up before dawn, and are off by daylight, and we get no good chance to collect, but have to do what we can in the heat of the day as opportunity offers. This a.m. we had our first experience, for this trip, stuck fast on a sand bar. We ran aground at 5:30 a.m. and got off, by the combined efforts of our own engines and the entire resources of a conveniently near river dredge (which also got aground and had to kedge off first), at about 11.

The nights are hot, and mosquitoes dreadful. To my great disgust, my net is too coarse, and about twenty force through every night, and I find them hanging like fat sausages to the top in the morning.

The river is fairly high, though falling slowly, and we shall have no trouble getting up to La Dorada. The crocodiles are as plenty as ever, and day before yesterday I went into the woods while we were tied up, and thought I saw a big red squirrel in a big tree. As they are 'desirable' I got up closer and popped my glass on it, and it was the hind leg of a big monkey. There were four of them; an old whaling big male, the mother, and two youngsters. They were red howlers and I didn't disturb them, partly, I guess, because I had no shot that would kill them, but instead watched them for quite a while with the glasses—a fine time was had by all! At Magangué, three days ago, they brought aboard in a cage a magnificent old male jaguar—a truly royal beast. He turned out to be part of a show, a performing animal, but nevertheless a native, and a beauty. Tom shot a big 'wa-wa' macaw, and daily we see both the red, and blue and yellow macaws. Big wood ibis, herons, horned screamers, and other striking birds are almost always in sight, and divide the interest with the capybaras (the biggest living rodent—about like a pig) and the crocodiles. I don't suppose there's a river in the world where there's more to see than on the Magdalena, as it is a big river, but still the boats run near the shores and you can see all the things. The Amazon, where Osgood was, is 3,000 miles long and so wide that most of the time you see only one shore at a time. O. saw nothing in his whole two months on the Amazon; we see daily things to stir a naturalist's interest to the depths.

The boys are all eager and good workers, and taking fine hold. The gang is perfectly solid, everybody getting really attached to the others, and the age-lines, I am happy to say, are not drawn at all except as to the matter of authority. Tom is a good-natured guy, funny as he can be, and a most naïve and genuine little scout, whom everybody likes though he always goes the whole shot, and if he didn't like anyone, he'd tell him so with the 'ease and grace which characterize his every move' as he puts it. Jeff is an earnest and modest boy, with great possibilities, and all are discriminating and intelligent, and all are gentlemen, and all are fine attractive fellows. Paul (Howes) is quite a good painter, and has a full kit of oils along, and has already done some very creditable little studies. . . . I think we shall really find it hard to break up, as we shall have to do, into two parties, as we are a particularly congenial crowd, and there are no dull moments. We've all been hot, tired, hungry, burning up with the insatiable thirst of labor in the heat, and at the same time, and didn't get on each other's nerves. So I think there's no danger, especially as everybody is absolutely game and there's not any shirk anywhere in the bunch. The real bad thing in such a crowd is a lazy man—and we've no such.

Perhaps you'll think I am talking a good deal about the congeniality of our crowd, and little about the work. I do think it is a little remarkable, considering the way the party was made up, that it should fall into its pace so quickly—and as for the work, it has not begun yet, and can't for some little time yet. Perhaps by Feb. 1 we'll get established somewhere.

The eastern Andes came into view the third day, after we had had a superb view, all unexpected, of the Santa Marta mountains, snow and all! The fourth day we saw the central Andes, and have been between them ever since, though to-day the valley is so wide that neither is in view, and the river is sometimes a mile or more wide, the channels running in queer directions, between islands, around shoals.

Looking out just now, I see the forest half a mile back, then nearer, a broad savannah. Then a shallow stretch of shining water, and about 200 feet away a flat sandy bar in the river. On it are nine crocodiles—three big ones—and among those on one end about fifty dozing black skimmers, and over the whole thing, and quite near, floats on spread wings and in the glaring light, a beautiful pink roseate spoonbill.

Honda, 5½°N. Lat., Feb. 3, 1913.

Yesterday I went out over a well-remembered trail, and had a bully time getting into the old places. But I followed it up much further, and got some fine things way up at the head of the stream, in a deep high pocket in the mountainside, with deep and tangled forest in a perfect chaos of rocks and stream-cut gulches. Got a pair of beautiful big motmots—the biggest kind, green and blue, with the whole chest, neck and head bright chestnut red, with the big black face-marks and a black tassel in the throat. (Sketch)

Frank and I and Howes are going up to the ridge to paint and collect. The weather has not been promising, as we have had some rain and much cloudy weather, and have seen no mountains near here, though they come close. But the rains are supposed to be over, and we will have to take a chance. So when the mules are caught and the election (yesterday) has worn off, we three will dig out. . . .

Honda, Feb. 9, 1913.

Frank and I and Paul Howes, who paints a bit, went up, not to El Alto de Sargento as planned, but to El Consuelo, only five hours away, where there's a superb view. . . . We had marvelous weather, and I painted three big panels showing the whole panorama—a perfect whiz of a view. The painting hours were from 6 a.m. (just light) to from 8 to 10, varying with the day. We only had three mornings, so we did well. F.M.C. is very happy with the pictures, and thinks 'em the best I've done and quite sufficient, so I am also relieved. . . . We feel we have done mighty well, for we have got the great thing we came for—the painting. I feel I have justified my coming, and we have got together about 600 birds as a by-product, and are just starting in.

RUFFED GROUSE. Ithaca, Nov. 5, 1912

TOUCAN. Puerto Barrio, Colombia, Jan. 29, 1913

Bogotá, Colombia, Feb. 16, 1913.

A lot has happened since I wrote you from Honda, the night before we left there. We got off, bag and baggage, about 10:30, and it was hot. We got up to El Consuelo, where I had made my painting the week before, at about 3, had a fine lunch, and pushed on only as far as Guaduas (bamboos) down in a deep valley, where we got in after dark, very tired. We left fairly early next day, about 7, I think, and went right up. The cargoes got out ahead of us, and we never caught them again till the end of the journey! at Facatativá. That day we got as far as a picturesque little old dead town called Villete, about 4 p.m., and as there was no other stopping-place less than five hours (seven for us) we decided to stay the night. A band of gypsies with two bears and two Gibraltar monkeys divided with us the honors and interest of the town. Contrary to our expectations, we had a pretty good night, and had few bites, though it was hot and we had no mosquito nets. Cherrie got the mule boys into action at 4:30, so we got off at 6. Villete is only 3,000 feet up, and we rode straight, sore and on heavy mules, up, up, up, for nine straight hours, only eating from the saddle some boiled eggs and bread and milk, at about 1. By 3 we were up the whole 9,000 feet, over the Alto del Roble, and the smiling plain of Bogotá was before us. We were too tired to enjoy it, though, and when, after an hour's wait among the gaping crowds at the station at Facatativá we got our seats and settled in the train for Bogotá we were very happy. . . .

It was only 54 the next a.m. and I got chilled, and had a reaction . . . and Paul Howes had picked up an intermittent fever. To-day, after four days' run of it, we both got up and went to Dubois' for Sunday dinner. [Mr. Dubois was the United States Ambassador to Colombia.] Had a fine time, and my doctor, a fine man with a Harvard training and Belleview hospital experience, says I'll be as good as ever tomorrow and able to go out with the outfit surely on Wednesday, as we plan. Paul no, as he'll have to wait a week for his relapse, which may not come.

Bogotá is a wonderful old town; this p.m. we rode all around it and had a fine time. Real people here . . . Mr. Dubois is a perfectly lovely, delightful, forceful, kindly man, whom the Colombians love and admire to the limit. . . .

Madgie, I can not tell you how bitterly disappointed I was to find nothing from you. Frank had a letter from Phoenix marked Jan. 15, and Tom one from Saginaw of the 11th. It is five weeks, and you haven't got a letter to me yet, and I can't help feeling deeply troubled.

[Bogotá, Colombia]
Feb. 21, 1913.

I've felt badly ever since I wrote my last, that I had scolded and fumed about not hearing from you, for I know the river was low when we came up, and has been steadily falling. They have had nothing come in at the legation for over ten days, and there are said to be seven steamers aground on the Magdalena! That's pretty nearly the whole fleet, and we may, six weeks later, have to help pull off the boats that carry our mail—to have it go clear to Bogotá, re-ship, and follow us home. Of course, in that case, I shall have no word whatever from you from the day I left you till I get to Barranquilla, and then only in case my letter down river got through all right.

There was a terrible fire at Giradot the night we were at Villete, on our way up here. We were afraid our old outfit was lost, but it wasn't. We now own ten fine mules. We had an interesting time with them yesterday, and it was soon evident that our two fine boys . . . didn't know the abc of packing, for they couldn't fix a pack so it would stay on a block. Finally Cherrie, who's an experienced man and not too long-tempered, flew into a fine old U.S. mad, fired out of hand the handsomer of our noble mule-boys, gave the other—to the great appreciation of the growing market-day crowd —a good lecture on what he was and was not, hired a good, dirty, capable, rough-handed and bare-footed arriero, with rags on and a keen look in his eye, put him over our handsome Manuel, and all sailed smoothly. This afternoon the boy came back for us, but we shall wait till the 23rd, as Paul's fever, if it returns, is due tomorrow, and I'd rather wait a day on the chance of having him go with us.

He is perfectly well, as am I, but his was of a recurring type and must be watched a little.

There isn't much to hunt around Bogotá, and we have all (but perhaps Tom, who *hates* to ride and likes town) been itching for days and days to get away. I confess to hating to send away those perfectly good mules and settle down to another day in town.

Our plan is to work, away from Bogotá altogether, the slope up over *paramo* and down to the east, going in relays, as far down as Villavicencio, on the *llanos*, for about a month or five weeks. Then return to Bogotá, and run down to Fusugasugá, toward the south, and work the slopes of the west there for about a week, then here again to pack up, ship, square away, and home as soon as possible....

You are not to worry at all about my little set-back. I have since then done a lot of hard work and to-day collected rails and galli-nules, etc., in water from knee to chest deep—cold water, too—and had no trouble at all. The altitude is just below where I begin to feel it, so I am in good shape to go after it.

Monte Redondo, Feb. 28, 1913.

I shall start this now, after a hard day of hunting and skinning (h. from 6:30 to 12 on slopes [like this]/; sk. from 12:45 to 6 without leaving my chair!) Got one or two fine things, but not much.

Tom and I left Bogotá Sunday, the 23rd, as poor Paul had his fever come back and couldn't travel. Left him in care of Mr. Dubois, who is a perfect *peach* of a man, and Dr. Montoya—also good.

Louis' letter is interrupted here to make room for an illuminating note by 'poor Paul' himself, now curator of the Bruce Museum at Greenwich, Connecticut. He writes:

I had come down, on the long ride over the mountains to this our base of operations [Bogotá] with a bad case of intermittent fever. I was very ill for a number of days, so the expedition minus P.G.H. was ordered on over the eastern Andes to Villavicencio, as time was valuable, and I was to join up as soon as I felt well enough, and which I finally did. I had financed nearly a third of this expedition, but when on the day the crowd left (having given all the money to Dr. Chapman and having little or nothing in my own pocket), I thought it very queer that Dr. C. gave me no ready cash to use, while ill, although of course I could stay at the *posada* as long as necessary, and later a horse was to be sent to me for the ride to join the others again. Louis saw at a glance how I felt about this matter. I was twenty-one, and this was my first expedition. I had no money and I was being left alone and ill. He put his hand in his pocket and after a bit came out with a five dollar gold piece. He tossed it up and down twice, then handed it to me. 'Here, Paul, I want you to take this, it's the lucky piece my wife gave me when I left home.' That is all that was said. I was too touched to answer. He shook my hand and that was all, until our happy meeting over the Andes some time later. We became very fond of each other, and I will never forget how he laughed at my crude 'funny strips' showing the trials and tribulations of the expedition and in which I always had him grossly caricatured. 'It looks just like me, darn it,' he would say, and then roar.

[*Louis' letter of February 28, 1913 is here resumed.*]

Before I begin to tell about these eastern Andes, I want to tell you that we learned Sunday, in Bogotá, that the seven stuck river boats were again afloat, and that two U.S. mails were in Honda, and would be in Bogotá Monday night. So you can perhaps imagine how we'll grab Paul when he comes into view: 'Hello Paul, Gottny mail? How are you? etc. etc.' . . .

I had to spend nearly twelve days [in Bogotá] . . . mostly lost time though I was only sick three days, so I lifted my head and yapped with joy like a setter pup with the hedgehog quills at last taken out of his fool chops, when last Sunday I got on the commander's bridge of a short snuff-colored mule and heard his little shoeless hoofs click under me. So far, over seven weeks gone, only 135 birds. Four weeks more to work in; got to do some collecting, and what's more, find some country, if the trip is to pan out anything like the last one. The eastern slopes are barren, treeless, hopeless, sad—and gosh how steep! For days and days, coming this journey, we've gone along little scratches on the mountains' flanks, where turkey buzzards looked like flies above us, and like other flies right straight below us. Such mountains I have never seen. Down, 2,000 or 3,000 feet so nearly under you, as you look off your sleepy ambling mule, that it makes even me gug to do it, a big river, roaring and white, lies as silent and characterless as a kink of thread on the carpet. The brown, wrinkled shoulders of the upper slopes rise, rise—get distantly green where the everlasting clouds hang and make the lofty fog-forest. Along the trails rare little farms, built so steep that they look like maps of farms tacked on the walls, harbor and faintly nourish a scattered people; the poorest, in every conceivable sense, I think, in the world. They know—of nothing, truly. They can hardly think at all, and stand in a blurry daze while you pass them, and probably for hours after. I have never been so touched by what man, God's creature, will do and do without, to live bare life, as here in these sad, huge, resourceless desolations of the eastern Andes. And I nearly cried, after thinking these and kindred thoughts, when the wife of the hotel-keeper in Chipáque (a town with a Plaza, fountain, a fine church [clock] that strikes by itself every fifteen minutes) said to me the last night we were there, after Tom had strung, tuned, and played the twenty-year old and still sweet guitar of the house: 'Ai, señor, la vida aquí está muy triste'—Ah, Sir, life here is very sad. Great God—what must these poor devils feel and think who in all their lives can never climb out of the eternal hole, heaven-high and hell-deep, in which their poor bug lives were chucked, and who have never, I almost really believe, seen another face, or cow, or pig, or any darn thing, but their own. It got my goat, and I here confess it. And I'm not such hell on my poor fellow-man, either. This is sure a different country. I'd like to (no, I wouldn't, but I could) hang myself up in its lost corners, for a year or so, and come out with a book that would make people sit up and yell! I have never seen such contrasts of people, of places, of natures and of nature. I must either have been asleep before, or else I was in the wrong places. But I've had sensations that would just pick me up by the neck and shake out the gasps!

For instance: Last night, when we were all here, and settled in the big room 'at our service' the young woman asked us if we would like some music. Certainly, what? Well, her brother had picked the art of playing the guitar, and sang. We hadn't seen any men around that looked like her brother, so: 'How old is your brother, señorita?' 'He's just gone five.' Well, a little somewhat old-looking babyish boy was produced in a minute. She sat in a corner and held the guitar, on her lap. The youngster stood beside her, and played, all on the neck of the guitar. He couldn't reach around it, so his thumb was only a nuisance to him, and he did the bass string with his little finger—never mind. I've heard the best 'tiple' player in Bogotá, and perhaps a hundred others along the streets; this little kid played with *perfect* precision, and had all the tricks of mute, and thumb, and hush and three finger four time (that makes your whole insides dance with them) that any I ever heard could handle. Then he sang. Madge, I would have given anything in this world to have had you (just for that hour, if you'd wished it) in this high square bare mud-floored room, lit by a candle, to see and hear the group of two in the corner. The girl was just setting. That youngster—two years younger even than Sum—sang songs, to the most moving and wild accompaniments, that were such perfect embodiment of romance that words were useless (although he had 'em) and not one but was the purest, most intensely characteristic expression of these places and people you could possibly get. He had a curious trick of hushing—then singing out like a purple finch, with his head back, everything rich minor except for an occasional line—for a question— in the major. Then that goat-getting hush on the minor reply. His sister said she had helped him with the words, *only*. He isn't a bit abnormal other ways, and when I set and baited a rat-trap in the corner he was in and out every three minutes the rest of to-day. But he is a *real* and certainly spontaneous musical prodigy, and should study—as she says he will. He sings with utter self-forgetful-ness, with the open tremulous manner of these people, but there was something in his tiny youth, five years, three of which were mostly unconscious, and producing, *in spite of this battering isola tion*, and never having been off this ten acres, a moving, powerful musical force like that.

I didn't know here, either, whether to laugh or cry, and was near

to both. He got *all* our change, which he solemnly looked over, and
then picked out all the little ones and gave them to his sister! She
laughed too hard, and I suspect she was touched rather roughly.
The *thing* is so much bigger than the kid; how in thunder did it get
in him? . . .

I started this, Madgie, with two candles, ten inches long. I now
have one candle, one inch long. The question is, can I get to bed
(some stunt!) before I don't have any candle any inches long?

VRMMMMMMMMM*** From somewhere out in the dark just
then came a sawmill-like hum, and *Bat*, right on the side of the
head, with a fine chill-bringing crescendo, landed a thing like an
elephantine junebug with a head like this (sketch) h'raus mit'em.
I jumped clear across the room. Candle now so (sketch). This can't
go on, for I can't hold the bug any longer, nor let go indoors—
good-night, more later.

Buena Vista, 90 miles S.E. of Bogotá.

We went out early next a.m., and up a trail-less mountainside
pasture, up, up, to reach some cloud forest that crawls over the top
of the range and drops in festoons down into the valley-heads. We
got there, separately, and met. I was sprawled on the stones at the
edge of the little stream, my cork so pulled that Tom said afterward I didn't talk sense. Be that as it may, for once in my life I had
nothing left, and had to quit at my goal, for I couldn't go another
rod. I sat in the sun in a little manioca patch right there for an hour
taking frequent drinks from the stream, and then, Tom having gone
on up into the forest (a mighty stunt of vigor and nerve, for he was
all but as gone as I), I picked a laborious and exhausting way down
the stream-bed to a 'water-trail' where they divert a small stream to
carry miles through fields and farms, for domestic use in distant
posadas, etc. Thence it was easy, for there's always an up-keep path.
I got back to Monte Redondo (only one house, a *posada* along the
trail) about 11, changed clo and rested till 12, asleep most of the
time, and was fit as a fiddle again by noon. Manuel had in the
meantime returned from Bogotá, with the news that Paul is still
sick and can't move for another week, and to cap it all, he had the

mail for the crowd, and after waiting all this time, not a thing for me. I can't tell you, possibly, how hurt and disappointed I was. . . .

Well, we left Monte Redondo the next morning at seven on our mules that were sent up from B. Vista and arrived the previous p.m. We passed all morning, like fleas along an elephant's belly, along the steep flank of bare or grass-covered mountains. We made an all-day ride of it, which I can't now describe, except to say that it seemed long, and we were tired by 4:30, when we got to Buena Vista, and that the last part of the way was through constantly improving forest, the first we have been in on the entire journey. B.V. itself, simply a biggish posada on the trail, is in the most commanding position of any place I've ever seen. It is at—or near—the end of a long hog-back subsidiary ridge of forested mountain, leading back to the great chains breaking from the Bogotá plateau. It is a little south of east of Bogotá, about ninety miles on the map, and it points south. So that in the morning we see the sun rise—like at sea—out over the perfectly flat llanos. A river with all its system of tributary streams lies about 2,500 feet straight below us and in the direct path of the sunrise. We never see a horizon from here; but a hazy sea of soft cloud veils the distant Venezuelan plains. We are on sizeable streams, all of the Orinoco system.

To the other side (and you only have to turn in your tracks, as we're on a narrow ridge) you look down and up into valleys and ranges, numberless, of richly forested mountains, towering away, bluer and bluer till you see 'beetling crags' of pale sapphire apparently resting on fleecy pinky white cottony clouds. At 5:30 to 5:45 in the evening, the sunset takes place in the lowest V formed by interlacing ranges, and I can't begin to give you any idea of the glory. This is a different country from any we have seen, and most miraculously beautiful; but its chief interest to us is that it brings down cloud-forest forms—of plants and birds both—and brings up Orinoco and Amazonian life to meet them. As an example: we went out, the five of us, this a.m., and brought in between us about 70 specimens of birds. This number represented about 42 species, and 38 genera!! We hardly had in the whole bag a species that was taken yesterday. I got two of my wonderful whistling birds—a slightly different species, but essentially the same thing—an enormous toucan, a fine dark-forest hummer, etc.

The forests are superb. There is a June-like climate, no mosquitoes nor flies, no dripping burning perspiration, just cool lovely pestless collecting, in enormous dry-floored forest. There are a number of trails leading through it, and you can go silently through aisles of gigantic trees and rich middle growth with profusion of hanging lianas and parasites. (Incidentally, we saw yesterday, growing wild in the forest, great sprays of the 'dollar apiece' lavender orchids.) If you hear something off the trail, it is open enough to work easily through in any direction. I criss-crossed the ridge beyond to-day in any old direction. Perfectly ideal collecting, in the richest fauna I have ever seen, and to me, *all new*.

Villavicencio, Mar. 12, 1913.

At last—at last!! Yesterday Paul turned up from Bogotá (having made the whole journey in three days—*good* going for a sick man) and brought me your first three letters. You will never know the joy of getting them. A mail goes to Bogotá from here Saturday the fifteenth and this will go by it, and take chances from B. down the river. Mr. Dubois left last Saturday for home. We shall miss him sadly when we get back to Bogotá; he *is* Bogotá to us! . . .

This morning I spent nearly an hour in a perfectly hellish thicket of weeds, about ten feet high and so thick I couldn't see five feet in any direction, and bearing the damnedest little burrs, in millions, that ever drew curse from human throat—so big *, and just long-pointed enough to prick and itch through such clothes as I wear. The bush has also thorns, or rather hooks. While in the midst of a most exciting still hunt (imagine it in such a place) for the author of an easily imitable bird whistle, my already burr-covered cap stuck and came off, and I turned my head in reaching back for it and got 'about a thousan' in my poor hair!! Before I was done in there I was so mad I could have cried; sweating like a July ice-pitcher(only feeling different), prodded and pricked at every turn, I called that little bird up to within probably fifteen feet three times—when he'd get wise without my having seen him at all and *run* away again. Never once did he even hop up on a stick. A mouse is a moose compared to the slick action of this thing. Finally, as a last resort, I tried a trick on him. I bulled my way, regardless of him, to a place where, in a low wettish spot, I could by squatting, see spots of ground for twenty-five or thirty feet around. Then I called again, and in about five minutes got an answer from perhaps 100 feet away. I pulled him up to about 50 and then, instead of doing it full strength I did it softly in the same key, hoping he might think I was farther away. And it *worked!* Immediately it came from only about half the distance; I sat tight and burned holes through the burr-bush with my eyes for the tail of a motion—or the motion of a tail—and was rewarded by seeing a ghost of a shadow move along a rotten branch. The direction seemed just right, and I popped my Aux at it and went in (it took five minutes to get thirty feet) and there lay the slickest little long-legged, stub-tailed, Jersey-cow eyed little shadow-bird you ever saw. It is a *grallaria*, related to my 'whistle' bird of Miraflores, but a little species I have never seen. So, just 45 minutes after I began, I came out with the prize bird of the day (and trip, no doubt) though to-day's lot included a *fancy* pigeon, one of the finest of the family, a new type of forest-dove, most lovely, and a little pale *blue* ground dove, with a black tail and a white head and neck, and trimmed with round black velvet spangles on his wings.

This stuff I did not intend to shove at you, but it got out just ahead of me! We all continue well, and I want to tell you that I can't get up to Bogotá any too soon for me, for I shall probably find another letter or two from you.

I've been pretty good about refraining from scratching my flea-tick-mosquito-blackfly-ant, and other kinds of bites, and the result is that I am hardly dug up at all. I usually look like those barber poles that have stars at the top and spiral stripes from the waist down! This time—but there, I won't tell you how I look just now. I've shaved several times, though I haven't had a haircut yet. My fancy clothes you fixed up for me have doubtless saved me something like 90% of the bites I would have had.

Bogotá, Colombia, Mar. 21, 1913.
Good Friday!

We're off again in the morning at 7, for Fusugasugá, some thirty miles S.W. of here, for the rest of our time—some two weeks.

Since my last note, Jeff and I have had an experience, which I will have fun telling you about when I get home. It was the funniest, and at the same time the most uncomfortable two days and nights('specially nights) I ever had. We stopped, and left the rest to go on to Bogotá, at a little lonesome *posada* or road house way up on the *paramo*, at 10,000 feet. It was cold and raw when we got there, about 3:30 p.m. Tuesday 18th, and a wet fog was blowing through the pass, only one and a half miles away, and the people— poor as dirt and covered with it—didn't want to take us in for a cent. Only Cherrie's smiles and diplomacy, and the fact that we took off our packs and sent the mules on with the others, made them take us. It was too raw and cold to hunt, and we couldn't see through the fog anyway. So we stuck around the place and got acquainted with our quarters. Quarters is the word, for they assigned us to a low platform in one corner of the one room in the shack—a mud affair with a bunch of grass thatch, no windows (thank God!) and one door: mud floor and mud everywhere else. We (and they) had no candles, so after dusk, when it settled down to be real cold, there was nothing for it but bed. So we put down our blow beds, fixed our blankets, and threw and pinned an extra double blanket over both beds, and taking off only sweaters and shoes, got in and passed a fair night. We had had cocoa and native soup for 'dinner.' Later, all the family, consisting of father, mother, some old female relation, two younger women, several youths, a little girl about eight, and an utterly, bitterly, putrescently filthy brat of two—innocent since birth of any cleansing influence—all crawled into a sort of hole in the farther wall for the night, where they snored, hawked, etc. etc. etc. till dawn, when they crawled snuffling and coughing out into the chilly fog for wet firewood, and the day began. We had cocoa again, and went out to hunt. Bitter business: *paramo* dripping, clouds driving drizzle, and birds as tight as Jamaica ticks to their hiding places. We got a few, and got in at noon. Dinner: potato soup, wheat soup, cocoa. Skinned birds, after a change and a rub, till it got so bloody cold we couldn't make our hands track. I spoiled three good hummers straight, because I shook so. Poor Jeff never stopped shivering from the time we got there till we left. But he put out a line of hopeless traps, just the same, like a man. It hailed in the afternoon, just lending the final touch of penetration to the cold. That night we had for supper potato soup, potatoes and a little rice. Early to bed with numb feet, that staid so till we left. But before we turned in a pair of sad old packhorses of women came in off the trail. They couldn't be turned out on the *paramo* at night (murder, no less) so they were shown into *the* room. They had a taller-dip, and made a pretty picture from our beds, lousing each other in the candle-light with claw-like hands, and grunting, snuffling, and hawking in the cold against the flickering background of smoked mud walls, their witchlike shadows dancing with the jumping light. By this time the dogs and cat and one of the turkeys were all in *the* room, and after the family had crawled into their den and the 'padrón' had *tied* on the door for the night, we were all ready for a real cozy night, laughing and talking until a late hour. The poor old dames grunted into their packs and shuffled out in the cold dawn. A roaring east wind, the sign of the rains, had sprung up, and the bare *paramos* whistled with it, and the thick black soaking fog slid over the pass and isolated us in a very short time after light. We knew we had eaten nearly everything they had, and that to hunt in this was out of the question, so, as temporary head of the exped., I told Jeff to go get his traps, hired the old man to take our packs to Bogotá on his mule, got breakfast started, packed up our outfit, and after breakfast started afoot with the howling wind behind us, for Bogotá. The breakfast deserves mention. First, cocoa. Then, a half hour later, a plate of soup, potato variety. Second course, soup—pomme de terre—overture by the donkey, to show breakfast was over.

So we got out—and just then the clouds broke and out came the sun! But we were packed and couldn't re-arrange in time to do anything, so we kept on, and had only been on the road three quarters of an hour when we met our boy, Manuel, with two saddle mules and a pack mule, sent up for us by Chapman, who had just got to the hotel in Bogotá Tuesday when the fever hit him. Rotten luck, but pretty fortunate not to get caught on the road. He hadn't a very high fever, but last night he had a beast of a chill, that absolutely exhausted him.

Bogotá, Colombia, April 9, 1913.

We are all well, and have had a very good and successful trip. The expedition has collected over 2,000 birds besides my 400 or more, and we have a very representative lot. Six men turned loose in a locality for a few days nearly cleans up the list of representative species. I doubt if any collection of 2,400 birds ever contained so many species, and little Rollo has just about everything that is of particular interest or that he didn't have before.

Barranquilla, Colombia, April 17, 1913.

Beginning where I left off in my last from Bogotá, Cherrie, Jeff and I took the mules down from Facatativá to Honda over the old trail we came up three months back, and got as far as El Consuelo, where we expected to spend the night, about 4 p.m. Here we found a special message from F.M.C. that if possible we were to come right through, for he had decided to take the 'express' boat from Honda next day at 9:30, so as to catch a Hamburg-Am. steamer for N.Y. Thursday. (That was Saturday.) So, though it's a six-hour ride from El C. to Honda, and the rains were on, we slid right along, and after a really pretty bad ride through the mountains in the pitch dark— letting the mules pick their way, and with a tropical thunderstorm brewing about us and blinding us occasionally with its fireworks—we at last got to H. at about 8:45, to our and others' great relief. Manuel, who was behind us, got the word we had left for him at Consuelo, and pushed on with the packs, and got in, drenched and a little frightened and excited, at just midnight. We got the express all right, with everything—twenty clothes boxes, two trunks and two big packing boxes of birds included—right with us; good business, as it's the entire collection. My share is almost exactly 400 birds, it would have been just except that I lost the little basket containing the few we collected on our Facatativá-Honda trip off my saddle in the dark, near Honda.

So Louis came safely home from his last South American expedition, an expedition attended by worry at both ends. Some of his wife's letters never did catch up with him, and he arrived before the letter telling her when to expect him. Laden with the baggage of his four months' travel, he stepped off a street-car at the corner of Thurston and Wyckoff avenues in Ithaca, and he was at once spotted by some of the Brauner children who ran joyously to him, shouting 'Uncle Louis! Uncle Louis! Go like a pig!' He obliged with a magnificent outburst of grunts and squeals that announced his arrival to his own family.

15

The Middle Years. The Studio

··

Louis returned from South America in May, 1913. Europe was
soon involved in World War I, and the activities of museums
were upset or interrupted. So for the next seven years he stayed at
home living the life of a family man, a neighbor, a citizen of his
community.

Our house, and the life that children take for granted, was full
of—shall I say the aroma—of tropical America. Mother thought my
father a considerate and imaginative shopper: in the coat closet
under the front stairs there was a slowly diminishing hundred-pound
sack of Bogotá coffee, and I was awakened for years by the morning
sound of its grinding; we used green and white pottery breakfast
dishes from Yucatán; ponchos were part of the family wardrobe and
vocabulary; there were panama hats around; a morsel of exquisite
Spanish lace and the bright embroidered edges of babies' dresses
bought in 1910 still survive after trimming many garments.

Less tangible souvenirs were Spanish songs sung or rendered with
style on the ocarina, Spanish talk, and names of people and places
heard in the grown-ups' conversation. Much in my father's nature,
and consequently in our family life, that was gentle, musical, whim-
sical, sympathetic, seems to me now to relate to his Spanish-Ameri-
can inheritance and travel.

Presently he had a letter from Mr. Thayer, almost querulously *asking what had become of the bird-skins Louis always brought home from expeditions for them. Here is Louis' reply and account of his own summer's occupation building a new studio, a separate fire-proof structure, in back of the house.*

L.A.F. to Abbott Thayer

Ithaca, N. Y., Aug. 29, 1913.

I was awfully glad to hear from you, and to have a chance (not that I really lack excuse, God knows!) to write you a long-belated letter. I had a fine one from Gra in January, just as I started for Colombia—and I had the constant longing that I always do when I'm in new countries, that you could be there to enrich the opportunity. We did have a splendid trip, and saw and got a remarkable collection of things. I just heard from Chapman yesterday that our Colombian collections number over 800 species, and that in the light of this fresh and well-labeled collection, many hitherto doubted or flouted species and forms show up even more distinctly, and that our work there has proved to be tremendously important— even more than we thought—in the establishment of true localities for a large proportion of the hundreds of species hitherto bunched as from 'Bogotá' which the world (particularly the continental and British ornithologists, where the collections are largest and oldest and richest but least complete as to data) must hail with great enthusiasm.

I don't know whether you knew that three of us got fever in Bogotá, or it developed when we got there, a sort of relapsing malarioid fever that has peculiar characteristics. Its worst one is that in severe cases its toxins, after recovery, are discharged through the vitreous humor of the eyes, often resulting in total blindness. Chapman, who was the most careful and the sickest, had the unspeakable horror of having his eyesight cloud and diminish to only about half-vision, and was desperate with the fear of losing his sight altogether. It is a little-known disease, apparently peculiar to the eastern Andes and their valleys, and the only treatment is to build up the general constitution, rest, and trust to nature to absorb the poisons and eventually discharge them altogether. That is what poor Chapman had to do, and he is just now—five months later—assured of his future, and beginning very slowly to take up the work of study and work on the Colombian collections. He did little with the first expedition's lot except publish the most obvious and interesting new things, for the collection was just rich enough to demand more; . . . it suggested rather than settled doubts. So he still has at the museum a large part of my first collection, and every bit of my second, and will have, probably, for some months yet. And that, Dear Uncle Abbott, is why you have seen nothing of my Andean birds. I am still afraid you will be disappointed, for the field was so enormous, and each day's work so varied, that it was almost impossible to get even pairs or duplicates. We used to exchange from each other's bags a good deal too, to insure as good a representation as possible in both collections.

I am sure I shall be able to send you quite a good lot of birds, and believe me, that one of the biggest pleasures of the whole lot will be picking out and sending you that box of birds. I will find out, when I get them here, what I have and what you would like. When we got down onto the east base of the Andes, in the Meta drainage, many of the formicarians, etc., were the same as the Venezuelan and Trinidad species.

You will be glad, I'm sure, to learn that I have at last taken the bull by the horns, and built for myself a little outside fireproof building—a studio, workshop, storage place for my collections of both birds and studies where everything will be safe. It has nearly busted me to do it, and I shall have to work hard to recoup on it, but I think the 'bird-artist' business is good for it, and justifies it, and I am certainly going to enjoy it a lot. It's a hollow tile building, no cellar, slate roof, floor of first hollow tile, then three inches concrete and dark red floor tile, ceiling 10 ft. 8 inches, room 24 x 18½, a bully fireplace, 6 x 9 north window and a shop room and wash-room with hot and cold water, and the whole business heated by hot water from my house; no ashes nor dirt nor coal gas—I had to buy a piece of land, adjoining mine, 35 ft. x 100, and the whole business costs about a half-year's earnings, and I'm trying to get it paid for this calendar year, but as I lost nearly half the year on my trip, and have been laid up till recently . . . with a bunch of strained tendons in my right forearm, the chances are not quite so bright as they seemed at first.

The strained tendons came from work on the studio where he enjoyed acting as a kind of carpenter's and mason's assistant and general handy-man. At one point in the process of its building he led my mother to the wall where the fireplace was to be and marked the level of her eyes. He then directed that the mantelpiece be set above that level, so she should never see the dust upon it.

I remember the maneuver by which the cases of bird-skins, too bulky to go down the stairs from the old third-floor studio, were lowered down the outside of the house with block and tackle and carried into the new one. The books and reference-library of field sketches, as indispensable to my father as the skins, he could then arrange more at large and surround them with the treasures collected on his travels. He hung upon the walls Indian baskets and bead work, dried snake-skins six to eight feet long, his pictures of Louis Agassiz, and the drawings of the Thayer children and Georgie Brush; he put on the floor or across chairs and benches Indian blankets and tanned skins of bear, jaguar, and kinkajou; there were cartoons, sketches, mounted birds, Indian bows and arrows, blow-guns and spears, and on the clock-case in the middle of the mantel-piece the skull of a flat-head Indian with the legend Hands and Feet off My Desk which had stood on the desk of Elliott Coues.

His own working place was a high and wide table under the large north window. Here, standing, or seated on a long-legged stool, he worked steadily fall, winter, and spring, starting right after breakfast every day. His painting costume was a soft shirt without tie, old trousers, and mocassins. (He paid no attention to his good clothes— was likely to go off on a lecture trip lacking one or the other half of his Tuxedo—and it was impossible to wean him from clothes grown old and shabby enough to be really comfortable.) The drawing table was full of clutter: paint boxes, dishes for water, brushes, pencils, bits of bark, leaves, flowers, twigs, the skins of several specimens of the bird he was drawing.

There sat Fuertes—a dried bird-skin in his left hand, a spray of wild morning-glory before him in a little vase, a piece of paper thumbtacked to an old drawing board in front of him—and the phoebe came to life before my very eyes. He held the phoebe skin while he worked, turning it this way and that, looking at it closely, counting its feathers with his pencil, blowing at it to make it fluffy, going to the window once or twice to examine its gape or eye-lid or rictal bristles in a stronger light. The specimen had been prepared in a special way—loosely stuffed; the head at a life-like, even a jaunty, angle; the feet sticking out or up, rather than lying flat as in approved cabinet specimens. He worked rapidly, putting down pencil stroke after pencil stroke without pause. Then he laid the phoebe skin aside, held the drawing at arm's length, took up his eraser, and rubbed the whole thing out. The bird wasn't placed right. He started again. This time, drawing it a bit off-center, he finished bill and face and wing-coverts in considerable detail. I saw it happen, every bit of it.

Thus wrote George Sutton, in The Audubon Magazine, January-February, 1942. He is describing the process as it occurred in a summer cottage; in the studio Mr. Fuertes would not have to go to the window from where he worked.

When the problem was a flight of birds against the sky he would quickly sketch, and sometimes color, a dozen or so little flying ducks or geese, cut them out with shears, and then move them around on his picture till he had an arrangement that he liked.

At noon he came into the house for lunch, bringing the picture or pictures he had been working on. He would stand them on the floor of the dining-room where the light struck them properly, or sometimes on the plate-rail, and ask my mother—and the children when we were old enough—whether the bird stood out, whether the water looked wet, and so forth. He depended on our criticism and trusted it more, I am sure, than we did. I remember his pique on one occasion when, knowing that he knew best, we failed to look at the pictures as critically as he wanted us to.

After lunch he went back to the studio for the light part of the afternoon. An errand downtown, work in the shop (he was an expert wood-worker and the best mender of household objects I have ever known), or more often visitors would claim the darkening hours. He liked to skate, and it seems to me now that often when there was ice on nearby Beebe Lake we would go over in the gloaming and join the students and the campus children for an hour or so before supper. Even at that period when companions of my own age were a necessity to me, I loved to skate with my father.

Closest to us among these campus children were the five Brauners (near neighbors until they moved to Buffalo Street and their house was taken by the family of Colonel and Mrs. F. A. Barton, no less loved) and the Breckenridges, grandchildren of Louis Agassiz' pupil and colleague, Burt G. Wilder. They were all devoted to my father, and he to them. Anne Breckenridge recalls as one of the joys of her childhood a day of deep snow when Uncle Louis came across the corner to her house and took her—chose her, one little girl—to go with him for a snow-shoe walk in the country.

It seems in retrospect that the weather, and our house, were often very cold. The house was warmed by a hot water system; the water would boil and overflow on the roof, there was running up and down stairs, hurry, excitement. The ceiling of my parents' bedroom was so elaborately stained by water seeping through meandering cracks in the plaster that my father, after lying in bed looking at it for some mornings, finally stood up on the bed with a pencil and finished the picture. It became elk and moose with spreading antlers.

Here is a letter written after one of the not infrequent March snow-storms to Courtenay Brandreth, his pupil who, previous to the date of the letter (March 8, 1914), had been his host in New York City.

Well, we are back in our old shack up-state, away from the brawl of Broadway and the roistering of Rector's. We may say, while we greatly enjoy the wild life, that we are glad of it! We have, in short, been sick more or less, ever since, as we were evidently unfitted to make the grade, owing to advanced years and ill-timed shortage of sleep and longage of hours, and were so made easy prey to the prowling streptococci of the Lehigh sleeper. Or thereabouts.

Which, slipped into words of one syllable, means that I've had a bad cold in my Bronix, which does not yield to the hair-of-the-dog-that-bit-me treatment afforded by our local salons-de-vivre. But now, after a week or two of somewhat pessimistic outlook—or in-look, which is worse—I am beginning to snort around a bit, and seek outside diversions. We are still blizzarded in, though trains are running; also city water, and an occasional trolley or delivery wagon, just to remind us of the good times before the big snow. So. If you tire of the gilded way, and feel like seeing the burdock tops sticking out of the pure but simple snowdrifts, put a couple of collars and your shoepacks in a flour sack and come up and see us. As we have no outlets, we have no dates, so any time will suit. . . . Whatever you bring in the way of frappé raiment, bring old things too, for I get nervous, sometimes, and want to do rough things that might tear a chiffon vest, or put a crimp in tin neck-ties and the like. And then, Mary might take another shine to you, and you'd want either chain-armor or your football clothes. . . .

Only occasionally did the brawl of Broadway interrupt Louis' life among the burdock-tops of Tompkins County, although more often each year he was invited to lecture and exhibit pictures away from home. A letter from Henry Dubois to his father, James T. Dubois, then United States Ambassador to Colombia, describes the effect of one such lecture on a sensitive young man. Mr. Dubois, senior, sent the letter on to Louis.

Louis Fuertes, one of those exceptional men whose soul and intellect have grown up together in perfect harmony to that stage of perfection where the voice of the being which holds them is an inspiration to those who hear it, has just finished pouring into me the most delicious narrative of your surroundings imaginable. In an illustrated talk here at the club, he has brought you thousands of miles nearer to me, and I hasten to tell you the good news. I feel as if I were standing on some island just off your wonderful coast, as if the marvels of the most superb colorings that the world's plant life produces were about to be unfolded to me in reality. And that beyond this wonderful garden of green palms and dense foliage, of warm mists and strange lights, of weird noises and myriads of moving and flying life, each clothed in its own brilliancy of a hundred bright colors, I could climb a range of mountains and find you sitting in all your ambassadorial splendor.

Having wandered thus far into the jungle I will now try to find my way out by telling you what I mean. Louis Fuertes has recently returned from a trip through Colombia from the west to the east, on which he sought strange birds. He found them by the thousands, and with his skill brought them home with him in picture and in salt. His lecture was a revelation.

Louis tried to group his lectures in time and place so he would have several on nearly consecutive days in the Middle West, or several around New York, and be traveling perhaps one week in six. This did pleasantly vary the routine of drawing and painting, but it would be hard to imagine a routine more agreeable than his. His time was his own to use while the light lasted, the new studio was as good a place to work as he could devise. He almost always had more orders than he could fill, and he lived among people interesting in themselves and congenial to him.

Professor William Strunk, Jr., has called Louis Fuertes' studio the best club in Ithaca. People were always dropping in: artists who wanted his eye on a picture, professors who needed a lantern slide or a drawing for their lecture, farmers bringing a snowy owl or a weasel they had caught, friends who came for the sake of his company or the fun that was generated in his presence. Naturally, some persons imposed upon him. But he could paint and talk together, or paint and listen, or paint and not listen. After a long-winded bore had finally taken himself off one day, Louis' by-then indignant friend John Senior said, 'Why do you stand for that fellow's talk, Louis? He's insufferable!' To which Louis, who had been painting right along, replied, 'I didn't hear him.'

Skinning birds and painting their pictures were activities that enthralled the natives of whatever country he was collecting in, and like them, the children on Cornell Heights clustered around whenever they had a chance to watch. I do not remember hearing him send one away, or seeing him show by any sign that he considered a child a nuisance. He behaved as if he and the child were both deeply interested in the same things—as indeed they were. The children, of course, brought him all the dead birds and 'critters' they found; Professor Needham remembers that Louis stopped his own work to skin a cedar waxwing his son Paul had brought in, giving a careful lesson in taxidermy as he did it, and then presenting the skin to Paul at the end. The Titchener children had live birds as pets, and when each bird finally died the owner took it to Uncle Louis to be made into a skin. When Alice's bird died, he was too busy to prepare the skin, but drew her a little sketch instead. She was disappointed then, but now when her sisters' birds are moth-eaten and gone, she has the little sketch. Another neighbor's child said that what he wanted most for his birthday was to be allowed to spend a morning in the studio and ask all the questions he desired. It was arranged.

Our house was at the corner of the block, where the street-cars stopped. You could see and hear them coming from the studio, and it was easy for my father to lope out the door and hop on a car going in either direction; all went downtown. Each car had a conductor and a motor-man, and these men were very fond of Louis Fuertes. Certain of them felt, as so many people did, that he was their particular friend. They had perhaps a vague notion that he was a 'bird man' and knew that he was a professor, which he never was. Once when he was sitting up in the front of the car, it stopped on East Avenue to let Professor Wilder Bancroft get off. As they started again the motor-man said: 'There goes an awful nice man, Lou. Why, he's just as common as you and me!'

One time when Uncle Louis went to the phone [Hugh Breckenridge tells the story] a country voice said: 'Say, Professor, I got one of them big old-fashioned hoot owls and I want you to take a look at him.' L.A.F.: 'Where is he?' Country Voice: 'I got him down here to Higgins Feed Store in the winder.' L.A.F.: 'Well, I wasn't planning to go downtown to-day, but if I do I'll stop and see him. (After discussing the tremendous size of owls . . .) Good-bye.' Later Uncle Louis had some business downtown and went to the feed store, and there was a male great horned owl in the window and a rustic in a mackinaw standing by outside with a proprietary air. As Louis looked at the owl the countryman sidled up and said: 'Big one, ain't he?' Louis said: 'Yes, and if it were a female, it would be even bigger.' The man bridled. 'Is that so? Well, let me tell you something, mister. Per-fessor Fuertes was here and seen him and he said it was the biggest one *he* ever see.' Louis slunk away.

Another kind of farmer was Foster Parker who lived at the swampy northern end of Cayuga Lake and raised wild ducks—to sell, and because he liked to have them around. As a result of hunting trips near there with E. H. Eaton of Geneva (author of the text of the Birds of New York) *Louis formed a close friendship with Mr. Parker. Forty-three letters written by Mr. Parker to Louis between 1901 and 1924 on lined paper carrying a handsome letterhead of wood ducks (designed by Louis) form a moving comment on the effects of draining the Montezuma marsh, on Louis, and on Foster Parker.*

Mr. Parker once spent a night at our house, and was heard walking back and forth in his bedroom (the old studio on the third floor) early in the morning. When asked at breakfast whether he had rested well, he replied: 'Fine! First time I can remember that I've laid abed till six.' Mr. Parker's letters are evidence of Louis' continued sympathy; here in one of Louis' to Dr. Chapman (Dec. 26, 1909) is a kind of epitome of it:

We all had a grand Christmas, and are pretty well in spite of it. I wrote my fine old farmer at Cayuga, Foster Parker, and got a pitiful mis-spelled and self-contained reply from him, saying that he thanked me for my good wishes, but his mother wasn't well, and he was veary sad, because he had bearied his oldest sister yesterday and her two sons were veary low, with typhoid fever, so it was a sad Christmas for them.

It's hard to tell what to say to such a man in such a case, and there's nothing to do. But it does make you wish you could divide up some way.

Louis did his best to divide up. To Mr. Parker, as to other men like him—guides, game wardens, museum preparators—he gave genuine friendship and all that goes with it of time and thoughtfulness. To the nuisances he was polite, though they often amused and sometimes annoyed him. The telephone became a bother—Mr. Fuertes was always accessible—and his mail increased in bulk from year to year. A letter written by Katharine Finch when she was taking care of his business affairs during his absence in Abyssinia in 1926 gives a notion of the nature, though not the extent, of his correspondence.

I have written the anxious school teacher that I didn't know what little bird woke her up at 6 o'clock every morning at Lake Maggiore in the month of August; have told the youth who wrote that 'I too am a lover of birds' that you didn't want to buy a live Mockingbird this winter; explained to the ardent Boy Scout leader that I couldn't recapitulate the heads of the snore lecture so that he could have local talent do it; told old grads that my influence with Rym Berry in the matter of football tickets wouldn't go as far as yours, etc. etc. —and now the Atkinson Press is printing 100 little cards which state succinctly that Mr. Fuertes is in Abyssinia. I'll still continue to write real letters to the prospects, but cards should do for the others. Oh yes, I forgot the lady who wanted to know if she could copy your 'Falconry in Elizabethen England' on a hooked rug, and if so could she sell the rug.

At least one man is anxiously awaiting your return to do him a picture of a grouse for a gift to a hunting friend. (I believe he hunts birds.) This person writes pleasantly that no one else in the country could do the picture so of course he will wait for you. Several want 'reproductions.' However, you know the line, or should by this time, and I'll leave the rest to your imagination, only saying that I have the more respect for your patience and good nature.

During the 'twenties Romeyn Berry lived distant from us the space of a vacant lot and was one of the frequent droppers-in at the studio. He recalls that when unanswered mail piled too high on Louis' work-table, Louis would simply cover it up with a sheet of the brown paper which he kept to wrap his pictures for mailing, and thus create a clean slate of sorts for the work in hand. But one of the characteristics that may be thought remarkable in an artist is that he did keep his business in order, he did answer his mail, and this meant that he must conscientiously reply to dozens of young people who wrote him of their pleasure in his pictures, sent him their drawings, asked innumerable questions, and confessed their own ambitions in his field. From a mass of such letters here is a series which possibly justified his patience with all the rest. For in these letters to George Sutton he wrote out more clearly than anywhere else the core of his artistic creed; in them he paid for his own education in the only way he could, by passing on to another young man what Abbott Thayer had so generously given him.

L.A.F. TO GEORGE MIKSCH SUTTON [aet. 15]
Ithaca, N. Y., Feb. 15, 1915.

Your very kind letter came to me out of a clear sky, and I cannot well tell you how much I was touched and gratified by your warm appreciation of my efforts to come at the truth in bird-painting. Much praise from the uninitiated means little or nothing: a rare tribute like yours, from those who have met some of the difficulties and know them by their first names, is an uplift and encouragement that means more than all the every-day, inexpert praise in the world.

So far as I now know, I shall be in or near Ithaca this summer, and if you should decide to come up, will be glad to help you in any way I can. My methods are not academic, and have been developed to suit the rather peculiar needs of the situation, and I might do you more harm than good.

In the mean time, if you have any study material, or pictures that you have done and would like criticisms on, I would be glad if you would send them on, and I will write you more fully than I can do now, as to their promise, the field, etc. etc.—all vital points if you are thinking of going seriously into it. Of course the field is limited, and must in a large measure be created by the one who is to fill it. When I started, about twenty years ago, there wasn't any field, but one developed, and now there is considerably more of a one than one man can fill, though there are not many who seem to combine the sympathy with nature, the specific knowledge of their subject, and the technical ability to paint, which are all necessary if their work is to stand up under the test of time and the inevitable competition that is ahead. Say what you will of Audubon (much of what you did say is just, too,) he was the first and only man whose bird drawing showed the faintest hint of anatomical study, or that the fresh bird was in hand when the work was done, and is so immeasurably ahead of anything, up to his time or since, until the modern idea of drawing endlessly from life began to bear fruit, that its strength deserves all praise and honor, and its many weaknesses condonement, as they were the fruit of his training: stilted, tight, and unimaginative old David sticks out in the stiff landscape, the hard outline, and the dull, lifeless shading, while the overpowering virility of A. himself is shown in the snappy, instantaneous attitudes, and dashing motion of his subjects. While there's much to criticize there is also much to learn, and much to admire, in studying the monumental classic that he left behind him. He made many errors, but he also left a living record that has been of inestimable value and stimulus to students, and made an everlasting mark in American Ornithology. It is indeed hard to imagine what the science would be like in this country—and what the state of our bird world—had he not lived and wrought, and become a semigod to the ardent youth of the land.

I had not meant to write an essay on Audubon—and shall not continue! I *do* want to thank you for the truly great encouragement of your letter, and to assure you that if there is any way I can help you to develop your bird-painting, I am anxious to do so.

Faithfully and gratefully yours,
Louis Agassiz Fuertes.

L.A.F. to George Sutton

Ithaca, N. Y., March 30, 1915.

I was somewhat chagrined when I received your letter of the 15th, to realize that I had not acknowledged in any way the receipt of your drawings. They came in due time and good condition, and I was waiting, before writing you fully, until I could find an hour of daylight in which to study and criticize them in such a way as they deserve, and as would be helpful to you. I have been greatly rushed this winter and just at the present time I am in the middle of a long series—some 72 little plates—of game birds, for a later number of the Geographic Magazine, for which the publishers are clamoring. Hence my present rush.

I very much appreciate your warm praise of my pictures. Of course I take them very seriously, and it would be insincere of me, under the circumstances, not to warm up under expressed appreciation of them. They are all far below the little pictures I have in my mind, and if they express any of the beauty or charm or feeling that I have in mind for them it is only because the imaginary picture is so surpassingly lovely that part of its charm penetrates through the heavy and stubborn medium of my clumsy hands, in spite of them. My only salvation is that nobody can see what *I had in mind* for my pictures! If we could paint without restraint or manual obstruction the beautiful pictures we plan, how we could make the world open its eyes!

To come at once to the criticism: First of all your work shows great promise, and you should by all means stick to it and work for the highest ideal you can summon.

Technically, I think you can work to advantage with a somewhat drier brush. It is impossible to exactly control either color or outline, unless your brush is sufficiently dry to avoid leaving a drop at the end of a stroke, and to distribute color evenly through the whole stroke.

Take a bird with a white belly and study, locally, the color of its shadow on the white. Put colored things so they can reflect in this shadow, and see what a mirror of adjacent colors white becomes in shadow. Your shadows lack in both color and in depth. It would be good exercise to paint, literally, a bird-skin or a dead bird, with the one aim of getting every point on it in exactly the proper relation in both color and value (value equals the relative amount of lightness and darkness, irrespective of color) to every other point. This will give your object—or bird in this case—solidity and rotundity, and is the only thing that will. Every object or landscape in the world—in fact anything you look at or isolate for a picture—has one deepest dark spot and one highest light, and every other spot has its exact relation between these and to every other spot. This is the main thing to know, in painting, and to properly recognize and master this analysis is the principal result gained by an art education. You are supposed to start with the appreciation and beauty-sense, and these things develop automatically as education progresses and experience accrues.

To take an example, let us analyze the fall magnolia warbler picture. Your drawing is nice, the conception pretty, graceful and very characteristic. The coloring is, locally, correct. But it so happens that local color (by which I mean the exact tone and color of a given part of the bird, seen in most favorable and analytical light) only tells at its face value and color rarely. On top, where much light hits it and sprays off, it is greatly lightened and 'greyed'; underneath, where an inevitable shadow falls, it is greatly darkened, and also reflects color and life from surrounding objects. If you realize at once what it has taken students all these centuries to wake up to; namely that all animals that are dark on top and pale below are so for the sole purpose of overcoming or compensating this inevitable top light and bottom shadow, your main difficulty will be solved. It is possible, and frequent, that white tells darker than black; that is, if white on the underside falls into sharp shadow it is apt to be actually darker in value than black on the top, shining in or bathed in much light. These things must all be studied conscientiously and with a wide-open mind, as all our natural ideas are apt to be violated when actual conditions are studiously examined. The way to do is to take any subject you want—preferably in simple design and colors at first—and do a picture of it three or four times, in different lights and positions, to accustom yourself to its changes, and get away from your traditional prejudices that a given surface is always to be represented by the same pigment or in the same manner. In other words, *loosen up*, be unafraid to try and represent what you see. It won't hurt anything if it does turn out awful; it may turn out right, and in any case you've learned something, either to do or not to do. And that is progress, while plodding in the track of prejudice without courage to kick out and see what happens is not going to develop anything better than it has already developed.

To point what I have tried to say, I have taken your own little magnolia drawing, and made a transcription of it which I am enclosing, with your other pictures, and returning to you in this same mail. It is not perfect—nor exactly intended to be—but it is designed to show you a little how white can look whiter when it's made of black and Prussian blue than when it is left blank (when it looks like a hole) and how black in shadow looks just like black in light, *not* when the two are just alike, but very different in order to take their proper values in surfaces opposing the light differently. Except for the *color*, the black on the upper wing-coverts equals the white under the tail. Compare the relatively adjacent white and black.

These suggestions should prove helpful to you. Work *all* for study, and none for either exhibition or commendation, at least for a while. As long as you fear criticism, you will hedge at making experiments and downing tradition. So don't work for anything but your own progress. Send me your results and I will help all I can. Send your mistakes *preferably* to your successes. If I can help you it won't be by praising you, but by showing you how to overcome your difficulties. To do that I must see what they are. Learn not to fear contrasts in the same field of color. They are hard, but *they occur*, and are consequently to be reckoned with.

I would like to know something about yourself. How old are you? What are your surroundings and circumstances? Do you wish, some day, to make this work your livelihood? And if so, have you any other source of income in case of tight times? These are all pertinent questions, though they may seem to you impertinent. I hardly think I need tell you that no other spirit than that of professional sympathy enters into my asking them. I realize, probably better than anyone else, because it is my *sole* profession, what its demands and emoluments are, and its risks as a livelihood. As an avocation I should put it beyond anything I know of in value; as a vocation I should certainly think long and hard, and prepare for many sacrifices in entering the lists. I have been able to command about the same annual income as I should have done as a college professor with the same grounding. I had the advantage of being early in the field and having an excellent teacher, in Abbott Thayer, to help me to overcome my early difficulties, and an excellent executive friend in Elliott Coues, who badly needed an illustrator just as I got ripe. I have, of course, no University connection to insure me a Carnegie pension when I begin to slide down the far side. I have been lucky beyond my deserts, and I have also worked hard and long and still am. That is no hardship in a profession of such boundless opportunities for the hand and the imagination to work together. But it is not exempt from the temptation to 'pot-boil,' and unless you are resolved to be for ever your own most relentless critic you won't be able to hold your banner high. I don't know, yet, whether you've got the thing in you so hard that it will prove your dominant passion right through your life or not. If not, I mustn't encourage you to give your life to it; if you have, I wouldn't be able to dissuade you anyway. I ought to tell you, probably, that I was considered mildly insane, although myself the only sufferer from the results of the malady.

I had not intended to write you a book on this matter, but I want only to impress you with my conviction that the field, as a sole profession, is a risk. As a pastime that may later develop into a valuable asset, provided you prove to have the persistence to develop the requisite skill, and above all, to have that insight into nature and that sympathy and understanding of birds which will make your pictures real contributions that the world *must* have, you may safely launch into the work and fear no rivals and no depression of your business. You'll never be rich, and you'll surely never be poor.

L.A.F. TO GEORGE SUTTON

Ithaca, N. Y., June 5, 1915.

I have delayed writing you for the same old reasons—I've been very busy and haven't felt I could write you as fully as your hard work and gratifying results warrant. And even now I won't be able to go far, but I want to tell you that I received your pictures, and to tell you that you are going ahead nicely. Do persevere, and work more from fresh material. The song sparrow is one of your very best.

The trouble with your shadowed chestnut-side is only that you haven't quite arrived—you are headed quite right. Shadow-color is not easy at all to analyze. You have to un-know everything you have always thought and start with a clean slate, or an absolutely open mind. *Analyze with a perfectly unbiased mind.* A good way to help is to take a piece of white paper, cut a small round hole in it, and study your color locally by isolating it from the rest, and comparing it with the white paper around the hole. Do this out doors, too, and see what surprises you get as to actual color of hills, etc., in the distance. Or tear a small hole in a big leaf and look at the skyline through it. All these things will help to clear your mind of preconceived notions of color—especially it will show you that local color (by which I mean the exact color, analytically, of any given part of your whole subject, isolated from the rest) is practically never unmodified by either warm light or cool shadow; in the latter case, too, it almost invariably absorbs color either reflected from nearby objects or blue absorbed from the atmosphere. You don't have to have blue sky in the latter case. That is why your warbler looks muddy. For exercise, try greatly exaggerating the colors thus reflected, as well as the lightness of the parts that *catch* light. I don't think it will be dangerous for you to do this, for your eye and hand are both sufficiently literal to hold you safe. But I doubt if you can grasp the extent of this effect of atmosphere (to lump the whole gamut of complications) unless you take a good swing out into it. Put your bird where the sun hits it, and paint it—exaggerate if you can the full relation of the light side and the shadow side first, and secondarily, work in the surface colors and markings. Take a fair-sized subject, so you can study it freely; a stuffed hawk is good. Don't be afraid to spread paint.

Your two chestnut-side studies are just the kind of thing that will help you; the same theme under different light conditions. If you have difficulty in adjusting your markings to your broader surfaces, half-shut your eyes, and thus exclude the complicating details both of pattern and of values. Divide your bird along its 'twilight' line, thus (sketch) and keep night from day.

Usually you will find the darkest line just beyond the line, *not* at the edge, for some light always comes around the other way, usually as a reflection from something else.

In sunlight, *everything* in the lighted side—black included—will prove lighter than *anything* in the shaded side, *white* included.

These are all basic principles, that I may have pointed before. I can't quite remember just what I have written before.

You are doing nicely, and must not be discouraged. At your age I did far less direct and sprightly things. Send me some more, and if you come to Ithaca let me know, and I will talk it all over with you.

L.A.F. TO GEORGE SUTTON

[Separate sheet probably enclosed with above letter.]

Here is a sketch to show some of the principles I have tried to describe. Notice that

(1) the darkest tone (except holes) comes not on the edge away from the light, but *between* the lighted side and the shadowed side.

(2) the reflected light on the shadowed side not only rises in value, but alters in color, due to the surface that reflects this light.

(3) *local* color is almost absent, and the whole thing is largely reflected or induced color from surrounding objects.

(4) high lights and deep darks: (squint for them if they are not apparent in the mass of details seen distinctly.) There is always *one* of each, between which every other part must take its proper

place in the scale. Here the high-light is the left eye-brow, and the nose holes form the deep dark. Excepting holes, *everything* in the lighted area is higher than *anything* in the shadowed area, and vice versa. The skull, by the way, is the artificially distorted skull of an old Flathead Indian, hence its flat forehead and stampeding brain-case. In profile thus—(sketch).

Take some unfamiliar object like this and make similar studies, as pure training of your eye. We are naturally almost blind to all but the most blatant and contrasting values, and even great painters—especially of the earlier schools and periods—never did get discriminating in this essential matter. Study, if you can get at them, the works of Geo. de Forest Brush and Abbott H. Thayer, in this connection. Many old-school painters understood contrast thoroughly, and played it like the masters they were. Few if any understood—or correctly rated—the importance of a perfect balance of values, and I think the reason many greatly esteemed works survive is because critics and amateurs alike are so untrained in the detection of this cardinal principle. Color subtlety is simplicity itself compared to value subtlety, which includes every possible element of color variation as thoroughly as does white light itself. Great pictures are often full of ingenious tricks of *color* to overcome the failings of the painter to achieve his *values*.

Your redwing study is a valuable case in point, and a difficult one. Do another, with especial regard for this matter of values. Don't be afraid of failing, and do it over several times. That is the best possible study, and should not prove a bore if the second is better than the first, etc. Study it all out, after you've made your drawing, and before you start to paint; point your high light and your deep dark, and adjust all the rest properly between, and then go to it.

When he wrote these letters Louis had not yet met George Sutton —in fact we saw him for the first time when he arrived to spend the summer with us in 1916—and they lack the warmth Louis was unable to suppress when he knew the person at whom his words were aimed. Perhaps this accounts for the difference between the personal letters and the articles and reviews he composed, wherein he did not permit himself the colloquialism and unexpected metaphor that make his letters sound just like him. Much of his published writing as a result is stiff and disappointing. An exception, however, is his series of papers on the voices of tropical birds, published in Bird-Lore in six parts beginning with the issue for November-December, 1913, and reprinted as a whole in the Annual Report of the Smithsonian Institution for 1915. Dr. Chapman had written in October, 1913, following their return from Colombia:

Glad you approve my suggestion for articles on the calls of tropical birds. My idea is to make it a series of short articles, each treating of three or four species with small black and white 'silhouettes' or 'vignettes' of the bird in the act of calling. . . . You have a special aptitude for descriptive writing particularly of this kind and could do this so much better than I could that I feel I should step aside in your favor.

Louis must have got quickly to work. Mr. Brewster reviewed the second paper (January-February, 1914) on the voices of tinamous, partridges, and solitaires with this comment, printed in the next issue of the magazine:

Having heard tinamous calling at nightfall in tropical forests on the island of Trinidad, I cannot help doubting if anyone not an artist as well as an ornithologist, and no less gifted with pen than brush, could possibly have characterized their utterances in terms at once so true and picturesque as those employed by Mr. Fuertes.

The sixth paper contains a description of the noises made by the red howling monkey 'which, though not a bird, ranks easily first as a maker of weird noises.' And thereby hangs a characteristic anecdote, told by Professor Harry Caplan. At Cornell University there is a club called Book and Bowl, at whose meetings students and faculty gather from time to time, someone reads a prepared paper, and all partake of liquid refreshment. Over the years, I understand, sometimes the Book, and sometimes the Bowl, has preponderated. At all events, Louis was a member and took his turn at providing the paper of the evening. On one occasion he read his description of the roars of howling monkeys, a vivid and exciting account that was much applauded. 'All right,' he said, 'you think that's pretty good, but now let's hear how a real writer does it.' He forthwith read, from the third chapter of Green Mansions, W. H. Hudson's paragraphs on the same phenomenon. Whether or not the members of Book and Bowl learned something about writing that night, they had an impromptu lesson in honest humility that one of them at least, Professor Caplan, did not forget.

Louis had no reason for humility in his capacity as raconteur, and the members of another Cornell organization, the Savage Club, enjoyed many of his amusing stories. William Strunk, Jr., a fellow Savage, once wrote of Louis: 'Whenever he told a story about some particular person, he always managed to bring in some little mannerism or characteristic gesture that in itself almost identified the person; . . . he always gave a graphic picture of anything he described; he must have looked at everything with the same observation that he showed in his painting.' Professor Strunk remembered 'a party given by the Savage Club one evening after the performance of The Hypocrites with an English cast including Doris Kenyon, Arthur Lewis, Reginald Denny's father, and other well-known people, for the men of the company, and Louis told the great story about the stuttering boy whose father twisted the tiger's tail till its head dropped off, and Mr. Denny declared that if [Louis] ever thought of going on the stage, he would make a successful actor because his sense of timing was so perfect.'

Impersonation, or acting, was the key to the humor of his stories. Whenever there was a rally before a Princeton-Cornell football game Louis was besought to t-t-t-twist the t-t-t-tiger's t-t-tail: in the story he was the timid boy relating the c-c-curious c-c-custom of the tiger, that when you twisted its tail its head fell off. He was about to perform upon a tiger he met behind his house, when it occurred to him that it might be some poor family's tiger. That's all there was to it; few of Louis' stories had more 'plot' than that. The character he portrayed in Old Ironsides was the familiar schoolboy reciting and getting stuck. In Martin, a well-known ghost story, he impersonated a superstitious itinerant darky preacher. His **Du**

Chaillu was a naïvely pompous liar; he could act to perfection the Italian organ-grinder, the old-time central New York State farmer, the whale fisherman, the circus barker touting a performer upon 'the horiozonteel baahs,' the professional lecturer on snores (created by his friend Robert Wildhack).

He told the story about a blustering tramp who, after peeping in the window of a lonely farm house and seeing only two frail old ladies, banged on the front door. When it was opened, too quickly, by a large and powerful-looking farmer, the tramp's bluff crumpled, and he stammered, 'Sir, I am a tuana peener.' He told an exquisitely long story about a man whose wife was clinging to a tiny ledge half-way down a cliff, one about a sailor who 'only required a little common civility, and damn little of that,' one about the Irish railroad worker who 'nivver knew me thumb was gone till I see a duck makin' off with it.' There was the Indian Chief who said to a sweet young thing asking his name: 'I am Big Chief Rain-in-the-Face, but you, my dear, may call me Drizzle-Puss' (for that gem I am indebted to Dr. R. C. Murphy), and there were many many more. If they have become bromidic now, it is thanks to their re-telling by the tongue of some less skillful artist; Dr. Murphy for one testifies that 'all stories by him were funnier than by anyone else.'

Such, then, was Louis' gentle life at home these years. Thus were the elements mixed in him.

16

Louis' Artistic Dilemma

·····································

THE DISTINGUISHED BELGIAN historian of Science, George Sarton, paid a visit to Ithaca in 1917, met Louis Fuertes at a dinner party, and afterward wrote him this note:

I wish to tell you how much I admire your work—at least the part of it which I had the pleasure of seeing in the Natural History museum of New York City. You have succeeded in devoting your life—at the same time and with equal success—to Art and to Science. You are happy indeed!

It is not easy to serve science well, or art well. Few undertake to serve them both, and of these few how many can succeed? There is no reason why scientific truth may not receive artistic treatment, as a historic event may possess the qualities requisite for poetry, but men have tended to separate art and science, with the result that the scientist is suspicious of an 'artistic' treatment of his material and the artist looks with some scorn upon a 'scientific' representation of his. At the highest level art and science can unite, and it was to this level that Louis Fuertes—and Charles Knight and Gerald Thayer—aspired.

Louis was conscious of limits imposed by his own short-comings as well as by the nature of the work he must do to earn his living, *but he did not lose sight of the ideal and was humbly grateful when a judicious critic thought him to have attained it.*

L.A.F. TO GEORGE SARTON

[No Date]
I think I have never received a letter which pleased and gratified me as much as did yours. You know, of course, how much both labor in Science and labor in Art are, like virtue, their own reward— and how the laborer in both fields reaps pleasure in the task itself, and comes to more or less discount the approval of the public, of necessity, if he will adhere to his own ideals and standards for advance and improvement. You may well imagine, then, the cumulative pleasure and reward I take from your very kind letter; it expresses my own hope of my eventual achievement, and I shall always keep it, a gratuitous word of commendation and encouragement from a source that I greatly value.

Louis' reply is undated. This was unusual for him, and creates the impression that he felt the exchange of letters with Mr. Sarton to be somehow apart from the business of the day. Indeed, at this time (he was 43) Louis seems to stand aside and assess his life as a whole. Although he had to face and overcome two immediate difficulties, the one technical, having to do with painting subjects not congenial to his talents or training, the other legal, referring to piracy of his pictures; and although he was aware of, and greatly distressed by, an apparent breach between his benefactor Abbott Thayer and himself; he still was able to see his work as a whole and understand its purpose; he recognized his true relationship to the men of his own generation, to the men—then youngsters—of the next, and to Thayer and Audubon who had come before. He steered as well as he could a straight course between opposite opinions of his work, guided by his own mature evaluation of it.

But 1917 is in the midst of the period next encountered. During the years from 1914 to 1920 or so, when Louis was chiefly at home, Gilbert Grosvenor employed him, and paid him very well, for eight series of paintings published in The National Geographic Magazine. They were: 'Fifty Common Birds of Farm and Orchard' (originally prepared as Farmers' Bulletin 513, U.S.D.A.), 'Birds of Town and Country,' 'American Game Birds,' 'The Warblers of North America,' 'The Larger North American Mammals,' 'The Smaller North American Mammals,' 'Our Common Dogs,' and illustrations for an article that he wrote, 'Falconry, the Sport of Kings.' Louis was grateful for this work, as will be seen; as he put it, pictures of birds are just about the last things anyone needs in war time, and without The National Geographic contracts he would hardly have been able to make ends meet. Also, it brought his name and work before the eyes of a great many people. These advantages were balanced by his reluctance to try animal pictures, particularly the dogs.

He refers to the animal pictures in the next letter. The kindly, well-disposed, and enthusiastic Mr. Brewster of Cambridge wrote one of his thorough-going eulogies on the animal pictures, which were pleasing to some of Louis' friends, but not, alas, to Abbott Thayer.

L.A.F. TO GILBERT GROSVENOR

Ithaca, N. Y., Dec. 11, 1916.

I saw the Geographic for the first time in St. Louis last week and am delighted almost beyond expression, both at the quality of the copy, and at your generous recognition on cover and title page. I have already received several most congratulatory letters, and hiding our blushes beneath our hand, really think that the number will prove a very acceptable one.

WILLIAM BREWSTER TO L.A.F.

Cambridge, Mass., Dec. 12, 1916.

What a surprise you have just given us—or, at least, me—in those wonderful mammal pictures! When Henshaw told me you had undertaken them I said, 'He'll fail, beyond a doubt. No bird artist can possibly draw mammals equally well—or vice versa.' Fortunately I was dead wrong in so thinking, as the current number of the Geographic triumphantly proves.

Louis was less happy about his pictures of dogs made in 1917-18, but once more he was able to please Mr. Grosvenor.

L.A.F. TO F. M. CHAPMAN

Ithaca, N. Y., Sept. 18, 1918.

I finished the dogs, and Grosvenor says he likes them fine. He suggested my doing the stars in a bright snappy way, to be of interest to the layman—but I thought there were a few things still on earth we hadn't tried, and balked.

And here, in striking contrast to the opinions of Messrs. Brewster and Grosvenor, is the reaction of Abbott Thayer to Louis' National Geographic Magazine mammal pictures.

ABBOTT THAYER TO L.A.F.

[Monadnock, N. H., Jan., 1917.]

If I were God and had painted those past-all-human-painter-powers true landscapes on the animal world I should enjoy seeing Louis Fuertes reveal the fact. The fact that a woodcock could sit on top of a church steeple doesn't make it either art or science to paint him there. It is the vast averages that art perpetuates. You are going to see the Am. Museum *et al* look pretty cheap, with most, all Europe following me, and merely through *studying* me.

I am coming out, soon, with a perfectly astounding confirmation of all my conceal[ing] col[oration] business. No one can know what a grief it is to me that your beautiful pictures are not devoted to their revelations.

But if you don't see them you can't of course, do them.

This brings into focus the artistic dilemma with which Louis was faced all through his career. He had been one of the first persons to understand and thrill to Mr. Thayer's discoveries in the coloration of birds and animals; he did see them. One of the great and continuing efforts of his life was to demonstrate, explain, reveal, convince other people of the validity of these discoveries. But he had to earn his living by painting illustrations of birds and animals that would show people what they looked like. Mr. Thayer in effect wanted Louis to paint pictures of birds so you couldn't see the birds, but Louis had to fill commissions as they were given. The illustrations for the Seventh Annual Report of the New York Forest, Fish, and Game Commission (1902) were ordered by Mr. Chapman, a given number of plates with a given number of birds upon the page, yet Mr. Thayer criticized even the combination of birds in each plate. As background Dr. Chapman had asked for 'what you term "a dash of environment"; at any rate a suggestion of haunt, something more than a silhouette against a clean white background.' When he received the pictures he wrote: 'The owl, I think, is about the best, most artistic thing you ever painted.' Yet listen to Mr. Thayer in the letter of April, 1903:

You've got to catch it about the owls. I send sketch to show my meaning. An owl, say a screech owl, is practically always to be found in a dim place, where you seem to see right through him, of course because he is graded, just as through a grouse in the same situation. You see all his markings sharp and clear and till you recognize them you mistake them all for forest details. If he can pass for a stub it is a secondary benefit, and probably he passes for a stub in his own background, not where he is. Side lighting as in yours is totally unrepresentative of the forest interior.

What does my Louis say? I long to see you. . . .

In an undated letter written before 1908 Mr. Thayer implores:

Oh Louis! won't you try once making a background wholly out of the bird's colors: Just his actual color-notes as you paint them. Some day you'll wonder at the present style of background painting. Both naturalists and artists represent the same demand in this case. When Merriam asks for a bird's natural surroundings he little knows yet that they are authentically given on the bird, and that nothing else can look right, any more to him, than to an artist.

Take a sora, for instance: dead, olive-colored sedge is just exactly as predominant in his background as in his color. He is not visible with bright green as any part of his background enough of the time to get any representation of it into his colors. The same of a savannah sparrow. His summer change is only a little grassy chrome on shoulder and eye-brow. The green covers these creatures, and you don't see them. And when you brush it aside, you find them against the dead stuff, or when autumn sweeps the green away, there they are, *ready*. This is wonderfully true of the partridge.

Here is the formula: In all cases where the human view is the same as that of the animal's enemy (or quarry, when that case is most important) the animal's colors dictate the only background the painter can put in, either for art or science. Of course the frog's view of the heron or the cricket's of a skunk or the crouching fox['s] of a hare's rear is not ours.

Do try it once.

Draw your rail's background details, and then make it all out of his colors—matched, value and all (sketch). What wet-spot-under-reeds-with-sky-vertical-glints rails carry on their flanks!

Try it once for me. . . .

Every time Louis tried it he met with the other horn of the dilemma, as in this letter from Mr. Grosvenor, written March 27, 1920.

I do not like at all your owl plate. I take special exception to the barred owl. I am very well acquainted with this magnificent creature, as we have had barred owls nesting in my woods for many years. I don't like the background that you have given the barred owl. . . . Altogether I think this plate is very inferior to the Fuertes standard, and therefore I am returning the plate to you herewith. It seems to me you have made a mistake to use such a dark background.

William Beebe, for whom Louis was working on large portraits of pheasants for a monograph to be financed largely by Anthony R. Kuser, complains as follows in a letter of May 7, 1912:

Kuser is very keen on making the birds stand out as much as possible and not merge into the background. Knight's protective treatment has rather augmented this and while I am perfectly satisfied, we must do what we can to fall in with his wishes.

Finally, here are some criticisms in a letter of January 30, 1923, from H. S. Morgan of the Forbes Lithographic Company, referring to little pictures to be printed on cards and distributed by Church and Dwight Co. with packages of baking soda. The remarks represent the opinion of the client, not Mr. Morgan, and illustrate very well the 'primary ignorance' against which Louis as an illustrator had to fight. His picture of a robin for this contract was returned because its breast was rust-colored, not the rosy red the advertiser expected a robin's breast to be. Louis sent him an actual robin skin.

Prairie chicken—very good, but lost in background.

Sharp-tailed grouse—pose uninteresting and a lack of color in the background.

Ruffed grouse—action good, but bird lacks modeling, looks flat, needs rounding-up, showing a general effect of light and shade as well as detail. Drop trees and foliage or have an opening in foliage so bird can be shown against sky. . . .

Valley quail—lacks detail in bird and needs a general light and shade on the body; body does not look round. . . . This bird is lost in the background.

Poor Louis. His most devoted, sympathetic, and acute critic, Gerald Thayer, had already found fault with him for trying to compromise, to paint pictures in which the bird could plainly be seen in a natural setting.

GERALD THAYER TO L.A.F.

Monadnock, N. H., May 24, 1914.

Your letter to Papa, telling how you thought the final verdict on your gifts and ambitions was going, made me a bit sad. You haven't sized things up just right, I think. Something that cannot well be ticketed lower than *great painting* is in your finest birdwork, I believe. Far posterity shall bear witness. Perhaps, too, you have achieved bird pictures with landscape which have the same rank—I rather think so. Rarely, however. Many wonderful birds of yours have mediocre backgrounds, as you know. And your timidity (?) about *going the whole hog* in the matter of concealing coloration has closed against you some doors to supreme achievement. Supreme birds of yours against *plain white backgrounds,* or at most with foreground sprigs against white, as in Audubon—that would be one thing. *True backgrounds,* bearing amazing testimony to the significance of those strangely beautiful bird-patterns which you and we so love—that would be another thing. Between those two things you compromise, as a rule. This compromise is not great. The concealing coloration thing is very much more, in countless cases, as you know, than a Thayer hobby. No man living could have done with it what you could. But you will not.

Possibly Gerald was right; the compromise was not great, but Louis had to make it. Gerald's ruffed grouse in the Concealing Coloration *book is a wonderful work of art, perhaps greater than anything Louis ever did. He took six months to paint it (he painted very few pictures in all), and he never made that adjustment to the world that would insure a normal means of earning a living for his family. The advice he gave Louis was good, but Louis could not take it and live. We must apparently make some concessions to the time, the society, the culture—Louis would say the state of ignorance—into which we are born, though this is a bitter truth, if true. Mr. Thayer made an Eden for his children that was not of the world, worldly, yet he left them ill equipped to live with that world, and without the financial means that would enable them to live without it.*

But let us go back to 1917, the year in which Louis seemed to pause and take stock of himself and his world. The letter from Mrs. Thayer that comes next in order caused Louis to write out as clearly as he was able his own view of the dilemma confronting him.

Mrs. Abbott Thayer to L.A.F.

Monadnock, N. H., Feb. 28, 1917.

As you probably know Abbott wore himself out trying to get the Allies to concealingly color their ships and men. At last they are to [a] large extent doing it. A friend, who spent last spring and summer at the French front, tells us that everything there, motors, bridges, derricks, the canvas used to cover piles of ammunition back from the front, canon, tents, and even white horses are painted with ruptive patterns, green, brown, etc., landscape colors. Snipers also paint their faces, and wear motley.

But all this came too late (in fact the English Navy have not yet got over the anti-white superstition, and make their ships light gray instead of white on the vertical planes) to save Abbott from getting so worn out that, though he has been sick a year now, he seems to make very little progress toward health.

He is pronounced sound, but excessively fatigued. His nerves are in such a raw state that he exaggerates every feeling. I ought first to tell you why I tell you all this. I want you, if you know Dr. Gould, to ask him if he can help Abbott.

L.A.F. TO MRS. THAYER

Ithaca, N. Y., Mar. 3, 1917.

Your letter came yesterday afternoon. Thanks for it. Dr. Gould has not lived here—nor been here—for a number of years. He knows all about Uncle Abbott's work, and we used to have frequent long discussions in which he was most keenly interested. I should be very glad to write him if you like, but I am sure that he would only have to have a word of reminiscence to recall Uncle A. vividly.

And now, Aunt Emma, I am enclosing a letter to Uncle Abbott. I wish you would read it, and if you think it entirely wise, give it to him or read it to him. If you *don't*, either destroy it or hold it until some more favorable time. I have suffered very greatly from the fear that he has found me an ungrateful and unworthy object of his wonderful kindness—those years you will so easily recall. And I have felt that he thought me out of sympathy, or unable to comprehend basically his wonderful contributions to scientific perception of coloration and environment, and in this way has lost the satisfaction in my friendship (and more) for him that would be a part of a more full and sympathetic understanding. I have always found it so hard to express any deviation from his idea without conveying the impression of total skepticism; to approach my problem as I see it from any other angle than his without implying disbelief in the great matter he has been crusading for, that I have come to feel that it is almost hopeless for me to try to alter things. Yet the fact is that I am perhaps in this country the *only* naturalist-painter with enough knowledge and experience, and with it enough optical knowledge, to appreciate even a small part of the enormous simple truths he has so ingeniously demonstrated, and I am, so far as I know, the one man among the present-day naturalists that not only believes in his truths but fights for them with the rest.

So I can't let the present misconception go to its final inevitable end, nor let myself be one of the unhappinesses that beset poor, intense, and high-strung Uncle Abbott, without at least trying to set it straight. Do please, dear Aunt Emma, think it over a little, and if you think my letter to him is not likely to be upsetting to him, read it to him, and give it to him. Otherwise, keep it till later or put it in the fire.

It is a very great misfortune to me that I am so busy and so circumscribed that I can no longer fly to the Thayers now and then. My happiest and most uplifting days: where would I be now —and what—if I had not had them; take, and give the others, our warmest love.

L.A.F. TO ABBOTT THAYER (under cover to Mrs. Thayer)
Ithaca, N. Y., Mar. 3, 1917.

It is very hard for me to go into the matter of my degree of understanding of your discoveries, partly of course because I have not seen you in so long to know their present development, and partly because of the function I conceive my power to paint birds and animals should fulfil . . . It is against such a vast *primary* ignorance of the very most rudimentary beginnings of natural history that most illustration is at present launched that I have felt it obligatory to assume that in nature only those individuals would be normally seen by the general *homo sapiens* which were more or less out of their most normal and assimilating environment—and I aim at painting the kind of *mélange* in which the half-blind 'normal' would be likely to perceive the creature in life, if he saw him at all. For my own peace of mind, though, I feel that I must insist that of all the men in the country with any experience in and knowledge of birds and animals alive and in their environments, I am perhaps the only one who *does* understand enough of optics to even thoroughly apprehend the value and operation of that most simple and all-underlying device of counter-shading: certainly the ruptive and others, sky-matching rumps and fronts of prey and predators are thoroughly intelligible to me, and you ought to know that I am at least *one* staunch defender and patient explainer of your wonderful crusade—and your book is nearly worn out from its constant use to that end.

I greatly hope that my treatment of the smaller animals, now nearly accomplished (though not to appear till next fall) will not be so depressing to you. Of course this is a new field entirely to me, and I have had to do a vast deal of research and study, and in many cases to go ahead with only all-too-meager material to work with. I am myself well aware of short-comings. My ambition, however, is to so represent these little creatures as to reach into the natural sympathy and curiosity of the 650,000 people who *take* the *Geographic Magazine* and the much larger number who see it, and educate them into a fair knowledge of the physical appearance of each animal, even if it is necessary to introduce sky, or a log, or stone, or something to act as a partially off-setting background. You must know that I could not possibly have failed to discover that the constant tendency (sometimes almost inevitable) is for the bird or beast to melt right into the picture, after having painted such subjects for so many years. And my work in South America and the tropics in general was just as plainly elucidating as to the ruptive value of toucan patterns, etc., as my work with ptarmigan in the Canadian Rockies was as to the value of gradation and mimicking pattern in combination. I can imagine no more luxurious activity than to paint every little creature we have beautifully availing himself of his many devices for obliteration (short of hiding)—in short, *just* illustrating your discoveries of concealing coloration, instead of the much less thrilling representation—as I feel I have to do—of their specific superficial appearance detached at least in part from their merging environment.

Nothing hurts me so much as the feeling, which has grown on me more and more, that you feel me out of harmony and sympathy with your enlightening labor and its discoveries. It may be that I can never live to assure you of the untruth of that feeling, for I feel so strongly that it is first necessary for me, with my gift, such as it is, to educate our 'fellow man' in the first facts of what these creatures we are thrilled by look like detached, so that you, with your special gift, can lead them to a deeper understanding of the beautiful *significance* of this specialized 'looks,' or surface pattern—whatever it may be—the sheer beauty of which when detached is so all-engrossing that its particular utility becomes lost . . . to the lay beholder.

It is particularly and increasingly painful to me to feel this way, for I know that you must feel that I have been unworthy of the devoted and altruistic labor you spent on me, and the unheard-of kindness you lavished on me when I was a youngster, and that I have failed to make the only return I know you would have valued: a development such as would have demonstrated that I had in me a spark of power and understanding that would, with guidance, shine with truth and light, and make my contribution distinctive among all others just by virtue of this inner fire. It is the greatest disappointment of my life that this has failed—and it has done so solely because I see so ordinary and un-thrilling a duty as that already described as the mission of whatever I can convey to my time and surrounding state of ignorance. You honor your contemporaries by presupposing an intelligence, and knowledge, and power of application of fact to fact, that I do not think has developed—nor can—until a vast mountain of indifference, ignorance, and worst of all, pre-misconception shall have been battered down by the means I have indicated. I may be—and presume I am—wrong. There is where my limitation sticks me—and there is where whatever misunderstanding there may be between us has started. I pray you to believe what I have said, and to believe also that I have for you and all of you the most genuine and undying affection, and the highest valuation of your labor and your sacrifice. No one else, I think truly, so well understands it, and the time will come when the world will realize it and wonder at the huge lack of perceptiveness that your contemporary world must have suffered under. If you can believe what I have written, which I deeply hope you can, you will know what I have never before been able to tell you: that I do sympathize and believe in your discoveries and that in the best way I know how I am trying to make it possible for others to come intelligently into possession of the fascinating knowledge you have opened the door to.

We all send our warmest love to you all. Please forgive me for writing you a book. It has been so long, and it flowed out so easily that I haven't realized till now—as I look at the pages—what I have inflicted upon you.

This year Louis was beset with difficulties; not only was he troubled by the artistic dilemma that faced him and the seeming breach with Mr. Thayer, but also he had external, material worries as well. The Birds of New York, at this time his major work, was being pirated by unscrupulous publishers. He learned of it through Dr. Chapman, who had been approached by the sponsors of a set of books called The Nature Lover's Library for advertising space in Bird-Lore. The publication they wished to advertise was a Book of 1000 Birds, illustrated by Louis Agassiz Fuertes. The illustrations were in fact reprints of the plates of the Birds of New York, and the sponsors of the publication had neither asked the artist's permission nor offered any payment for the use of his name.

L.A.F. TO FRANK M. CHAPMAN

Ithaca, N. Y., Oct. 8, 1917.

The *Book of 1000 Birds* is getting to be one of 1000 troubles. They reached through the lustful hands of the State printer and landed on the full set of *Mem. XII* plates, and are now exploiting their Nat. Hist., using my work and reputation as a fulcrum. I fancy I'm perfectly helpless as to the use of the plates, which were not copyrighted. But I'm going to fight them on the exploitation of my name and position, which, as I see it, is inalienably mine, and the more I get into it the madder I get. I'm going to get the best counsel I can, and go to it: enjoin them a while, if possible, and let somebody else sweat. I can't thank you enough for letting me know early, for I got the jump by so much, and may catch them before they are on the market.

L.A.F. TO F. M. CHAPMAN

Ithaca, N.Y., Oct. 11, 1917.

Your whole-hearted letter touched me very deeply: I don't know what I'm really going to do, as I hate a fight and shall in all probability lose if I enter the lists against the wily publisher, especially when backed up, as he is, by the herpetistic State printer, than whom, etc. etc. I have an engagement with Col. Sackett (the *Tribune's* lawyer) for next Thursday, when I shall lay everything before him, and we'll see what can be done.

I shouldn't want you to delete the page advertisement from *Bird-Lore*, because, first, you don't know that it's a steal until we decide it is one, and second, because the only thing I've got now to land on is their advertising and use of my name to sell the book. So they can't advertise too much to suit me, especially if I can slap an injunction on their output. They don't even know I'm displeased, and Col. Sackett is going to tell them so, not I. At least that's my present idea: it may change, and I may write them a stiff letter giving them a chance to come through, and if they don't, land on them then. Personally, I think a diplomatic adjustment is better than war, where everybody is bound to lose, besides getting a grouch for life.

L.A.F. TO F. M. CHAPMAN

Ithaca, N. Y., Dec. 19, 1917.

The N. Y. papers have lavished considerable unwelcome attention on my suit; I suspect somewhat that the defendants have had a hand in it, seeing that if inevitable, it might be better to have it thick. The more I learn, the madder I get, and the more I become convinced that they were all along counting on my easy-going simplicity to get by with it. One evidence that they were expecting a possible withholding of the State plates is the duplication by Brasher and Horsfall of most of the conspicuous species.

Enough of that stuff, though: I'm already sick of it. As far as I'm concerned, say whatever you want to about any and all of it. It's a punk, amateur, cheaply visioned thing; a pure attempt to put over a sub-mediocre Nat. Hist. and get away with it at a profit: it's the third attempt to make the old Standard Natural History pay expenses. Go as far as you like, and don't consider my share in the least; I didn't contribute it, and I don't acknowledge it, so it mustn't hold or handicap you in the least, and it is certainly my wish that you review it entirely as if you didn't know anything about how I was included in it.

Late in 1918 Louis won his action against the University Society and the Nature Lover's Library. The case did not come to trial but was settled with a judgment in his favor and a payment to him of $2,500.

So this particular difficulty worked itself out, and the ruffled surface as well as the disturbed depths of his affairs resumed their accustomed calm. As a Christmas gift he received a copy of Audubon the Naturalist by Francis Hobart Herrick, inscribed 'To the Audubon of his day from his friend Frank M. Chapman.' This scholarly biography, the first complete study of Audubon's life, is now the standard work on a subject unfortunately much re-worked, popularized, and sentimentalized. The subject was fresh when it came into Louis' hands and was deeply exciting to him. Here is his thank-you letter.

L.A.F. to F. M. Chapman

Ithaca, N. Y., Christmas evening, [1917.]

As usual, you send me some touchingly appreciative remembrance; I had read of this new Audubon, but hadn't seen it. It is a splendid thing to have, and I have already started to read it. I shall make it a part of my 'historical background'—but in spite of your more than flattering dedication I could never arrange myself against it in a really convincing manner—me with my 1917 clothes, notions, shotgun, means of getting to my inspiration and field—as against his romantic and picturesque day and experience.

I don't know whether you knew that here, in the town library, we have one of the first 175 copies (the orig. output) purchased by E. Cornell from the orig. subscriber, and used as the nucleus of the 'Cornell Library' which antedates the university by 18 or 20 years. This set was for ten years or more my daily bread; by it I was thrilled so that it melts me now to remember it, and many—so very many—of the plates are still as familiar to me as the wall-paper in the hall of the first house I remember living in! By those lovingly done things I was moved—and still am—in a way I would find it hard to express. For most of them bore the authentic stamp of the *fresh* bird. Frequently their strained positions are at variance with my point of view, or what characterizes the species to *me*, but I drew myself, for years, by his method of laying the bird on the paper and tracing *around* it, in true profile—and his ardor was so transparent to me, and mine so responded to it, that I could never do other than admit the enormous influence on my almost aching ardency to 'go and do likewise.' If he hadn't been so patently and helplessly stormed by his love of the form and beauty of birds, I should have followed *him*, blindly, instead of his inspiration, for I was too young to differentiate, except for the very positiveness of his real *source* of inspiration. But I doubt if I should ever have had the stamina to work as he had to; I should have failed to stem the tide of adversity—and I *know* I could never, in his time or mine, have negotiated the great folio reproduction and its attendant enormous financing. What a monumental thing for a reed bent by the faintest breath of emotion, as he was, to have accomplished. That, to me, is quite as wonderful as his actual response to his creative lust—for nothing else expresses the desire to perpetuate the evanescent beauty of bird or flower for future enthusiasts to respond to.

I've written you a wordy dissertation on a flimsy pretext, like a sophomore trying for an exempt in English II! But it's partly your own fault, and you may be easy in your mind as to my deep appreciation of the books—and the spirit behind their coming to me. Thank you, Frank, from my heart.

He wrote on February 7, his birthday: 'I have finished the Audubon, and have enjoyed it more than any book I ever read.'

17

The Middle Years. Sheldrake

································

TWENTY MILES NORTH of Ithaca on the west shore of Cayuga Lake there is a point of land called Sheldrake that extends east for several hundred yards from the general shore line, pointing into the lake a long finger of loose gravel that shifts to north or south away from the day's prevailing wind. Inland from the gravelly tip, but still on the point, stood two identical brown-shingled cottages comfortably far apart with a water tower between. The cottages faced north; in front of each the lake washed scanty soil away from a weathered oak at the edge of the beach, and behind them both stretched an even row of huge-bolled willows, once stakes on which to dry fishing nets. Inland a little way were a country village store, a few farm houses, a rambling white clap-board hotel—old-fashioned in 1914—and perhaps a half-dozen comfortable summer cottages. For nine years (with the exception of 1918) Louis brought his family to spend July and August in the 'point cottage'—the one farthest out. He seems to have thought of the place in terms of the birds nesting there, as he wrote to Dr. Chapman in June, 1915, that he 'spent Sunday down at Sheldrake, and got all demoralized by the country freshness of it. The point is super-birdy: m. larks, Carolina doves, cuckoos (y.b.), bluebirds, redwings, grackles, robins, song sparrows, phoebes, w. pewees, cat-birds, chippies all have young around the place.'

I did not think of Sheldrake in this way, but rather in terms of what a child handles, sees, and hears. The beach was an endlessly delightful place to play, with stones of all sizes from sand to small boulders, full of fossils and glacier-given treasures: 'lucky stones,' 'turtle-backs,' 'elephants' toe-nails,' and, among the assortment of colored pebbles, scraps of flint from which my father was always willing to strike sparks for our pleasure with the heel of his jackknife. Beside the house grew tansy, wild caraway, burdocks, and poison ivy. Our view was the lake, with the long hill on the other side tapering away to the north where the sudden frequent thunderstorms came from. They came right at us, a black line of wind followed by a white line of rain on the green-lit water. There were dramatic sunsets, and we went to sleep to the sound of small freshwater waves breaking just beneath our windows as the wind died down.

I do remember the birds that were there: sandpipers getting their feet wet as they run along the water's edge always appeal to children, a great blue heron sat on the oak tree, and the point was a favorite place for herring gulls—I recall objecting vociferously when my father grabbed his pistol and went to shoot a Bonaparte sighted among them. The characteristic sound by day was made by mourning doves, in the evening by screech owls that my father brought very near, calling to them with their own voice.

For a few years my Grandmother Finch had the other point cottage, and those summers were colored by the activities of my Aunt Katharine and her friends, Sheila St. John and a graduate student from Scotland, David Kennedy-Fraser. Mrs. George S. Williams of Ithaca lived in the center of a group of houses farther up the beach with her daughters and their families on either side. Each of these families—the Fitchens and the Robinsons—had six children; three English cousins, children of Mr. and Mrs. D. C. Lee, often spent part of the summer with their Grandmother Williams, and for several years four Wyckoff children were in the other point cottage. There was apt to be a tent set up near us sheltering a Breckenridge boy or a student of bird-painting. Besides these and other constant summer neighbors there were week-end incursions from Ithaca of summer-school students, often Alpha Delts bringing the daughters of Professor Titchener and other friends—all glad of a chance to swim and enjoy the truly delicious place.

For some years my father took work with him and tried to paint at Sheldrake, but after a while he frankly settled in to 'do nothing' —except give us all a good time. On the Fourth of July he would always fly for the children huge paper balloons that rose and sailed for miles by heat from their own little fires of straw—a delicate operation with delightful result. He mentions this custom, which he must have enjoyed, in a letter of January 19, 1912, before the Sheldrake era. A. K. Fisher, for whom he was painting a series of portraits of hawks and owls, had told him of the shooting of a fine duck hawk that lived on the Post Office building in Washington.

I am indeed sorry to hear that the Post Office peregrine has been murdered. I forget whether I ever told you that a pair yearly raises a brood in one of our enormous gorges, twelve miles from here. . . . Fourth of July, two years ago, I was flying a paper balloon for the local kidcrop, and one of the old peregrines saw it and came dashing up to look it over, and having satisfied himself that it wasn't good to eat, lined away for Taughannock, where the nest is.

My father liked to swim as much as any of the children. One of the feats they admired was his swimming underwater, on one breath, all the way around the Fitchens' breakwater—an L-shaped affair about four feet wide and possibly ten by twenty long. Many years later when an aged assessor was trying to make my identity known to his equally aged fellows (to prevent their placing too high a value on our house) he said: 'She is the daughter of Louis Fuertes.' There was no reaction on the part of his companions. 'You know, the bird man.' Still no response. After a somewhat protracted and embarrassing pause, one of the old men brightened. 'Oh, wait a minute,' he said. 'Wasn't he the fella that was such a good underwater swimmer?'

He was also expert with canoe and sailboat, and he was a first-rate woodsman and picnic cook. My mother thought he was imposed on, as he was always chosen cook at community picnics, but I don't believe he objected. She was certain he was imposed on, however, when the Ithaca Rotary Club used Sheldrake point as its picnic ground. She was always less than enthusiastic about this organization that existed (it seemed to her) for the purpose of taking men away from good luncheons at home once a week and making them buy poor ones in company with the local undertaker, and the disgust with which she went about the yard impaling cigar-butts on a wire the day after the Rotary picnic is vivid to me now. It must have been so to my father, too, for he wrote from Holland in the summer of 1924: 'I'm sorry we had to miss the Rotary party, but another year, dear, we'll be there.'

L.A.F. to WILFRED OSGOOD

Sheldrake, N. Y., Aug. 3, 1921.

To-day I cook corn and coffee for 150-200 Rotarians and its wife, so you get short shrift.

Damnear got drowned Sunday; hellofa gale out of the n[orth], swimming on the point in the roaring, bellering surf. Got yanked off the end by the extraordinary current, and snaked up-lake at four miles an hour in the big he-waves and spume and just got out by the skin of my teeth, after a rotten frightening and weakening struggle. It was small comfort that all the others—young strong swimmers—were nearly as all in as I was . . . All next day the water was running back over the point so you couldn't push a canoe over it from the n[orth].

It was through his influence that some of the Sheldrake children took to collecting geodes, moths, and butterflies, though he did not set out to teach them in any formal way whatever. He was, simply, there; his interest was infectious, and normal children were susceptible. I'm afraid his own son and daughter were immune; if I had any reaction at all it was a kind of unrealized sense that the birds and other creatures were being taken care of, they didn't require my notice.

As barker, my father was the chief attraction of the amateur circus, but he never performed upon the tennis court, or took

: 230 :

part in the after-supper baseball games. Instead, he repaired to what was called the 'sitting tool'—a frame effecting a compromise between the contour of the beach and that of the person—whereon we put mattresses and reclined to sing. Often there would be a little driftwood fire at our feet, and always the Big Dipper in the sky beyond.

In the autumn of 1915 he was thinking back to the summer and forward to an opportunity to go duck-hunting on Lake Erie.

L.A.F. TO F. M. CHAPMAN

Ithaca, N. Y., Sept. 18, 1915.

Just now moved up from the lake. The mercury is trying to ape the soaring white pelicans of Pyramid Peak, and I already wish I was back at Sheldrake, splashing in the pellucid shallows with the playful perch. But I ain't; I'm sweltering in the shimmering sunshine with the shrinking sunflower—I stick to everything I touch (and conversely) and drip on everything I get over.

Just had a marveelious invitation from 'Senator Sage' to spend a week or ten days in October at Long Point, a-ducking. Insofar as I have a double-head date in Dayton for the eighteenth and nineteenth and he asked me commencing the twentieth, it looks like a bet. Whatchagot up your own sleeve?

He accepted the invitation.

L.A.F. TO MRS. FUERTES

Long Point, Lake Erie, Ontario,
Oct. 22, 1915.

Well, your first letter, Mary's letter, and the thermos bottle all came to-day, and I got 65 ducks, so little remains to be desired but 24 hours of sleep and rest concentrated into eight hours.

. . . The marsh is the most beautiful place, at all times, but at sunset, and the hour following it, it is beyond description. Just now a perfectly full moon, almost blue-white, begins like a ghost to show in the east just as the glow from the west begins to reflect across. Then it brightens as the sunset progresses, and the serene and calm violet east and the flaming red and orange west both seem too beautiful to be real. The flat blue-black horizon of sparse trees, the ruddy beds of quill reed, and the rustling rushes that the boat slides past, and the vibrant and brilliant air cut everywhere with the swift steady flight of ducks, ducks, ducks,—some sifting straight overhead, silent except for the icy whisper of their wings, only heard for a second or two when they are nearest, others lining their straight course into the sunset—the darting teal, going as if they were hurled out of a gun—the frosty marsh smell everywhere and a cool wind in your neck, all gets to you in a wonderful way. Then, when it is almost dark, suddenly there is a roaring, rushing, splash, all over in less than a second, and dimly against the darkening sky a broad line of velvet, silent birds deploys, rises, and falls into its formation and melts into the sky beyond.

L.A.F. TO MARY FUERTES

Long Point, Lake Erie, Ontario, Oct. 22, 1915.

Dear Mary Lamb:

I am having a lovely time, and when I came home to-night, after a long day out on the marsh, hot, cold, tired—sun-burned, lame-shouldered from shooting, and worried because I hadn't heard from home—and found your nice letter and one from Mother, I forgot I was any of those things I said I was, and everything was perfectly splendid and I was very very happy.

You were a sweet little Mary to think about me and write to me, and it made me love you more than ever—so that it almost hurt.

It's very late now, as I've written a long letter to Mother too, and Mr. Sage has got *his* letter all done and is waiting patiently by the big log-fire till I get through—then we're both going to bed.

Good-bye, Mary dear. Give my love to Summy too, and remember that your daddy loves you always, and more than ever when he knows you are thinking of him.

Your own and only
Dad.

And once more Dr. Chapman was tempting him to go to South

America. Mrs. Chapman, their son Frank, and George K. Cherrie were in the party. Louis resisted, but not without pangs, as this next letter shows.

L.A.F. TO F. M. CHAPMAN

Ithaca, N. Y., May 29, 1916.

I was greatly tickled to get a parting word from you, and the card from Panama among the spigottitos which came a few days ago. Of course by the time you get this you'll have had all sorts of grand experiences, Cherrie will have taught several *cargaderos* their native tongue, Frank will know how to spell *aguacaliente*, and my dear Aunt will know at least one mule by its first name— 'Anda.' ['Go.'] All of which stirs up in my jealous nature a turbid roil of green-eye, for I am still on the old mud pavements of my native town, listening to the common sounds of squealing trolleys and neighborhood carpentry, waiting somewhat listlessly for my peonies to bloom and my new vines to 'catch' on my studio. Working very hard, having finished the mammals, plus eight added species, making a thirty-two page number. Mary has the whooping-cough, and Sum to play—a nice outlook for June and July.

L.A.F. TO F. M. CHAPMAN

Ithaca, N. Y., Oct. 24, 1916.

I'm just taking up definitely the second series [for *The National Geographic Magazine*] small mammals, for a year from Nov. I hope they make a success, for it was a bold bad stroke on my part, and will be monumental, whether a success or failure. I am not divorcing myself from birds, as a glance at my schedule for the winter will show:

1. 9 plates for a beginner's book, by Dryden Kuser (done.)
2. 9 plates of water fowl—Grinnell and Swarth, California.
3. Backgrounds for three magnificent Habitat pheasant groups— (Kuser.)
4. Several large duck paintings—*variosos individuos*.
5. *Ducks of the World*, monograph by J. C. Phillips—ad. inf.
6. *Birds of California*—to replace Brooks, at the front. This seems too bad, but they cannot wait.

These are my major contracts, not forgetting

7. 32 plates (=58 half-plates and 4 full plates) of small mammals. Does that look like a winter's work to you? If not, add

8. *Birds of Massachusetts—Forbush.* (=*Birds of N. Y.*, Eaton) which will in all probability be voted by legislature the first of the year. To me, it appears like brain-storm material from now till about 1922.

Nevertheless, I think I shall not let it force me to work too continuously, but break it now and then for lectures, A.O.U., and other chances to change off that may come up.

He kept at the brain-storm material—indeed he was still working on the Birds of Massachusetts in 1927—and alternated Sheldrake summers with busy winters spent for the most part at home. An August letter to George, an October one and scraps from January letters to Dr. Chapman give bright glimpses of his seasons' occupations.

L.A.F. to George Sutton

Sheldrake, N. Y., Aug. 3, 1917.

We have been down since June 26, and have had the same kind of a time you are familiar with. Swallows are packing for their flight. Great blues are numerous; four came along recently and one stayed on my big oak for a few minutes. No interesting shore birds yet.

I have three tame skunklets that we operated on for aromitis, successfully. You'd be crazy about 'em, as we are. Doves abound on the point, and night herons and screech owls also.

Send me more pictures when you can; I'll try to be less dilatory.

I've finished the 'small mammals' which will be out next January, and am now collecting material for a series of dogs; not as much to my notion as wild things, but not to be despised in war times, when my field gets, apparently, very flat.

L.A.F. to F. M. Chapman

Ithaca, N. Y., Oct. 16, 1919.

I've been swamped with a lot of interesting and beautiful fresh material, which in this hot weather means work, work, work, or have it rot on you (or me, which is worse, as I'm more sensitive!) Three peregrines, all different, from Fishers Island, a ruffed grouse, and the regular amount of small stuff have kept me out of mischief and away from my writing desk for some time.

Ithaca, N. Y., [Jan., 1920.]
Florida seems far away now. It is zero and blowing great howling guns right off the pole.

Yours with a bark and a snuffle.

Ithaca, N. Y., Jan. 22, 1920.
It's colder'n the devil; a forty mile gale to a zero thermometer our portion the last few days—roads blown full, and etc.

I'm, as usual, way behind, because I can only do one man's work. So don't carp if I don't write long letters. Please do up a small package of Florida climate, plus a little hot sunshine, and the Florida smell, and send C.O.D. I like winter, but *Gosh* how I like summer!

L.A.F. TO F. M. CHAPMAN
Sheldrake, N. Y., July 24, 1920.
We're all down at Sheldrake, and very well. I saw all the Thayers a few days ago, when I went up to get Mary (my little girl) who was visiting near Dublin. I was greatly shocked and touched by Abbott, who shows very unmistakably the ravages of his break-down last year, and his present condition, while far from what it was, is still very pitiful and moved me very deeply. Still, he is painting strongly and his work is in vast demand, which encourages him a lot, and I think he is pretty happy just now. The family is all together, and it is a busy outfit, which is in itself a blessing. . . .

Why does the memory choose this to hold and drop that into oblivion? Is there meaning in what we remember? Do we retain the immortal, essential shapes of truth and significance, discard the confused and superfluous? Often it seems quite otherwise, but sometimes it must be so. From this summer visit with Anne Breckenridge I can still see the contour of Mount Pac-Monadnock across the valley and the set tubs in the cellar where we were made to do some laundry as an enterprise in character-building. I recall rides in a chauffeur-driven car and prying interest in the love-affair of a young lady pianist. There were porcupines in the wood-shed and incessant midnight whip-poor-wills. When my father joined us he took us on a walk through the woods, and we came out from their shade into a fragrant, sun-soaked meadow that I can still joyfully smell and feel and see.

I don't know how we got to Monadnock where the Thayers' house was, I don't remember the appearance of the place. I read with shock my father's words: 'I saw all the Thayers,' because I cannot raise any recollection except of Uncle Abbott. I had seen Gerald before, and I felt him to be a special person from another kind of world. How could we have seen him, and Galla, and Aunt Emma, and I not remember them? Is it because the one sight I retain is lit with all the brilliance of a stroke of lightning that casts the night around it into darker dark? In that flash I see the interior of Abbott Thayer's studio, and on a huge canvas a half-completed painting with heavenly figures of heroic size and charging horses. My father stands next to me, and Uncle Abbott, beyond him, is somehow in the world of his picture, which he explains with all possible intensity. I was distressed by a livid lump, or goose-egg, on his temple.

The dark descends. I have further just a glimpse of us walking down hill on a wagon road where the long grass of mid-summer was yellowing. I asked my father if Uncle Abbott had hurt his head; he replied almost in tears, no, that he was old and not very well.

That is all. Recently I asked Anne what she remembers; it is chiefly the awareness that Mr. Thayer was someone Uncle Louis loved very much. We agree that we had not been prepared for what we were going to find, nor given any explanation afterward. Perhaps my father's own thoughts and emotions were so absorbing that he simply didn't notice us, perhaps he had the right instinct to know that we would not need to be told to remember this.

The Thayer story is drawing to its close; Mr. Thayer died May 29, 1921. In the early spring of the next year the Metropolitan Museum of Art in New York City held a memorial exhibition of his work, consisting of most of his major paintings (with the exception of the Freer collection in Washington which, under the terms of the will of its founder, could not leave the building in which it was housed) and an entire room full of his pencil drawings. The artist Carl Burger, one of Louis' devoted friends, wrote the following eloquent letter after he had been to see the pictures.

CARL BURGER TO L.A.F.

New York City, April 15, 1922.

This afternoon I spent at the Metropolitan Museum steeping myself in the superb beauty of Abbott Thayer's paintings. There is, as you must know, a special exhibition there of his work, comprising most of the important things he did. I have never been so profoundly moved by pictures—they are more than pictures—they make me realize what a mite I am. They are better than any sermon I ever heard. They seem to me the acme of beauty and truth and sincerity and goodness. I am thankful to have seen them and to have known him, though ever so slightly. To you, who knew him so well, they must seem like old friends, and I am sending you a catalogue . . . If you haven't seen the exhibition, you must do so.

I know that he did go, because my mother went, too, and still speaks about it. She had not seen much of Thayer's work before, although she was a staunch admirer of the Concealing Coloration book, and the exhibition was a revelation to her. Also Alden Hadley, in his article called With Fuertes in Florida, wrote:

More than a quarter of a century after our camping trip to North Indian Field, and on the occasion of my second meeting with Fuertes since that, to me, most memorable experience, he told me of having just seen an exhibition of Thayer's paintings in New York City. With deep emotion, he spoke of the work of his master, remarking that no one could look with understanding upon these paintings without being deeply sensible of their profound mystical and spiritual qualities. In fact, he said, 'tears came into my eyes as I looked upon them.'

Louis offered to write an expression of his debt to Abbott Thayer at the time Mrs. Thayer was collecting materials for a volume of his letters. She had asked to use the ones Louis had saved. She thanked Louis for his 'kind permission' to use the letters and said she did not need any new expression of his feeling; she already had it. 'I cannot imagine your doing better (or anyone's doing better)' she wrote in August, 1923, 'than you did in the spontaneous thing you wrote; the spontaneity is part of the charm of it. Here it is, taken from two different letters.'

Such teachers as was Uncle Abbott cannot die, in truth, for his life was in itself an all but holy light, and those that fell within its beams can never again go wholly into shadow. . . . My whole youth was sweetened and deepened, more than any one can know, ever, by the close and lovely contact of those two years under your hospitable roof.

No human being ever gave me the disinterested and unmeasured affection and priceless help that he so voluntarily gave me.

Louis knew only one way to discharge his debt to Mr. Thayer: to hand on to another generation whatever he could of the training given him. He had written to George Sutton (January 21, 1916):

In case everything goes as you hope, and you come and I'm here, the matter of 'lessons' needs not worry you at all. I have no secret processes or other patents on this profession, and I should consider it a privilege to pass on to you what little of the help and encouragement I could of all that has been so freely lavished on me by my good friends in days and years now past, and if I should myself seek reward for so poorly doing what was so richly done for me, I should in truth feel like a worse parasite than I hope I shall ever have to feel!

He was thinking of George's summer when he wrote to Mr. Thayer in April of that same year.

I am always made happy when I hear from Monadnock—how far away, to me, those happy and inspirational days seem. I am very sure you can't ever realize—unless some such dream-thing fell into your own impressionable youth—what an enormous thing you did for a kid in an only half-right environment, when you made me your son-for-a-while, and emancipated my eyes and brains from habit to real seeing. It probably does not seem to you, from your lofty look-out on such things, that I have gotten much ahead in this emancipation. But to me, when I see the lovely (and before unseen though beheld) adaptations and ingeniously contrived fusions of sheer beauty and tricky obliteration that constantly present themselves, it is painfully evident that I shall go on from year to year getting deeper and deeper into debt to you. The only way I can think of to even up the balance at all is to pass on when I can, to other boys who come into my reach with any kind of eye-hunger for these things that get so deeply to you and yours and me, something of the help that you so wonderfully and freely gave me when it was so necessary for me. And I know that, if I could do that, it would suit you as well or better than anything else I could do. . . .

Love to you all. I find I feel very sentimental and far away from a very dear and cherished part of my life, and when I write to you it rushes over me very powerfully.

From the correspondence with Conrad Roland, another gifted young man who spent a summer with us at Sheldrake, comes a letter written some years later. It is an answer to a plea for advice on his career as artist, and in it Louis sets forth the essence of what he had learned from Mr. Thayer, the very core of his artistic theory.

L.A.F. TO CONRAD ROLAND

Ithaca, N. Y., Sept. 15, 1925.

I'm sure I don't know what to say to you about your work and your attitude toward it, and the ideals that prompt you, except for God's sake be honest, and strive for what seems to you true and lovely. I should say that more high aspiration has been egoized into mediocrity than has withstood the terrible ordeal of passing through a human soul for its interpretation. Art, as a means of expression of the ego, is like playing a symphony on a jewsharp, in nine hundred and ninety nine cases out of a thousand (count 'em), and I think a man in our field . . . can well go on to sixty plus with pure study and representation before beginning to get fancy. I am aware that ninety-nine percent of the artists and *all* the critics, who earn their living by their vocabulary, are agin me in this, and would scorn such art as I like as photographic (as if it were a scrofulous imitation) but I still stick out for knowledge—good, sound, deep, and appreciative knowledge— as the one fundamental basic pre-requisite of all art, and particularly of naturalistic art. There haven't been ten people in all history that have had it, and the outlook isn't too bright for the future, but that is no detriment to the pursuit of it, and the fellow that *lands* will eventually have the world at his feet, which will probably bore him to death. Great lovers have all had their admiring audience; great lovers of natural truth perhaps less than others. But that is my simple credo: it's easy, however, to 'believe' in truth, as an abstract conception; quite another thing to discover and crystallize this truth into visible and permanent form. That's a hard job, and most artists would rather pass the buck, and in place of hard-wrought unadorned truth, present the gog-eyed world with the decorative by-products of their efforts, not so much for truth as for originality. *As the vehicle for truth*, originality is fine; as the mere expression of half-baked ego it is a flop, as witness any fall exhibition after the silly season.

The notion is that truth, before it can receive visible and permanent form as a work of art, must pass through a human soul. The individuality, the personality, of the human soul is useful as a vehicle for truth; when it tries to express itself alone it fails, 'egoizes the truth into mediocrity.' This platonic thought, with its scorn for 'art as a means of self-expression,' was basic with Louis. He loved all nature as a manifestation of truth and tried to represent it in his pictures so that truth should have a visible and permanent form. We hear again the Thayer letter of 1897:

All that true training does is to purify one's powers till they no longer *refract the truth* in its passage through.

This was the kind of training he had received, and the kind he endeavored to give.

Louis never saw any of the Thayers again. He received one more frightening letter from Gerald that foreshadowed his tragic end in mental illness, and this, from Gladys:

GLADYS THAYER REASONER TO L.A.F.

[Woodstock, N. Y.] July, 1925.

What part of the globe are you *at*, just now, and whatever has become of Kippy to whom I've written a number of times in the last three years? In the midst of my joyous duties of this overwhelming new life, with a brood of three, up to date, and Dave who is dearer and finer than words can tell, I still have moments for sadness at the grim way life has of scattering friends and families to the four winds, till through their crowding preoccupations they little by little lose touch. The Thayer-Fuertes bond of old was too vital a thing to be allowed to flicker—and I presume you and Gra still hear from each other.

Well, even our blessed Addie has now left our sight. I had the impulse to write you at that time, but like many other promptings of that nature it was never acted upon. Addie [this was Mrs. Thayer, called by Louis 'Aunt Emma'] died as she had lived, cheerful, soldier-like, planning for others to the end. I could not get to her, on account of the babies, and David was the only one of us to be with her. (She in Peekskill with her sister.) My keenest pang was her leaving without ever seeing my second baby, Jean. Allen she already loved, intensely, and was longing to get back home to them and us.

Papa of course never saw either. It's all a strange, strange dream, and we are marched along through chapter after chapter of shifting experiences, with that great intricate volume of the past folding behind us as we go. . . .

Oct. 26, 1925.

This was written one midnight last summer while waiting for Dave to come home. . . . Louis, let's all cling tight to the great sacred old times. How few people knew Papa as much as you did. How much you were to him, and what a big part you played in our happy youngsterhood.

And finally long years later, after she too had gone, her husband, himself one of the young people who had lived and worked with Thayer, wrote in a letter of November 29, 1949:

Of all the young people who lived with or worked with Thayer, Louis was the closest and most beloved.

18

1920-1926

....

T HE SEVEN YEARS that followed 1919 were full of creative work, of quiet—he called them humdrum—pleasures at home with his family and friends. The years were honored by a formal connection with Cornell, varied by travel to Florida, Holland, Wyoming, and capped by a nine months' collecting expedition with one of his oldest friends, Wilfred Osgood, to the plateau in central Africa then called Abyssinia, the richest remaining dwelling-place of birds new to him.

The most important works of this time were The National Geographic Magazine article on falconry and hawks, several large paintings of flamingos, two or three very remunerative orders for advertisers, and, filling in the gaps—always there to come home to—the seemingly endless plates for the Birds of Massachusetts. There were the usual small jobs for educational publications, personal orders for friends, and sometimes pictures painted simply to take advantage of lovely sky or a fine peregrine falcon that happened to come his way.

This is Louis Fuertes' book, and far less than justice is done in it to my mother, his wife. She was neither by taste nor training a naturalist, but in wit, in charm, in skill at the business of living she was his perfect equal. If he was quick at repartee she was not one jot behind him, and she could always relish a situation such as this: one summer at Sheldrake an unhappy young man from Ithaca was much at our cottage and with us at dinner in the hotel. A dowager at a nearby table suffered in curiosity as long as she could and then asked: 'Louis, who is it that M—— comes down to see? Is it Madge, or is it you?' 'Me?' said Louis, 'Why, I scarcely know the man!'

My mother had to cope with the wrath of several jealous wives who thought their husbands spent too much time in the studio, but never with a jealous husband. She endured a good deal in the way of house guests, not only unhappy, intense, or just boisterous young men, but also strangers who had known Louis in some far distant wilds. Most of them were people she was delighted to know, but there was an occasional bore to be listened to, or a difficult wealthy wife who made it clear we were not entertaining her in the style to which she was accustomed. Our house was small, and we never had more than one family helper, always an excellent cook but not an impersonal trained servant. They were generally country neighbors: Eida Andrews Duncker from Eaglesmere, Ida Boyer and Walter Van Sickle from Sheldrake. At different times and for periods of many years, each shared our family life and contributed richly to it.

People were not by any means the queerest guests Mrs. Fuertes had to live with. Early in their married life she came home to a house ringing with screams like those of some mortally tortured child. It seemed to be upstairs, the bathroom door was shut, she could hear it splash . . . it was in the bathtub. Where else could Louis put a loon to keep it happy until he had time to study it? There were pet skunks at Sheldrake; there were rats and mice brought to the front door by Boy Scouts as food for the owl in the studio; there was for a long time Bombay, the African gray parrot whose cage hung in the dining-room and smelled and could only be cleaned by Louis (too busy) because Bomb bit the female members of the family whenever they drew near.

But she had her reward in a life she would not have exchanged with anyone. When my parents entertained more than one or two persons they did so, most informally, in the studio. Alpha Delts were welcome there for tea on Sunday afternoons, where they were kept amused by pretty sprightly conversation, as well as by looking at the curios around them and trying their skill on South American Indian *blowguns. A letter by Katharine Finch describes another kind of gathering.*

I am just back from an amusingly cosmopolitan tea party at the studio—mostly archeological, the *pièce de résistance* being a Hungarian-Polish count who is to lecture on the ruins of Carthage tomorrow night. Mrs. Coonley Ward, the old lady whom I visited this summer with Madge and Louis, has taken him under her wing and brought him here. She was also very much among those present, with three secretaries etc. Then there were the Pumpellys, Gene Andrews, Schmidts, Mrs. Comstock and a smattering of students, also Maude Radford Warren who is an old friend of Mrs. Ward's.

I had an interesting talk on politics, British and American, with a Miss Murray, an English girl, an interview with the count, and poured tea in intervals. The guest of honor had Byron among his other names and proved rather sentimental, wherefore I was amused when Louis shocked him. He told L. that he had heard [that] the American eagle, upon losing his mate, pines away and dies in a very short time, and wanted to know if Louis as an ornithologist could verify this peculiarity of the noble bird, whereupon L.A.F. remarked that the eagle, instead of dying, went and got another mate in about ten minutes.

There were late-autumn dinner parties to enjoy the game from Louis' hunting trips, at which a few bottles of red wine were served with the wild duck. These were the days before cocktail parties, when alcohol was not in the social picture in the way it is to-day. Louis only played cards when his refusing to do so would spoil the pleasure of three people who wanted a game of bridge, and with all his good intentions he could never keep his mind on the game. Once after trumping his partner's ace, when she mourned, 'Oh Louis that was my trick!' he replied, 'Well, now it's ours, my dear.' Louis rarely smoked and then only to seem inconspicuous when everyone else was doing it. He did not achieve his end, however, as he would light a cigarette and then forget it, on one occasion thus burning a hole in his hostess' embroidered and lace-bedecked table-

cloth. He was distressed, didn't know what to do, couldn't afford to buy her a new cloth, and finally painted her a picture, signed in the lower right-hand corner with a cigarette burn.

Pictures were his usual gifts. He had an inkling once, when certain rather stodgy people made special point of an invitation, that an engagement was to be announced, and he painted a little picture to take along. When he and Madge arrived he found his guess more than confirmed; there was an altar contrived before the fireplace with a smilax-covered arch above, and lo it was a wedding. Later on at home when he was asked the cause of his sudden fit of giggles he answered that he had just realized that the picture he had given the bride and groom was two geese going south.

The neighborhood activities changed as the children grew up and as the families around us went and came, but to these families Louis was always useful as a husband at home during the day who could be called on in crises of plumbing or furniture moving. To all the children he was 'Uncle Louis.' One of the Sterretts, spying him among the members of a chorus at a music festival in Bailey Hall, spoke up in that childish treble so audible in adult gatherings: 'Look, Mother, there's Uncle Louis. I didn't know they could use him for this.' When the corner lot was 'location' for the movie company in the days of Pearl White and Francis X. Bushman they used him whenever they needed an extra. During the war years they used him to paint street posters, make bond-raising speeches, take the Cornell Heights Boy Scout Troop whose leader had entered the service. They used him to make butterfly wings for the children in a pageant and masks for the dramatis personae of Alice in Wonderland. Neighbors and University people with out-of-town guests to entertain shamelessly used him at any time of day, appearing at the studio door to be shown pictures, bird-skins, and his collection of trophies. I don't remember that he complained of this treatment but I do recall the stream of visitors, and his letters tell how much he needed daylight hours for painting.

Louis' first opportunity for southern travel since 1913 had come in 1920 when he went to the Bahama Islands again. This trip was related not to museum activities but to private orders for pictures, and it is chiefly significant in that it introduced to Louis the possibilities of the movie camera in bird study. It marks the beginning of a period during which the studio was filled with enormous canvases depicting flamingos in their habitat. Before the murals for the Flamingo Hotel in Miami Beach were completed, he was heartily tired of the subject, and the birds' long necks and legs seemed to compose themselves only as giant pink S's and K's.

Among the ornithologists Louis must have encountered at A.O.U. meetings from time to time was Allan Brooks, the artist from British Columbia, who was working on pictures for a Birds of California in 1916. When he entered the army, Louis was asked to take over the work, as the publishers did not want to wait. Louis was more familiar with Brooks' illustrations than with Brooks at this time. In the first draft of a reply to William Leon Dawson, who had asked him to take over, he wrote:

To come at once to the matter of my opinion of Major Brooks' work. I can only say that I have been greatly pleased by it always, although our experience and consequent interpretation have been different. I think he has achieved more success at pleasing and restrained landscape in his pictures than I have, and I think I have been longer a student of the comparative anatomy, appearance, and general 'personal looks' of the birds than he has, and probably have spent a larger proportion of my time since boyhood in the direct study of birds, and seen more widely varied types in life than almost anyone I know—and all with the one idea of learning and visualizing their typical appearances.

The two men came together in Washintgon, D. C., at the A.O.U. meetings in November, 1920, and Louis persuaded Major Brooks to come home with him and stay at our house until after Christmas, when they went briefly to Florida to collect together. From this time forward Major Brooks was among the best of my father's friends. The slight difference in manner of work placed no barrier in the way of their appreciation of each other; on the contrary each admired the other's particular skill and took deep delight in his presence. I think every member of our household, and our particular friends, loved him as soon as they knew him. Certainly I did. He took me on winter bird-walks, he gave me Kipling's Just-So Stories for Christmas, he filled a booklet of sample drawing-paper for me with delicate pencil sketches of deer, moose, mountain sheep, and goats; my father made me a companion-piece with birds of prey. Twenty years later he wrote:

Do you remember the horned owl in the cage in the studio the Christmas time I spent with you? It had a good appetite and ate what bodies were available, also any rats, etc. that the boy friends of Louis brought in. Then there was brought in a live chipmunk which was kept for a model. We both drew this and Louis became so attached to it that he could not give it to the owl, so after much consideration he took his collecting pistol and shot the owl, which I still have in my collection. I wished later he had decided to sacrifice the chipmunk as it got out of its cage and destroyed every skin it could find lying on top of the cases, tearing open the skulls to find only cotton instead of brains.

What would I give to have a holiday like that again!

The holiday was followed by a steady exchange of letters. An answer to Louis' letter written when he heard that Major Brooks had suffered a serious fire leads to others in which the two artists compare their experiences at the hands of those who order pictures.

ALLAN BROOKS TO L.A.F.

Okanagan Landing, B. C., Aug. 16, 1921.

It is fine to hear from you, for you are almost as bad a correspondent as I am and my burns have brought me something anyhow. My fire was in an outbuilding—work shop, store room, and summer kitchen—and I burnt my hands on the last two guns I saved. They were nearly red hot and I don't think they are safe to fire now I have saved them. The doctors promised me a pretty serious time but I fooled 'em and was in swimming less than two weeks after my accident although they were pretty horrid looking hands. . . .

I am just finishing the California books (2). Grinnell still sends me large photos of sequoias etc. for backgrounds for weasels, kinglets, and the like, and worst of all prefers those pictures in which I use his heroic backgrounds to the ones I implore him to let me use.

You can pretty nearly fool everybody all the time and the normal man is incapable of observation. You ought to see the old horsemen raptly admiring those stretched-out atrocities of the last generation (sketch) you know the kind. Tell 'em they did not know what a galloping horse looked like and what sort of a chance would you have?

I sent some pictures to Chapman and Pearson for *Bird-Lore*. The best was a little blue heron done from life—background, pose and all, done on the spot—shot an adult and young and did 'em and the little mangrove sprouts right there and then. Result: all the other pics. accepted, this one sent back to me—first the iris of a little blue was yellow not grey-blue, 2nd. the bill was green not blue and black, 3rd. mangroves always had branching roots. At least Pearson says all this and Chapman backs him up. I refused to change the blue-grey iris to a yellow and all the rest, and they hand the pic. over to Sanford and refuse it.

L.A.F. TO ALLAN BROOKS

Ithaca, N. Y., Sept. 19, 1921.

Your good letter has lain too long unanswered. I can't tell you the relief it gave me to know you could still write and had the full use of your hands again. Did you lose all your birds? You said you had them stored in that building. If you did, you'd better move here for a while and use mine and my studies, which, as you know, are always most gladly at your disposal.

Your little blue heron experience is almost as amusing as it is exasperating: I've so many times had the same or similar brushes with those in high places, matching definite first-hand knowledge with long-standing notions. Nobody not visual-minded can possibly know how much gets by unobserved and unnoted by those, even, whose business it should be to discern and record the common things—much more the difficult or rarely encountered ones. Any bird- or animal-painter knows, with anguish often, what a stubborn and exasperating thing prejudice or preconception can be.

Louis was painting herons for T. G. Pearson himself—four colored plates for the Audubon Society bulletin on the heron family—and he also ran afoul of Mr. Pearson's idea of how a heron should look.

L.A.F. to T. G. Pearson

Ithaca, N. Y., Oct. 5, 1921.

So far I can report no material progress on the heron pictures, but you are on the right track. I hate nagging, so to avoid it I'll do almost anything. . . .

Wish I had time to gossip awhile, but I have too many irons hot, and am off in a few hours for Chi., Cleveland, and Pittsb'g, where I severally sing, squeak, squawk, beller and and hoot like Mother Nate-yure's little creat-yures, etc.

Louis finished the pictures and received from Dr. Pearson a letter of thanks and approval qualified by these remarks:

T. G. Pearson to L.A.F.

New York City, Jan. 24, 1922.

I suppose you drew the dark reddish egret from a skin, yet the bird looks a great deal lighter than the birds I saw in the field. I wonder if you would object if the printer attempted to darken the bird just a little as he has suggested he can readily do?

L.A.F. to T. G. Pearson

Ithaca, N. Y., Jan. 25, 1922.

Regarding the reddish egret, the pallor or darkness is due to the amount of 'bloom' or powder that is present. This is an accurate tone for the bird I have, both from comparison with the skin and with the study I made on Andros when I got him, and seems, in my rather wide experience with the species (I've seen hundreds of 'em, in Andros and the Keys) to be quite typical of the bird in life. Like the Louisiana and little blue and most dark herons in fact, the tone is much paler in life than appears in skins, due to this

CORY'S BITTERN. Ithaca, May 17, 1913

Northern Shrike. Ithaca, Jan. 20, 1922

delicate and fugitive powder that the birds produce, I think in the epidermis. T. S. Palmer calls it 'Fuertes powder'—but F. P. or T.N.T. or Dupont—there it is, take it 'r leave it, and in live herons, marsh hawks, swallow-tail kites, and many pigeons it is the chief element in their living looks, and the first to disappear when made up into a skin. If you want to bother, just get out some of these birds sometime and carefully lift the feathers of the back or wing, and see how each feather has protected the underlying ones, leaving them gray and bloomy, in contrast to the dark (even *black*, as in s.t. kite) exposed part.

So if you care to have the engraver deepen the tone no harm will be done, only the bird will then resemble the typical mounted rather than the typical live bird, or the live bird whose feathers are old and dull. A *fresh* Louisiana is the most lovely thing in the world, the colors of Isabella and Catawba grapes before you touch them—as if a silver frost was laid over all the pigmented parts.

Pardon, please, this poetic dissertation on a fact you can blow off with the unaided breath—but even if it should happen to be one of my few discoveries, as I've said, there it is, and like Savonorola and Joan of Arc, I'll *deeie* for it if needs be! Only I don't care whether anybody else cares about it: I dare say no dynasties will fall or rise on it. Still, it is an almost unknown feature, of great interest, in that it gives a totally new appearance and beauty to the critters that have it, and to me the fact that it has heretofore been unnoticed does not seem an argument for continuing to ignore it.

Livingston Farrand had come to Cornell University in 1921 to be its fourth president. After he had held the position long enough to get his bearings he called Louis to his office one day and expressed to him his surprise at learning that Louis had no official connection with the university. When he had been offered the presidency, Dr. Farrand said, he had known only two things about Ithaca: that it was the home of Cornell and that it was the home of Louis Fuertes. He naturally supposed the two were associated in some way; he thought it a shame they were not. In short, wouldn't Louis accept a professorship? Louis thanked him and asked for time to think it over. At length he declined the offer, possibly for reasons similar to those he had expressed in a letter of February, 1922, to Joseph Grinnell of California. He had said:

While my own job is always uncertain, I generally find that it is remuneratively above the average of full professorships here, and at least I don't have the depressing pastime of blaming trustees, etc., which so often crystallized my poor father's unhappiness at his limitations. Still there are worse heritages for our children, as I now see, than a good education and the spectacle of respectable (in its real meaning) economy in the material things and fine opportunity in the things of the mind.

Dr. Farrand extended a counter-offer: wouldn't Louis give an annual series of lectures, any number, on any subject he chose at any time of year convenient for him, and accept the title of Resident Lecturer? Again Louis asked for time, and consulted Dr. Chapman, who replied (December 2, 1922) as follows:

If you do not get change, rest, stimulation, incentive etc., from your rushing-about talks here and yon, cut them out altogether, and take the lectureship. Take it anyway—and if need be cut the others out. You should have a connection with the university, nearly everyone thinks you have and you ought to live up to your reputation. Once you have your course prepared it will roll along by itself. It's a good thing too for everyone to have some more or less fixed dates in his calendar. A good thing for your children to have this honor come to their parent. Beyond all this there are the students —you can do a good bit for them. So I'm all for it, particularly if you can cut out the peripatetic stuff. Lectures designed primarily for instruction not entertainment are far more interesting to give than popular ones, and a course develops this interest. Well, when are you coming down?

Louis accepted the appointment; notes of congratulations from widely different kinds of people were unanimous in their expressed opinion that the university was the chief gainer.

Louis gave a series of seven lectures in the spring of 1923; the next year he expanded it to ten, with the following titles as announced in The Ithaca Journal of March 12, 1924:

(1) Flight and Migration of Birds; (2) Songs and Calls of Familiar Birds; (3) Zoological Art and Artists; (4) Coloration of Animals; (5) Coloration of Animals, continued; (6) Coloration of Nocturnal Animals; (7) Coloration of Animals applied to Camouflage; (8) Nature Writing, Good and Bad; (9) The Naturalistic Viewpoint; and (10) Species Recently Extinct or Verging upon Extinction.

Several undated sets of his longhand notes for these lectures were saved; there seems to be no complete set for any one year (he gave them four times) and the notes are fragmentary, consisting simply of reminders to him. But it is possible to get from them the gist of his matter.

The first two are self-explanatory from the titles. Lectures 4 through 7 deal with Thayer's discoveries and their application. Lectures 3 and 8 begin with a historical sketch of the subject, (3 deals with painting, sculpture, photography of natural things, 8 with writings about them) and then proceed to detailed criticism of specific painters, sculptors, etc., seen from Louis' point of view, which he discusses at length in Lecture 9. This leads naturally to Lecture 10, since the species now becoming extinct are disappearing because of a lack of this naturalistic viewpoint, or because of the prevalence of its opposite, the humanistic viewpoint.

A paragraph from one of the sets of notes on Lecture 9 is full enough to define what he calls the naturalistic viewpoint. It is given below, followed by the final paragraph from Lecture 10, a challenge for respect for all life that sounds to our day like the voice of Albert Schweitzer.

The naturalistic viewpoint . . . [is] a sane approach not only to the study and portrayal of nature, but as well to its simple enjoyment. Quite unconsciously, man takes himself so seriously, and becomes so engrossed in his own special creation and specific individuality that all the rest of the great creation falls into secondary importance if not oblivion. We view it as something put there for us to enjoy and waste, exterminate, destroy—or utilize as long as it lasts (pigeon, antelope, buffalo, forests, etc., etc., etc.). The more sophisticated and artificial our lives, the less we realize our physical dependence on nature.

How get? Subdue the subjective and induce the objective.

Parallels—Rats no more wasteful than man.

Ask a rabbit about man? . . .

Everlasting 'human interest' entirely unworthy, and naïve commentary on our intelligence.

Honor whatever God you have by an appreciation of and respect for the world he gave you *as he gave it*, and devastate not. Leave all consideration of commercialism, economics, aesthetics, even, out of the argument, and if only on the grounds of human decency to the world that sustains us, let us honor ourselves as well as our common mother by seeing that no creatures become lost to our successors through our selfish or heedless negligence, but rather, by our efforts and sympathy with and respect for *all* life, and an increased understanding of it, see a return of the now vanishing wild life of this great and unique land, for all posterity to enjoy.

I have difficulty imagining my father delivering himself of anything so solemn as this last long sentence: humor would keep breaking through. But here is what Arthur Allen, writing for Bird-Lore in 1927, says about these lectures:

Fuertes was not an orator—his manner of speaking and frequent digressions often made it difficult for students to take notes on his lectures—but so vivid was his personality, so original his vocabulary, so humorous his metaphors and so warm his human sympathy, that notes were never necessary. Students left the classroom inspired. They remembered everything he said and discussed it among themselves as though it had been a baseball game.

It may be that Louis' lectures prompted Martin D. Hardin, minister of the First Presbyterian Church in Ithaca, to send him the sermon acknowledged in Louis' next letter. It would be the only way to have his message reach Louis, who did not attend any church (*except during several seasons when he and Mrs. Fuertes sang in the Cornell University Choir under the exciting direction of Hollis Dann*).

L.A.F. TO MARTIN D. HARDIN

Ithaca, N. Y., June 5, 1923.

Let me thank you most cordially and heartily for your sermon which I have received and read with the warmest feeling of admiration and—though this may mean little to you—approval also. It would be hard for me to outline to you my own substitute for the creed: I never can force myself to stand and go through with the Apostles' Creed, which I learned from a dear lady in my early and well-directed youth. I try to so live that, reward or no reward, I can leave behind me a memory as of one who had better lived than not, and to take advantage of no man, and teach wrong to no child. I shan't bore you with a recital of what I hope to make my life mean: indeed I doubt if I exactly know myself.

MARTIN D. HARDIN TO L.A.F.

Ithaca, N. Y., [June, 1923.]

Thank you so much for that letter. I do want to have a talk with you about these things. I am sending you another sermon preached not long ago which sums up my own idea of all the creed which is needed. To my mind it's the spirit of love and service which counts, and you have got that as few people I have known.

In a key more normal for him, he writes of a kind of life he liked to live and before long would live again.

L.A.F. TO WILFRED H. OSGOOD

Ithaca, N. Y., Sept. 12, 1923.

I confess to a strong resurging of the old tropical longings, that are, I fancy, a sort of atavism with me, I feel so dam natural when I'm in 'em, and the remembered smell of the first land-whiff, the first roar of the surf on coral reefs, the jangling bells of medieval Catholicism and the childlike philosophy with which it drenches the lands—all sort of boil up in me every once in a while, and I look out at an approaching winter and remember how easily one slips out —for a time—of all these contacts and gets steeped in the romance and delight of new-old scenes, and hunting and working in all the enthusiasm of discovery.

Hell, it's hard, sometimes, to have a temperament at all, for in the midst of blessings comes this damned 'fallacy of the elsewhere,' and balls you all up. I, too, get fed up after two or three months of it, and the feed lasts for five or six years, but then it all comes back on me, and I want like hell to miss a winter, and get winded on an Andee, or sweat quarts in a hot, mosquitoful, death-quiet river-forest, or poke around in the sub-temperate zone among tree-ferns after trogons and formicarians, or have my guts turned over by an unexpected gang of howlers overhead.

I would certainly admire to have you sot down in front of my fireplace with your pipe going, and something to warm the cockles with, for about an evening, and get you talking. Then I'd probably sit down and book up with Frank and Fred Walcott for Peru this winter and let the *Birds of Mass.* migrate whither they list.

In the spring of 1924 Louis had on exhibition one of his few flights into sculpture, a gorilla seated, looking bemused at a butter-fly on its hand. It was cast in bronze, (also in pairs to be used for book-ends), exhibited at the Pennsylvania Academy of Fine Arts, and very favorably reviewed in two French art magazines.

Louis had a lifelong interest in the big apes. In 1895 at the Savage Club in London he heard the African explorer Paul Du Chaillu give his account of a gorilla hunt, and Louis retold the story himself to the delight of many audiences. His contributions to the Cornell Widow, made when he was an undergraduate, were an-thropomorphic cartoons known as 'Louis' Monks.' He signed his letters to college friends 'Monk,' which John P. Young explained by saying: 'Lou could imitate the common organ-grinder monkey so well that it became one of his best-known bits of color used in entertaining the world in general.' People still remember him as the center of fun at a fancy-dress ball he attended not as the monkey but as the Italian organ-grinder with drooping black mustachios, 'spigotty' talk, a hand-organ on a wooden leg, and a real monkey borrowed from our neighbor Irene Castle Treman. My mother went with him as the little girl who ran into the crowd collecting pennies, with her curly hair down her back, dressed in rags, and a pair of her own little girl's tan cotton stockings which she had undarned at the knee.

There was a stretch of years during which Hendrik Willem van Loon had been our neighbor, living first alone in an apartment in the other side of our house, later on with his family near by, and always adding color and fun to our society. He had lived away from Ithaca for some time, however, when out of the blue one day in the summer of 1924 he sent Louis a telegram reading, in substance: 'Come for six weeks' bicycling in Holland as my guest start Monday.' Surmising that his considerable bulk would not have decreased with the years Louis replied: 'Only on condition I don't have to ride with you tandem'—and went. Besides these two, the party consisted of Mrs. van Loon and Mr. van Loon's eighteen-year-old son Hansje. They did bicycle a good deal, though the weather was persistently cold and rainy; they sketched; they visited the van Loon relatives who royally feasted and otherwise entertained them.

L.A.F. TO MARY FUERTES

Ithaca, N. Y., Oct. 17, 1924.

I have been meaning—or trying is a truer word—to get a letter off to you for ten days, ever since I got home. But I found such a pile of obligations and immediately important business letters to attend to that I have really not had a minute to write the letters I like to write or do a bit of painting. . . .

Mary, I was so disappointed that our boat got in too late for me to see you in N. Y.—I rather hoped I might. I missed you all the time in Holland; you would have loved it, and every day I would see something that made me just long for you. I'll never go abroad again without you. And as it has only been 29 years since my last trip, you might as well be picking out your clothes!

Yesterday was the last day that Herbie and Mabel Williams (Herb's folks) had in Ithaca, so I stole the day after 11:30 and we all four (your mother completing the party—she was a Sumner, you may remember) hopped in the Rollin with a frying pan and coffee pot and rolled lollingly along in the lovely October air—just haze enough to make the orange and red hills all soft with lavender shadows—and finally ended up on Bald Hill, at Jesse Cornell's, and loafed on the warm hillside, talking and watching the hawks ring round and round and up and up until the sky burned our eyes. The lavender hill shadows up the Caroline cut got longer and bluer—not dark but light cool blue, and I really have not had such a heavenly day, it seems to me, in years. Herbie and I used to ramble all over that territory as kids, hunting hawks' nests, and chestnuts, or ski-ing in winter, and all the same old feeling I had for him when he was the king of our gang—full of ideas and inventions and fun—seemed renewed and vivid again. I almost never, now, can recall and re-live the friendships of my youngsterhood in their old vivid colors, even when the old friends are there, (a somewhat pitiful confession, Mary) but I got it yesterday—and now I don't know whether it makes me feel younger or older! But anyway it was lovely, and I am grateful that I had it.

I'm afraid this is a very sentimental letter—perhaps if I waited till tomorrow it would be all business!

H. W. VAN LOON TO L.A.F.

Westport, Conn., Dec. 27, 1924.

Dear Loowee, the more than magnificent lap-wing hangs in my room and looks as if he would dearly love to act as an amateur eagle for my own Prometheus and partake of the fat morsels that stand in front of his frame and belong to the corporeal entity known as HvL. This is a complicated sentence used to express a somewhat complicated feeling. For you have worked so many invisible things into that dead bird that I feel a little ashamed of the gift. Because in a thoroughly selfish fashion I dragged you through the island of Walcheren and the lakes of Friesland is no reason why you should have burned the midnight juice and remind me of my obligation *per avis beatissima.*

The climate was against us this summer and the eternal flu which overtakes me whenever I enter my native mudpuddle. But now that said flu is a thing of the past I look back upon the five weeks as a very diverting entre-acte. Just little glimpses. The funny meals on board our noble yacht, the evenings spent in the parlor of Lucie's house, Lange Jan deedledeeing his eternal deedledee, rain or shine, moon or sun, wet or dry, the incredible complicatedness of life in the Dutch metropolis and the strange champagne bath of Lier, the British watercolorists painting the . . . canals of Bruges and the Breughels of the Brussels museum—in short a special little attic of my brain filled with strange bits of color and humor. . . .

And so, before the year is over I thank you once more for having done more than your share in accumulating these stray bits of spiritual ornament without which this house would speedily perish.

Another opportunity for vacation travel came the following year. John L. Senior, a favorite friend since boyhood, invited him to bring his family for the summer to the Diamond G Ranch near Brooks Lake, Wyoming. Louis accepted for himself and me, and we had a wonderfully good time on horseback among the mountains. On an overnight pack trip I for the first time heard the Du Chaillu gorilla story; at the end he leaves the role of the hunter, and assuming that of the wounded gorilla attacking him, crashes forward to the ground. My father's performance by firelight in the primeval forest was properly thrilling. I must have shown adolescent signs of shame at his excitement over the birds he saw or collected, for I remember that he apologized for being what he described as an 'Oh! and Ah!' father. I submitted with interest to his demonstrations of bird-skinning, however, and formed romantic schemes of accompanying him on future collecting expeditions as his field assistant. Judging from my letters home, I might fairly be accused of having been an 'Oh! and Ah!' child.

Among the people we met there and particularly enjoyed were Mr. and Mrs. James E. Baum, Jr., and their children. Mr. Baum was an ardent and expert hunter and fisherman, and from the congeniality of this summer's experience sprang the suggestion with which the next chapter of this book, and the last of Louis' life, begins.

19

Preparations for Abyssinia

....

JAMES E. BAUM TO L.A.F.

Chicago, Ill., March 17, 1926.

If a man should come to you and ask: 'What is the strangest country in the world to-day? Where is the bird life the most curious and plentiful?' You would unquestionably answer both by one word—Abyssinia.

All right. Now that we have established the desirability of your going there what do you say to going with me next September? Here is the picture:

I am taking the family to Europe, sailing May 14th. We will spend the summer in France and England and in the fall I will leave Marseilles for Jibuti in French Somaliland. From there take the little 500-mile railroad to the capital of Abyssinia, a burg called Addis Ababa. It is high and comparatively cool country, being 8,000 elevation; very much like California in climate. From the capital I will take the saddle and pack horses and make a three months' hunt. Can you come? . . . Here are the advantages of Abyssinia:

1. Cost.
2. No game laws and licenses.
3. Accessibility and saving of time.
4. Climate.
5. No tse-tse fly.

6. Going horse-back instead of foot.
7. Myriads of birds and all kinds of game animals.
8. Curious customs of the country.
The Field Museum will give me credentials that should enable us to get permission from Ras Tafari . . . to go everywhere.

Louis was in Chicago soon after receipt of this letter and went with Jack Baum .to Wilfred Osgood's office in the Field Museum to discuss the suggestion. Dr. Osgood was interested, and almost without knowing when it happened Mr. Baum found his private hunting trip changed to a scientific expedition that might be financed by the museum. The three men talked with the president, Stanley Field, before Louis left to go home.

L.A.F. TO WILFRED H. OSGOOD

Ithaca, N. Y., April, 1926.

In my hurried and hectic laying down of the Ab[yssinian] proposition before Mr. Field, I had no time nor chance to outline my personal requirements and share in the proposed cost of the ex. so that will have to come, I fear, from you or by letter from me. Let me be kept in touch with the progress of the matter, and I'll do all I can to render it an attractive prop. to the Director and Mr. Field, of course. *Now Careful! If you go, I'm plumb sold on it:* otherwise I fear I shall be likely to get a hoof boil or something! This, young man, between ourselves. Not that I doubt anybody's resourcefulness and loyalty, but you know and I know how different are the needs and viewpoints of a work expedition and a play expedition, and we can neither of us, alone, afford the latter. . . . It had to be said, as well first as last.

WILFRED H. OSGOOD TO L.A.F.

Chicago, Ill., April 13, 1926.

The steering committee wishes to report progress, at least enough for you to take the matter right seriously. When we bite, we bite hard, and once we put our hand to the plough, the sparks will fly and we'll hit the line a mighty wallop regardless of what happens to the metaphors. I am speaking now of the [museum's] little combination composed of the President [Stanley Field], the Director [D. C. Davies], and the Curator [Wilfred Osgood] and it is by way of preparing you to realize that in hitching up with us you'd better relinquish all idea of doing this stunt in a small way. Jack and I got together with the Director to-day and I think we put it across with him. He will take it to the trustees next Monday and we'll know definitely whether we do or we don't and how much money we'll have by the middle of next week. . . . You probably know Jack Baum better than I do but I was looking into his blue eyes to-day and they looked pretty good to me.

WILFRED H. OSGOOD TO L.A.F.

Chicago, Ill., April 15, 1926.

I've a date in five minutes more or less, but here's a line to say that we've sold our proposition. In fact it is oversubscribed and the privilege of backing us was near to becoming a matter of contention between bidders. My boss says keep it dark for the present, but you can count yourself elected and we'll put it over in big letters.

TR and Kermit are here to-day covered with jingle bells and I'm in the thick of it.

JAMES E. BAUM TO L.A.F. [Telegram]

Chicago, Ill., April 16, 1926.

Everything arranged stop News will finance whole expedition to the extent of twenty-five thousand Hooray   Jack Baum.

This dazzling message was telephoned to Louis during a studio dinner party. Excitement rode high that night. What had happened was this: Mr. Baum, a writer as well as a sportsman, had aroused the interest of Walter Strong, owner of the Chicago Daily News, in an expedition to a country remote, little known, and yet replete with historic and literary associations (not only the Queen of Sheba but also Prester John and Johnson's Rasselas were Abyssinian rulers) and offered to act as historian of the expedition for the paper, sending in the narrative of the trip as it occurred. Mr. Strong welcomed the offer and volunteered to support the expedition to the sum of $25,000.

L.A.F. TO WILFRED H. OSGOOD
Ithaca, N. Y., April 17, 1926.
Of course now you've got to stop here, for there are matters upon which we must confer. I labor till then on hum-drums and banalities, to get 'em out of the way . . . (Done hastily, in a snow-storm, before breakfast . . .)

WILFRED H. OSGOOD TO L.A.F.
Chicago, Ill., April 19, 1926.
I'm not much at these before-breakfast-snowstorm efforts, so all there is left for you is the tail end of a hectic day and evening. The Ovis Polis left this morning and the atmosphere began to clear for something else. Yessir we right up and asked for $25,000 bucks and that is what we got, but I can assure you that we can spend it quite legitimately. I am long past the old Biol. Survey days with V[ernon] B[ailey] and a starvation allowance. One of the first things Jack and I decided was to raise your wages at least 20% and hope you won't object. If you don't turn out worth it, we'll never never speak to you again.

As soon as I can get a little time, I think the plans will resolve themselves pretty easily. I've just outfitted the Conover-Zimmer bunch for Africa and know pretty much what is needed. . . . I've lost all conscience, modesty, prof. ethics, etc., and if publicity gets results and especially if a newspaper is our patron, I'm for seeing their end of it as well as ours. I've had no time to look for an *Ovis poli* from Ab., and perhaps there isn't one, which means taking some other tack. But Beebe has his Sargasso Sea, Andrews his dino-saur eggs and missing links, Roosevelts their *Ovis poli*, and by Gosh, if we can do no better, I'm for the good old Queen of Sheba.

The Ovis poli was Marco Polo's sheep, the object of an expedition from which Theodore and Kermit Roosevelt had just returned and the peg upon which they hung their publicity.

L.A.F. TO WILFRED H. OSGOOD

Ithaca, N. Y., April 20, 1926.

I think the whole thing was handled most admirably, and am glad I was not there, with my spattery enthusiasm.

L.A.F. TO MARY FUERTES [about to sail for Europe]

Ithaca, N. Y., June 28, 1926.

This will be the last sure chance to wish you a bien viaje (as we Spaniards say) and I certainly do wish it you. Everything has been very quiet since you left, and a lot of food has gone back to the pantry, on two counts: we've had small appetite to eat with and you weren't here to do your share. . . .

I've finished 20 of my 40 little picturelets and am going strong.

No news has happened since you went away. I hope you will find time to scribble us a last minute bulletin before you sail, just to tell us you're all well and have been a good girl . . . and remember what

I told you about the $\begin{cases} \text{Purser} \\ \text{Doctor} \\ \text{Radio man.} \end{cases}$ Ask the captain how many

times up and down the mast is a mile, and here is Mother saying I've got to stop so's to catch the mail.

A roseleaf, my dear, off one of the peonies—

Hastily, and with much love, honest-true.

L.A.F. TO WILFRED H. OSGOOD

[Pencil. No date.]

It's too dark to paint, bein' a rainy day, so I take Dixon (or is it Venus?) in hand, to get in tune with youall. It's about settled that we close the house—or rent it—and that Madge comes with us as far as anyway Parisfrance, to take on Mary for the winter. So please include space for her on the Mauretania. . . .

I'm beginning to get itchy, and my daily stint is becoming less intriguing, if you get what I mean, and I tremble lest it be the

beginning of the end of my usefulness as an ornithological illustrator, *pro tem*. I would like one month to do nothing but prepare
myself for this job with books and specimens, but I'll have to go
it blind, and do my best.

WILFRED H. OSGOOD TO L.A.F.

Chicago, Ill., July 31, 1926.

Dear Lou-lou Fou-fou:

Having spent the day talking about GooGoo [Mt. Gugu] and
JamJam [Jumm Jumm] etc. I am starting this off abovely. Your last
letter arrived just after Dr. Lambie, and I scarcely took time to
more than identify it and be sure it contained nothing tragic or
sensational. The Dr. is a peach and it's a shame you couldn't have
been here. I'd been wiring him all this week and when I finally got
a reply he was on his way. . . . I am much bucked up by Lambie's
dope and think I know what we should do in every little way. He
says we're in for a great trip and we surely are. If you want to know
any thing at all, just ask me.

L.A.F. TO ALLAN BROOKS

Ithaca, N. Y., Aug. 7, 1926.

My dear Major:

Yours of July 29 came yesterday; the Sc. Method Pub. Co. re-
quested me to do that piece of work, but as I was trying to finish
the Mass. job and also 40 little single pictures for an advertising
job that was very good and prompt pay before leaving, Sept. 1, I
took the liberty of suggesting that they write to you. Yes, you are
certainly right: not one person out of 10—or 100, I guess, could tell
a quiet bird out doors from a stuffed one, which is why so many
rotten faked-up photos get into good papers. It is certainly hard to
understand the visual dumbness of your man on the street. For one
thing, the open is to them a closed book—and *only* a book. The
difference between the outlook of a city-bred and city-youthed man
and one who has had the open country for his early background is
to me perfectly astonishing: I meet it more and more and find it
continually harder to understand what there is to live for [in the

city] with nothing but struggle and competition and trying to beat someone else as an objective.

ALLAN BROOKS TO L.A.F.

Okanagan Ldg., B. C., Aug. 16, 1926.

Just a line to wish you good speed on your trip and to thank you for your kindness.

You will have a wonderful trip to the healthiest part of Africa north of the Transvaal, and I know you will enjoy every minute of it. But take care of yourself, old man. We cannot afford to have anything happen to you, and all bird lovers will be anxious until you are back.

L.A.F. TO WILFRED H. OSGOOD

Ithaca, N. Y., Aug. 22, 1926.

I had an amusing passage with a binding concern in Washington re special bindings on two books for Ras and Zaidi [the National Geographic Book of Birds and Book of Animals]; they suggested a modest red morocco full gilt extra special in box-to-match for only $70.00 each! I called attention to the absurdity of calendered print-stock in a $70.00 cover, and said that about $10.00 ea. was the top of what I had in mind, and as far as I can see they are doing the same for 10 they suggested for 70!!

Keep a-swinging, and fust news you know we'll all be saying Oh see the Whales! Isn't the Atlantic Ocean dear?* . . . . .

* The answer is yes.

The party gathered in New York and sailed as planned. Leaving Mrs. Baum, Mrs. Fuertes, and the children in Paris, the members of the expedition went to Marseilles by train and took ship there for Jibuti in French Somaliland.

Dr. Osgood was director of the expedition, which included besides Jack Baum and Louis Fuertes a young mammalogist, Alfred M. Bailey, and C. Suydam Cutting. During part of the time they split into two groups, with different objectives; Osgood and Fuertes going after small mammals and birds, Bailey, Baum, and Cutting on the trail of bigger game. Mr. Baum sent his narrative in to the

Chicago Daily News whenever he had the opportunity; the articles were syndicated and appeared in The Ithaca Journal, among other papers. Later they were re-worked and published in book form, first as Savage Abyssinia (J. H. Sears and Co., 1927) and then as Unknown Ethiopia (Grosset and Dunlap, 1935).

20

To Abyssinia

....

L.A.F. TO MRS. FUERTES AND MARY
About ¾ down the Red Sea, Oct. 3, 1926.

Dear ones on land—*Pos.* hot, *Compar.* hotter, *Sup.* hottest. Life is one B.V.D. after another, with a splash of Red Sea water between.

The ship's company is highly cosmopolitan and rather second-class; entertaining rather than interesting. The days and nights have gotten successively hotter and we've had that scourge of the hot seas, a following wind of about our own speed, most of the time.

But for the birds that are apt to turn up any minute it would be exceedingly dull. The old Red Sea is 1,300 miles long, and it seems interminable. With luck we'll get to Jibuti about 4 p.m. tomorrow, and have two days there before the Wednesday train goes up to Addis.

We came through most of the canal at night, but in the early a.m. were still in the Bitter Lakes which form its middle, and as it narrowed saw many herons, cranes, hawks, some bright little jewel-like kingfishers (sparrow size), and—best of all—three flamingos were feeding only about 200 yards from the boat, and didn't fly or seem at all disturbed, and gave us a great thwill. Since leaving Suez we've been continually out of sight of land, but almost always swallows, wagtails, wheat-ears, kestrels, terns, or a fine big dark eagle with the whole crown and nape cream white have been about the ship. This a.m. half a dozen tiny migrant quail, half or less the size of our bob-white, have been wearily following us, lighting occasionally on the deck or awnings, and getting chased off before they caught their breath. Yesterday we had four kestrels (a small falcon) and at one time four eagles sailing about in the wake. Three of the k[estrel]s spent the night aboard and are still with us. They are holding high mass on the after deck, singing and intoning—we've a score of priests and nuns aboard—and I'm in disgrace at the other end of the ship, but not quite alone. There are other unregenerates aboard too.

L.A.F. to Mrs. Fuertes

Addis Ababa, Oct. 8, 1926.

At last we're here, after a most wonderful journey. You know that the endless Red Sea was hot, and we were all intensely relieved to get to Jibuti, especially after the ship's gang had all gone back on board. We had 2½ days there, and none too much to get the baggage and transportation muddles unmuddled and see the place. The last afternoon Bailey and I hired a terrible old hack and a little rat of an old horse and went out to Ambouli, an oasis two or three miles from Jibuti, and in less than an hour I had collected seventeen birds with my pistol, every one of which we skinned and put up before going to bed; a good job.

Early Wed. a.m. the train pulled out for Addis, with all five of us sumptuously established in the Salon car by ourselves. All a.m. we passed through Somali country, saw many dik-diks—slender little antelopes not larger than rabbits—most engaging little things that dash away for a few rods and then stop and look back over their shoulders. Tall grass hides them!

It would take a week to tell you all the things we've seen. We spent the first night at Dirredawa, where it was hot, being only 2,000 ft. or so; the second at Awash, where the R.R. crosses the river; the third day, to-day, brought us to Addis Ababa, up on the plateau at 8,000 ft., where it is cool and lovely. Last night (this is the a.m. of the 8th) the thermo. registered a low of 48°, and sleeping was intense and delicious after the two weeks straight of hot nights.

There is no describing Addis, so I'll try! Crowded aimless streets —full of people of all sorts, cattle, sheep, goats, camels, horses, burros, and more of the same. Our auto journey to the British Embassy was a triumphal procession, honk-honking every second, going at 1st or 2nd speed, parting the throngs, in which the panic is equally enjoyed by all the various elements therein.

The hotel is a great rambling place with huge high rooms, a lovely garden all around, several yards and outbuildings on the slope behind. At 6:30 kites, crows, a big white-bibbed crow, a great thick-billed raven with a white nape, a stumpy-tailed small crow, and a couple of huge vultures were all around (sketches). When a servant left the hotel with a tray he carried a knife which he waved over his head, in spite of which a kite swooped down and tried to snitch the food from the tray!

Coming across the plain a harrier (marsh hawk) sprung a quail and it dropped to earth to hide; the hawk dropped too, chased it out of the grass, but the quail got off to a quicker start and pulled away, on which the harrier quit and flew off. But a small falcon had seen the whole business, and instantly wheeled, doubled his speed, and hauled the quail down in less than 100 yards, picked it right out of the air as neatly as you please and carried it off. This all happened in say 10 or 15 seconds, but the action was all parallel to us only a few rods away, and was seen by all five of us. Five minutes later we saw two lanner falcons try to catch a swallow, but they weren't good enough and a timely twist at the last moment put the swallow twenty yards out of the line—more than the hawks thought worth diving over.

We haven't had a drop of rain nor even a cloudy day since leaving Ithaca. We shall be here for at least ten days, getting our stuff out of boxes and into packs, assembling men and animals, etc. A mail goes out to-night, which ought to get this to Paris in twenty-one days, or about Oct. 29th. So I shan't wait to tell you about our reception by the Ras; we may not be recognized by the Empress, as she is becoming more and more of a religious recluse. But we are all in Grade A extra broad health and raring to go. We passed along by the Arusis, to the south about 60 to 100 miles—a great elevated region, with peaks up to 11, 12,000 ft. This is our first objective, and is the home of the Nyala antelope and many interesting birds and animals, is not very far, and will serve admirably as an introduction to the country and its ways.

As I write, a strange sparrow chirps on the veranda railing, kites glide swiftly to and fro—their shadows usually preceding them. Vultures are always in the sky. The city, from a distance, looks like a great eucalyptus forest, but from within is unlike anything you ever dreamed of. We look across a little dip to the Queen's palace —of curious Ethiopian-Byzantine-railroad-shed architecture, the silver dome of the church (her special interest) almost in her yard.

Our first night was too weird and eerie for words. It gets dark soon after sunset, so when we finished dinner and came up it was pitch black. An old crone was working by a lantern on one side, her great black shadow chasing all over the white wall behind her; across the court a servant was watching his master's horse, also by lantern light, and singing the wildest queerest minor Midway chant you ever heard, full of quirks and quavers, now falsetto and now down an octave or two.
[On reverse side.]

Don't mind a 'carbon copy' now and then: time is so hard to find that I'll probably do most of the newsy ones this way, and send one to Mother and one to you, using the back for that personal touch. Between notes, moving about, seeing things, collecting, etc., it is going to be a hard matter to find time for much letter writing. . . .

Jack's typewriter is clicking away like 20 sets of new false teeth. You'll get his stuff soon after you get this, I fancy. He's already sent off several batches.

My best love to you, Madgie, and to Mary and Barbara [Barbara Wyckoff, a friend of my age who spent the winter with us], and Mrs. Baum, I'm sure, would appreciate being remembered! I 'wished you was with us' all the way from Jibuti to Addis; the Red

Sea would have killed you off. We saw more beautiful things than I ever saw before in my life, and I wonder what kind of eyes and minds the people have who say that this is a dull desert trip, hot and uninteresting. It beats anything I ever saw, and I wouldn't have missed a mile of it for anything. The long slim straight black Somalis, in rags and a long spear, and a hellish knife stuck in their belts—then the Danakils, not very different but usually with a rhino-hide shield, watching sheep, herding cattle or goats, leading long strings of tawny camels—*always* armed with spear and knife, were in themselves enough to make you glad you were here, they are so different from *anything* you ever saw before.

Addis Ababa, Oct. 11, 1926.

We rec'd word this a.m. that we were to meet at the British Legation at 3:30 to go with the *chargé,* Mr. McLean, and have our audience with the Ras Tafari [the present Haile Selassie, Emperor of Ethiopia] at 4. So we hired the hotel's two cars, put on clean collars and started off. It was really a most interesting thing. The audience was held in a small room at the Queen's palace, not Ras T's own throne room, and was rather democratic, though formal and austere at first. His Highness was only accompanied by his own personal waiting man. There were the five of us, the British *chargé,* an interpreter, and the Ras's little silky brown dog. The lion was in a big cage outside, having outgrown the throne steps.

Osgood was presented, and he introduced each of us in turn. The Ras shook hands warmly, and smiled, but said nothing. He sat down, and we did, and after a little pause smiled at O., who started in in English, and through the interpreter outlined our plans, expressed the amenities, and did a very good job. We all felt that we had been cordially received, and that the Ras was interested.

Personally, he is the color of very old ivory, with black close curled hair, beard, and moustache. Black eyes, large, expressive, but tired-looking; his face perfectly non-committal till something pleases him, when it breaks into a most engaging and friendly smile. One feels that he doesn't get too many chances to use it, though. He is about 36, slight, not tall; I doubt if he weighs 130. He was not dressed differently from any other well-born Abyssinian —black burnoose over white shama and trousers, very nice French shoes. He has slender, soft, but very firm hands, like a painter's ought to be. There was no Oriental flurry nor pomp. While there were hundreds and hundreds of civilian retainers all over the place, we didn't see an armed guard anywhere.

I suppose we were there half an hour. O. presented his letter from Dr. Lambie. Tafari smiled and said quite simply, 'He is my best friend.' After outlining the plans roughly, O. explained the purposes of our work and presented the two books of photos of the Museum and Chicago, and I gave him my two books with the request that one be passed on to the Empress. O. said, 'These are not expensive gifts; merely evidences of our gratitude, and an explication of the nature of our work.' Ras Tafari then smiled his nicest (which is very nice) and said, 'The thought ahead is worth a great price.' While O. was talking, he looked each one of us over, in some way entirely without rudeness; he was a little stumped at the radio proposition, but said, 'I will grant permission to use it on trek, but not in Addis Ababa,' at which the British attaché nearly fell dead, for he was sure it would be categorically refused. Then, after all business was concluded, the Ras said, 'I will see you again before you leave,' and soon after, we came away. We felt that if we had impressed him as strongly as he did us we should have no trouble. Our application for passes must go formally through the British Embassy. It will take two weeks at least to assemble our men and animals.

After the Ras visit we all went to call at the German legation, where we met most of the English here and a lot of others. The ambassador is a young man—40 or so—a Swiss by birth, and was much amused to find I could talk Swiss to him. He has quite a zoo—2 hyenas (they run through the grounds every night) $n+1$ monkeys and a lot of birds. We're all fine, and most of our stuff is here—

[On reverse of letter.]

I didn't want to tell Mother, as she would worry for months about

'Poor Louis' but the one piece of bad luck thus far has fallen on me, for when we came to check up on our outfit, neither of my pieces—the trunk nor the duffle bag—were among them. The probability is that they got side-tracked in New York and have never been sent at all, though Cutting says they were there before his, and I had receipts before I left Ithaca. It is pretty tough, but doesn't wreck anything except my painting. Clothes I can get, blankets and beds are furnished, tools are in duplicate, and guns also. But I am handicapped by having to use untried and unaccustomed tools, inadequate clothes for the uplands where it gets really cold, no painting nor even drawing things at all, and the loss of a whole trunkful of conveniences—drying trays, skinning tools, etc., that I had carefully planned. We have cabled to the Museum, but of course only as a matter of record and protest; it won't do any good. But I can get along, and it would take a lot more than that to throw me.

Our expedition stuff is splendid; excellent saddles; the pack-saddles, to everyone's great surprise, are pronounced fine by the local mulemen.

L.A.F. TO MARY FUERTES
Addis Ababa, [Oct., 1926.]

Here are your little friends the dik-diks, with some of the other beasties and birdses that gladden the eye when plastered on the landscape extending from Jibuti to Awash—from sea level to say 5,000 ft. (Sketches on other side of paper)

You would have loved every queer sight and sound not to say smell (or ároma) that percolated to our avid senses—of all of which there were many, all new.

This (or these) are probably the longest letters I'll have a chance to write for many a day, as we are just now marking time till the arrival (through customs) of our outfit at the hotel, when serious and arduous work commences. Then first you know we'll be up and at 'em. By the time you read these lines, we should be in camp in the alluring Arusi country, on the trail of the wily nyala and etc.

I must, even now, cease firing, as there appears to be a down and out Hungarian Count who taxidermises for a living, and a chance offers to look over a few if not many Abyssinian birds and beasts, and now's the time.

L.A.F. to Mrs. Fuertes

Addis Ababa, Oct. 16, 1926.

A mail goes out to-night, and early Monday a.m. (this being Sat.) Bailey and I go out to Col. Sandford's for a week or ten day collecting, while Cutting goes alone up to Debra Libanos, a holy place where everything's tame, to get movies of the great baboons that throng there, and other things, and the rest (O. and Jack) stay here to oversee the assembling of our horses and men, and repacking of all the outfit. The London shipment is in Jibuti, and comes up Wed., getting here next Sunday (the 23rd) and I may as well relieve you at once by telling you that I was able to find very good colors, a box and everything, paper and all, here at a little Greek shop in Addis! Also good strong shoes; a Hindu tailor made me some swell riding pents and legginks, so I am only out a few non-essentials, and can learn on this short trip what I may need later on for the big trek.

To-night we raz the Ras, as it were, and are mildly excited. Then we have to have all our outfit ready tomorrow a.m.—10 a.m., I guess, as it takes two days; we ride out early Monday morning, and do it in one.

3:30 p.m. Just back from a long walk with O., down to the horse market. We missed the market, but saw so much, in the way of strange humanity, that it seems impossible to even commence on it: a wide wide street, native mud houses all along both sides, and an endless procession of men and beasts going both ways. All the women from 5 to 95 are loaded full and bent down with burdens, but are jocular and happy, apparently. Black boys carry burdens, but your Abyssinian, of whatever station, carries his head high and his hands free except for a staff. I enclose a daylight flashlight head-light highlight Bailey took the other day, thereby causing great disturbance and much excitement; you see it was nothing much to get excited over.

The State dinner was marvelous, and we all enjoyed it hugely. We were the last to arrive—just on the dot. The British chargé and wife, all the American Hospital crowd, two Americans who trek west tomorrow, the Belgian Minister and wife, a Belgian consul from Dirredawa and wife, the French Minister, and ourselves. A plan of the seating was on a table; I'll have to describe the rooms later. Snifters were served by black Abyssinians in white dress suits, gold buttons and skin tight trow. Bare feet, for once, were not in evidence, of course. After the amenities, we were shown into a large brightly lighted reception room, and the line proceeded to the far end, where Ras Tafari, in white with a close-collared long cape of deepest purple, with a gold throat-latch, stood beside his large and dusky consort, dressed in white soft cotton embroidered á la Maya. This part was very formal and whispery, and as soon as everybody had been received and passed on, with only the briefest pause, the Ras led off very slowly and, ladies first, we all filed into the state dining hall. An imposing room, with modern pictures (hunting scenes were pronounced Old Baltimore Rye ads by Cutting), a long table with solid goldfish and gold service, no kid, and cut glass in half dozens for each. The Ras sat in the middle of one side, the consortina opposite, and the conventional black concentrated at the ends.

The food was marvelous, a most ingenious mixture of European dishes with native confections, three kinds of wine—red, white, champagne—and—tej. The latter was the first we have experienced, and wasn't s'much. It is usually milky buff-colored stuff in old jars or dirty bottles with a bunch of leaves stuck in for a cork, and plumb unintriguing. It was here a 'clear amber liquid,' tasting a little burned or smoky. We all tasted it and smiled appreciatively, with loathing in our hearts. I raised my glass to the Ras's son-in-law, who knows no word of European talk, and he smiled a luminous smile and lifted his champagne glass—which was a relief, because I could change and did.

After dinner we returned to the big room, and the Ras at once singled us out, and came over and joined us in the most democratic manner, and talked with us generally and informally for fifteen minutes, in the lovely soft French that Amharic seems to engender. He was friendly, interested, asked all sorts of questions about birds and animals of America, the size and age of our cities, etc. Then, after some general conversation, we all went back to the dining room, where a screen was put up, and we all saw the movies we brought, and Rosita Forbes's reels also, after wh. we came home, and found it was 12:30—very late for us.

We go for tea this p.m. to Col. Sandford's [in Addis] and our two mules loaded with stuff left to-day noon and will be out there [at his ranch] when B. and I get there tomorrow night. We'll stay anyway a week, maybe 10 days or more, until the whole show is ready to go on the big trek south. Cutting also goes, alone, a three-days' journey north to Debra Libanos. He has to take six horses and five men. Of course his is a regular trek; we are 'visiting,' and don't have to cook and camp en route.

The fleas have found me, alas, but Zonite helps by relieving the beastly itch. I hope for better things outside the town.

Yours till I return, anyway.

Col. Sandford's farm on the Muger River,
35 mi. north of Addis Ababa, Oct. 21, 1926.

Monday, Bailey and I rode over here, with a change of horses, over the Entoto hills (10,000 ft.) and across the great savannah of the plateau. Great cranes, herons, three kinds of ibis, two of geese, and countless small birds abounded. I had my pistol handy, and collected 17 birds on the ride, four of which were none other than the mysterious horned lark (*Otocoris poli*) himself! That, you will remember, is the bird-objective of the trip (I now have six) being represented by a single specimen marked only 'Africa.'

We got here very tired, at about 2:30, and as soon as we got partly rested were called to tea! Fresh cake, and fresh (don't faint) strawberries and cream!! We were soon bucked up, and I got most of my birds skinned before dark.

This 'farm' is apparently just a ménage—every luxury at hand.

We are here all alone, with just the house servants, who do us beautifully. I've been here three days and have 45 birds (including three eagles, two of which I got right and left) and B. has 46 mammals, mostly rat size, but two 'klipspringers,' and to-day he got objective #2, a huge great 'old man' of the Gelada or 'decolleté' baboon. I saw three specimens in London, but nothing like this old veteran. He weighed about 60 lbs., and is covered from ears to tail with a great shaggy mane twelve to eighteen inches long, and has the most individual character of any beast I ever saw. Osgood will go crazy when he sees the photos and skin.

The farm is on the very edge of the plateau, where it breaks down into the great cañon of the Muger, a tributary of the Blue Nile. The cañon is 2,000 ft. deep, and we plan to spend a day and night at the river before we go back to A.A.

Just now we are working very hard, as this is only a brief opportunity. . . . Up at daylight, dawn, rather, and on the trail by 6 or 6:15. By 9:30 or 10 we've covered several miles, each on his own hunch, and are back at the house with an all day and evening's job. A silent, good-natured Galla boy follows our every step, and carries not only our game and an extra gun, but a basket of fresh strawberries: tough, *I* calls it!

Each day is jammed full of thrill and discovery. To-day I shot a most beautiful little eagle, all pale rich tan with heavily black and gray barred wings and tail, and a full soft crest on his nape. He was very lean and slender, with an awful lot of style; I never heard of one like it, nor saw a museum specimen. Those gorgeous gleaming glossy starlings are common. We sit on the porch skinning, and toss the bodies of birds and mice into the air; none has yet hit ground, for a dozen graceful kites sailing around nip them on the fly as daintily as can be. At lunch yesterday a great form slid by the window; Bailey grabbed the .22 rifle and went to the door and there on the edge of the garden sat a magnificent eagle, a true *aquila*, like our Golden, only this one was all pale buff with dark tail and primaries.

We have so much work to do that we can't stop to paw over

and study the things we get. As each day's hunt gets us birds we never heard of, often of great beauty, that is rather too bad, but inevitable.

I'm glad of this chance to get 'gradually' hardened up. I'm already in fine shape, and now do my morning's hike over hill and dale (and hills and dales are hills and dales here!) and feel fine. All my essential outfit has been replaced, so my only worry is that the shells won't hold out, and we'll have to come home because we've no more ammunition to shoot with!

I must stop now, as it's almost an hour past my bed time. I go to bed here at first-yawn time, and sleep like a log in spite of hyenas and pi dogs—until just before dawn—up and at 'em, breakfast over and on the trail by 6.

An earlier finish than usual, and the fact of a runner's going in tomorrow, were a combination I couldn't resist.

I expect letters when I do go in, about Mon. probably, as two or three mails will have come in by then.

Love to Mary and Babs—and I hope you are not skimping on your opportunity because the money seems to slip. I want you and Mary to get the very most of everything; another chance may never come.

Don't worry about me; I'm going like a new Ford—and I hope to do as well as an old one. Good night.

Addis Ababa, Oct. 26, 1926.
Just in from a marvelous week at Col. Sandford's ranch, I find your good letter enclosing Katharine's breezy letter and the clippings . . . All your news is good, and I don't believe wife ever told husband before that she had too much money!

Bailey and I rode in to-day in response to a letter from Osgood, and leaving this a.m. at 7:45—not bad to be all packed up by then —changing horses half way, we were back in Addis—30 miles—at 12:30, feeling fine. We plan to get off on Fri. a.m. for the Arusi country to the south, on a long swing that will take till December anyway, but we'll always be within a week of the mail, so don't slow down! I'm glad you're learning French; now we can talk when

Miss Ida's in the room. [Miss Ida, who cooked for us, was absolutely deaf.]

Except for the damn fleas, which treat me here as ever, I'm having a wonderful time. I'm as hard as I've ever been, can climb and work hard all a.m. in the rocks and hillsides and skin till bed time without undue fatigue, sleep like a child and wake up pink and refreshed, at sunup, ready for the new day! Put up about 85 skins in the six days, including eleven of the *Otocoris poli*, and on the way in collected the nest and eggs!—the first ever recorded, several large hawks, etc., and Bailey got nearly the same number of mammals, including three klipspringers and four huge baboons. So you see we, too, have not been idle. And the stuff is all A1, no junk nor half-done jobs in the lot, either.

Mary, how you would have loved the ride in over the twenty-odd miles of savannah land. We had splendid ponies that ride like Diamond G horses, fifteen miles and then fresh ones for the last half. Sacred ibis, a black crested ibis, herons and geese let you ride almost up to them, but the most exciting are the great cranes— standing as high as the little humped cattle—that let you ride up to perhaps 50 or 60 feet before they spread their glorious black-and-white wings, drop their long necks, and 'run up' the speed necessary for a take-off—trumpeting loud and long as they pick up, and with a stately rhythm fly up and up, until they can sail, like angels, if I picture them right—wheeling up and up and up into the sky till the long line of neck and legs gets lost to the eye, and they are just transverse lines wheeling in the burning blue of noon. I'd rather be able to do that than anything I ever saw done—but an ear-splitting engine would spoil it: it's the most serene thing any living thing does.

Well, my trunk and roll have been found—in the Brooklyn warehouse of Turner Davies—and are on their way, due in Jibuti Nov. 20. I can make out with what I have until we get back from Arusi.

O., Jack, and Suydam just came back from a state visit to old Fitaurari Hopta Georgis—War Minister, Governor of Arusi, and leader of the advance guard under Menelik when he defeated Italy at Adowa in 1896. They describe him as a black old lion of a man

—now quite sick, and old, but a broad-chested erect old warrior. He hates everything European, won't enter a motor car, and his house is surrounded by three circular stone walls with loop-holes, a regular old feudal stronghold.

This will be my last from A.A. for two or three months. Don't expect much from the field—I'll write when and as I can. Don't worry about me—I already feel ten years younger, and have no doubts at all but that I shall go on stripping off the years. I'm all black but my nose, which is a rich royal purple, with scales, which I leave on for protection from the tropic sun! You've seen it thus before this.

Addis Ababa, Oct. 26, 1926.

This has been a big day, any way you look at it! Two letters from you (Oct. 10 and 12) with K's and Shub's enclosed. I am so darn glad that Shub [his son Sumner] got his math., and that Hugh has subscribed for the *N. Y. World*. Now Bombay can read all about the trip, for that paper carries it. [Hugh Troy was taking care of the parrot, Bombay. The newspapers were for the floor of his cage.]

From daybreak till near sunset this has been one long series of conflicts, jabberings, bucking mules, broken noses, exasperating delays: reason, getting an unwilling safari of thirty men off and out of town when they wanted to stay over Sunday. But we got 'em off and follow ourselves tomorrow, on the train that starts this to you-wards, as *** used to pray it.

It was a long ten hours of constant pressure. If left alone these people sit or talk and chatter and accomplish absolutely nothing. They have *no* idea of consecutive effort nor of forward-looking, thinking only of each thing as they need it. Being unable to understand, mutually, a word, doesn't help. One Negadi (old Mohamet Naji), demanded a spade. 'What in the devil do you want of a spade?' 'Well, suppose somebody might die on the trip, how could we bury him?' Vetoed, but he turned up later with two just the same. Without Jack, we'd still have a caravan on our hands. He wrastled with sulky mules, showed a few western tricks to subdue buckers, and finally the conservative old mulemen fell for everything, and seeing they were beat, they fell to and as the shadows were lengthening, led by Jack, the first twenty mules filed out of the yard and down the road, followed before long by the rest. We still have all our personal stuff to arrange before morning, and will have to take a lot of stuff with us by train. . . . You'll probably get both of my letters together; if you are like me you won't mind.

In camp, on Mt. Albasso
(10,000 ft. alt.) Nov. 12, 1926.

This is the first time I have sat down to write since we left Addis, now twelve days ago. We went by train to Mojo, getting there 24 hrs. before our caravan. We fell right into the hands of a most efficient and helpful German settler, who had lost his all in German East Africa in the war and was starting all over again cheerfully and already making a good go of it, largely (as he readily averred) due to his rugged and capable wife. We picked up quite a lot of birds there, all different from foregoers, as it is only about 6,500 ft. Ever since then we have trekked, making one-night stands, off by 8 a.m. next day, 35 men and 52 mules strong. We spelled the mules (and men) one night at the Kalata River (where I got Menelik's oriole, *inter al.*), in the Awash drainage. That was a fine wild place; hyenas yapping around and a leopard's fresh trax in the creek bed; big steel traps yielded—an eagle! Then up out of the valley and onto the southern plateau of Arusi. After a couple of longish marches we finally arrived at this beautiful place—the head of one of the many little (but very troublesome) gulches, with a small local forest, a purling stream, and square miles of grass for the animules.

It was an experimental location, largely determined by the condition of the animals, who could go no farther without risking saddle-sores, etc. We hadn't been in camp four hours before Bailey came in, his men staggering under the load of a fine young bull nyala skin and head! About 5 p.m. Jack came in (no, that was next day) having shot two more, one a fine, the other an enormous bull, seven or eight miles from camp; I saw a very fine one at 150 or 200 yards, loping rather slowly up a draw, his great lyre-shaped horns held back at about 45°. He was a beautiful and stately sight, and in the smallish verdure of these highland pastures looked very large, and was long in sight. That second day here both Bailey and Osgood got fine cows, so the series is complete, and *nyala* an accomplished fact, unless a calf or an *unusually* fine bull should turn up.

Yesterday, out ten days and all O.K., we bought two bullocks (a Christian one and a Mohammedan one) for the men. Last night they had a grand raw-meat feast, and to-day the camp looks like a N.Y. back area-way with all the red stockings in the world hung out to dry—rods and rods and rods of strings of 'jerky' with squealing kites and great croaking thick-billed ravens swirling constantly above, not *quite* daring to snitch the meat.

We are sending in the specimens thus far collected to Mojo, thence (per Mr. Ehm) to A.A., for storage till we come back; hence this letter. From here on we probably shan't get many chances, for two reasons; the large heavy stuff is nearly all in hand, and the boys fear to go back in ones and twos, account of 'robbers' etc.

O. and I just got back from an all a.m. ride looking for our next camp to the south—and found it, about 12-15 miles around on the ridge on the south face, looking across the great plain of the plateau—laid out like a huge lavender-spotted leopard skin (spots= cloud shadows) far below us, its far edge breaking down in stupendous gorges and 'jangles' to the valley of the Webbi Shebeli some 25 miles away. An enormous and beautiful sky hangs over all this, the clouds draping themselves around the great peaks of Zuquala, Gugu, and—in the far pale-blue distance, the highlands of Jumm Jumm, 50-75 miles to the south. There is a small forest there (a great rarity in this country, especially at such an altitude). We will leave here as soon as the skins are dry enough (a day or two more) then wait at the new camp, working that region till the men and mules come back, four to five days, and then say good-by to these glorious and delicious heights and drop down to the lower levels to collect the far more diversified (but not more interesting) things of the wider spaces.

Here the characteristic things are ravens—great croaking buzzards with a white nape and deep heavy bill (sketch) that light on the backs of sore mules and eat the raw live flesh of the poor things; eagles of several kinds, vultures, and the great 'Lämmergeyer,' a bearded vulture, one of the largest birds in the world, and a most monstrous-fine flier; kites, a large white-breasted hawk; Bateleur eagles; on the barer parts of the hills francolins like huge quail, of two kinds, give most beautiful shooting and delicious food; doves of several kinds hoot, grunt, coo, or rattle in the boscage, according to their individual wont (or will).

Of little things there are many; snap-shots at wiggles in the low bush yield new things almost daily, and several of them should prove *really* new. By far the loveliest of all are two kinds of sun-birds, tiny slender things that replace hummingbirds in this continent. One is black, resplendent with shines of purple, green, and bronze; the other is *all* rich iridescent *emerald* green (blue toward the sun) with a little fan of dandelion yellow feathers in front of each wing.

Our health has been of the busting or vulgar variety. We eat three square meals a day, our cook (Hussein Mohamet) being a bang-up good one, and our stores opulent and swell. It is black dark by 6:15 and stays so till 5:15 a.m., so we eat our dinner after the day's work of hunting, skinning, and note-writing, and by 7 or 7:30 it's too darn cold to do anything but crawl into our blankets, so we knock off an average of 9 to 11 hours sleep nightly! I haven't found the altitude a handicap. To be sure, one gets quickly out of breath climbing stiff hillsides, but I've had no distress, and walk miles daily, up and down over rocks and 'nigger heads' and feel splendid all the time—as does everyone else.

I have skinned and put up just 200 birds—almost 100 per week of being in the field. At this rate (which of course will fall as we assemble the characteristic fauna) we'll have a very big and representative collection of Abyssinian birds when we're through. We go still south from here, toward Jumm Jumm, then swing west, through the pass south of Lake Zwai (big game country) and back north to Addis Ababa. Then we'll probably take a trip north to Gojjam, in the arm of the Blue Nile, the upper heights of which have been but scantily noticed by naturalists. If our luck holds we'll certainly get a bunch of things; almost all the desired things are already in camp, O. topping it off yesterday by shooting a fine dog wolf, the peculiar red wolf of Abyssinia, *not* heretofore taken south of the rift—a really fine animal, rarer than the nyala, and even more local. This may well be an undescribed form.

Our little group wears beautifully, all busy as possible, and each able to do his own stuff in his own way without criticism or suggestion. We don't have time here, to play or get clubby, much, as the days shoot past before we can grab off the good thereof. But it's a *swell* ex., and so far very successful. No troubles with outfit or natives, and help at every hand. So we are *quite* unworriable-about.

Over.

There isn't much to add to this mimeograph except to tell you that *just* as I left A.A. your letters and Shub's and K's all came, and started me off free from all the things I might have worried about.

Of all the amusing, pathetic, and interesting things that daily happen with this motley crew of men and mules I can't even make mention. I *hope* I can remember a lot of them later.

For example, my 'personal' boy's name is Tecla—he's no pearl! and my syce (gun-bearer and hostler) is named Abeba—which means flower! Abeba is a fine, shy, faithful, brave fellow: I *wish* I could talk to him. Tecla (whom I picked at the last moment because he looked unsophisticated and was spotless) is rather stupid, a town-boy of no use in the field, who *reeks* of garlic or its Abyssinian equivalent (or better), keeps my tent neat, and does my washing and greases my shoes; otherwise he's a cook's assistant, and my service from him is thus vicarious.

I had a bit of bum luck at Mojo; an acacia branch snapped back and drove a half-inch thorn way into the back of my leg, just above my leather legging, and broke it off flush with the skin. Before I could get back to the house it had worked under and away from the hole; I dug for it, but without effect, so had to leave it. It literally gave me hell for two or three days, as I couldn't bend a foot without pulling all the muscles crossways, and I couldn't straighten my leg without pushing it in, and hurting like the devil. But now it's O.K., and I hardly know I have it. Whether it's absorbing or what I don't know, but it's not even sore any more, for which I am truly grateful. For a while I was terribly worried lest I have to leave the ex. or hold it up, but nothing of the kind happened, for which I thank Mary's little brass rabbit, which I hung on my Ingersoll strap that night!

We've got a bully camp, only the nights are really pretty cold. Frosts occur, and up where Jack and Suydam went the other night for an overnight, the water froze and the ground got hard.

The best part of this opportunity of getting a letter off to you is that the men will bring back the 'accrued' mail with them, and I'll have more word from you.

The sun has slipped behind the shoulder to the west, and a chill spreads instantly over everything. So I'm going to don my Zebra coat (a life-saver—gosh I'm glad I didn't pack it in my trunk!) and make a holler for supper. Hussein has been low to-day, due, no doubt, to a tummy-full of raw beef. You should see the technique: they grab a big hunk in their teeth, then with a deft upward stroke of a 12-inch knife they separate it from the parent hunk, and repeat. I will say, from my recent butchering experience, that raw meat is *much* tenderer than cooked. But I didn't prove it by eating.

L.A.F. to Mrs. Fuertes and Mary

Addis Ababa, Jan. 20, 1927.

Yesterday afternoon O. and I pulled into Addis Ababa ahead of our caravan, which arrived this a.m. about 10. . . . We weren't looking for it much before tomorrow noon. First of all, to relieve any possible anxiety, we are both well and fit. I am ten pounds lighter and ten years younger than I was. O. is on his feet and his feed, has almost forgotten his insides . . . and is well on the road to complete and permanent recovery. We'll take up the details of our saga later. The first thing on arrival, of course, was to get the mail. So as soon as I could get hold of one I jumped an auto and popped out to the hospital after it. Met Dr. Pollock on the first corner, and he came in and we went out together, and I got a double armful of mail, and O. and I sat, 'thus, far into the night'—and I can't begin to tell you of the comfort and joy your letters brought me. I have never been so long (three whole months) without a word of home news, and I was half afraid to read your letters, but as only good news, both from you and from Shub and Mother developed, I finished at last and went to bed with a feeling of content and happiness that was little short of elation.

You will want to know of our doings so here goes. After my last letter, from old Chilalo's chilly slopes, we all hung together till Thanksgiving, parting the next day on southern Chilalo, Baum, Bailey and Cutting going s.e., to cross the Webbi Shebeli to Sheik Hussein after lions and big stuff; O. and I heading for Lajo crossing of the W.S. (s. and w.) to work the Gedeb Mts., then go down through Bale and Sidamo to Allata in the Jumm Jumm district—a type locality for a lot of Neumann's new mammals. I turned into a pretty fair rifle shot, and became head monkey-hunter, and got by with some distinction, getting eight guerezas—great black and white plumed monkeys, a fine old male of the unique jamjam monkey (known only from Neumann's type) and later a ♀, and several smaller ones of almost equal value. Besides this I painted 50 or 60 field studies, many quite elaborate, and collected and preserved 559 birds on the trip, in over 40 different camps! So you see I wasn't idle *all* the time. O. got nearly 300 mammals, including several big antelope—hartebeest (sketch) etc. 'The wild hyenas round us howled,' but we'd no adventures of a dangerous kind, and came through sound and still friends in spite of our hardening arteries and peculiarities, and are ready for more.

We found Mr. and Mrs. Rey (author of *Unconquered Abyssinia*) here at the hotel yesterday, to our great surprise and pleasure. Gave them a nice young wild guinea for their dinner; we weren't fitten to ask them to dine with us, our clothes all being locked up and we ourselves right off the mules. The other boys get in this p.m. on the train. As we have had *no* communication, they don't know where we've been, nor we they. You can imagine there will be a wild pow-wow, with chianti and everything, and all five talking at once like Abyssinians! They come up from Awash station with their stuff by rail, the caravan following light, due to arrive in about five days. Quite remarkable, I calls it, to connect so close to our schedule as laid out last Nov., arriving on consecutive days. We know they are O.K., as our A.A. agent (not stuttering!) had a telephone talk two days ago with Jack—but no details as yet. . . . xxx Those x's stand for 24 hours, in which much has happened. Of course the absorbing thing is the arrival, safe and sound, on the train yesterday, of the rest of the outfit. We had a grand reunion. They also had a fine trip, got a lot of stuff, but no lions. Bailey killed a leopard, *in* the air, as it jumped his 'boy,' thus undoubtedly saving his life, but not in time to save him from being badly clawed up about the face. As cool and collected an act as any old-timer could possibly achieve. . . .

My chief sentimentality on this trip was that being so far away and in a place with *no* communications, I couldn't send you any word at Christmas. We had a party, made a little speech to the men, and gave them each a dollar and a jounce of rum and had a nice warm feeling—but so different from any in my life before! On the Abyssinian Christmas, two weeks later, the Christians all came up in a body with my Abeba as spokesman, wished us a Merry Christmas, and asked for another!! As we were then (due to visiting chiefs) out of both rum and dollars we had to pike.

I've had a few minor and innocent adventures, but mostly we've gotten by with no distracting loss of time. Our state visits to local governors, etc., were so interesting that we couldn't really grudge the time lost, except once, when, having got behind the caravan to hunt some red bee-eaters, I was haled by a small chief in passing his gibbi and held a 'social' prisoner for 2 hours while he looked us up. . . . I'm crazy to see you both and hear you talk French. After I'd conversed, as I thought fluently, in French with my captor in Wando, I was much chagrined when he said: 'It surprises me that you don't speak French. Why, French is the polite language of every country, and *tout le monde* speaks French!' Can you beat that for a squash?

Addis Ababa, Jan. 30, 1927.
[Misdated Dec.]

We all went to tea at Ras Tafari's, quite informally, and were rec'd. quite alone and had a fine time. We took his and the Princess' pictures—still and movie—met, personal, the latest lion cub and cheetah, and I showed him my field studies and asked him to choose a subject for a picture which I wanted to paint for him, to remember our expedition by. He chose a lovely trogon, and I've finished the picture and shall have it framed tomorrow.

Re-packing, discarding used-up equipment, re-distributing our stuff, etc., etc., takes much time and effort, so we have hardly been out social at all, aside from [the] Ras's.

Feb. 3, 1927.

The Ras had us all to dine again last night, this time just us five, Mr. and Mrs. Rey, two other American boys, and the Jap. Consul at Cairo, here for a few days. . . . I presented him the picture, which I wrapped in scarlet silk and tied with gold braid—pretty doggy. He seemed pleased, but didn't come through with any lion-mane capes, etc. I've not waited for such things, but bought what I've needed—a shield, some spearheads and other nicknacks, a little old ivory, etc. There's nothing really nice here, as these people are practically without possessions, and make nothing but the articles of daily utility, which are generally plain and quite smelly, and wouldn't appeal to our friends as gifts. I've bought a suit of clo. and a shama—just for such occasions as Bozar Balls etc.—blowing about $3.50 for the toot assomble.

Tinish*, our baby baboon, has perked up a lot and lives on our porch, getting most of his care from me. He's a little mick among monkeys, a plebeian from head to tail, but so darn appreciative of a little care, and (like most micks) so perfectly abnormally smart and quick to learn that you almost expect him to grin and talk back to you. But he never does either. He's as scrawny as a spider, has hair that's too big for him; his skin hangs on him in folds and wrinkles and he looks a thousand years old. He'll get about as big as Terry, but now he's only about as big as a kitten—all shanks and big solemn head. I don't know what he's doing now, but I'll go out and sketch him at whatever he's up to. Here he is: (sketches).

* [*Tinish* is] Amharic for *little*.

Fri. p.m., Feb. 4.

The Reys gave us a dinner party last night here at the hotel, and it turned out to be a bang-up slick affair. The Zaphiros (Oriental Sec. at Brit. Legation), two American boys and ourselves, and an Englishman—very nice—at the bank were the party, and we laughed and talked and sang and enjoyed ourselves till 1 o'clock, so you know it went. . . .

Having picked off and killed all of Tinish's many fleas, I now allow him to follow his strong desire to curl up on me, and he is now asleep in the crook of my elbow as I write. He's quite the most appealing little rat of a patient and pathetic sporting gent I've ever seen (more sketches).

L.A.F. TO FRANK M. CHAPMAN

Addis Ababa, Jan. 23, 1927.

Osgood and I just got in two days ago from the first long leg of our trip, and I found in my letters (three months' grist of them!) your fine one of Oct. 28th. . . . Also the sad news of poor Ake's death—a man with dreams half-fulfilled, and with a great work half done. [Carl Akeley, the creator of the famous African Hall in the American Museum of Natural History, had died November 29, 1926, on an expedition to Africa.] Both O. and I have felt much depressed, and even in this overbusy time of re-organization, re-packing, and the thousand distracting details of each day's work have felt the shadow of our friend's death back of all our work. It was his hope, though, that when he did die it would be in Africa. . . .

My best congratulations, *Old Man*, on being a grandfather! I had a shock myself when I let my whiskers grow out summat, to find that they are snow white, and I look 75 in 'em. But O. let his grow, and aside from looking a little sacrilegious, they are very becoming to him.

This is a wonderful experience, and I only hope I don't get tired and thus lose my enthusiasm for it. We have had about three months of it now, and our outfit of 50 mules and 50 men has covered over 1,000 miles, made over 80 camps, and collected about 1,850 specimens all told. Divide all these figures by two and you'll have approximately the saga of each of the two parties, as we split on Nov. 26th and foregathered yesterday. Without a word of communication since parting, the two outfits got back to Addis Ababa just 24 hours apart. . . .

We had, of course, many picturesque experiences, my topnotcher, perhaps, being a late afternoon swim in Lake Sh'ala with the hippopotami coming up to huffle and blow every few minutes, often quite near by. They were not at all alarmed, and we had a very nice swim together! This lake is heavily saline; I was surprised to find hippo in it. They seem, locally, to prefer salt lakes to fresh—there are both kinds adjacent.

It would be hard to pick out the 'high spots.' In the high mountain forests of huge cedars and 'olive' trees, a band of blood-winged leaping turacos is no flat affair. The morning water-flight of sand grouse is a stirring sight and a very sporting event of the hot dry lowlands. Five hundred flamingos that don't even move away as the caravan skirts the salt-encrusted beach doesn't need boosting with you as a bird sight, and the same thing, doubled or trebled, seen farther up the lake from a mile-distant camp, swinging up and around and back and forth with the rising sun on their backs and a still-pink sky beyond the mountains across the lake found me short-winded as I forgot to function for the time being. I was afraid I'd be a bit jaded on fillymingos, but there's no danger. I had the same almost unbearable thrill—wide, deep, and full—that my first glimpse gave me, so many years ago, at Grassy Creek. This bird has a different charm—perhaps less wildly beautiful than ours—but it gets you in the same place. . . .

From here we go north to the country of Gojjam, a mountainous region in the great arm of the Blue Nile, and the big game gang there splits off for a shoot to distant Simien, the home or habitat of *Capra walei*, the last untaken desideratum, and by far the hardest to get. O. and I will work around Lake Tana [*miscalled Sh'ala*] then west to Gallabat to collect in the sudan fauna until the boys come back and all together again to Khartum and down to Cairo— Europe for the families of us who's got 'em and home somewhere around June 1, I figgers.

L.A.F. TO MRS. FUERTES AND MARY

Bichana, Gojjam, Feb. 23, 1927.

An unexpected chance to get a line to you, as Col. Sandford has a Somali agent here at Ras Hailu's new town, and returns P.D.Q. to Addis.

After leaving Mulu on the 11th we struck right north and camped that night at the Muger River, 3,000 ft. below the level of the plateau, and had our first and only hot night since we got on the plateau in October. We came out the next day, trekked three days to the top of the Blue Nile cañon—5,000 ft. deep and about eight or ten miles across. Camped halfway down, crossed and climbed halfway out next day (starting in the moonlight at 4:30 a.m. and descending the steepest and most spectacular part in the swimming pink glow of sunrise), camped about 2,500 ft. below the top, and out the third day, without loss or injury to man or beast—and all felt well satisfied. Ras Hailu, apprised of our approach, had sent a large escort to meet us beyond the Blue Nile, but they went to another crossing ten miles away and we missed them. But he had couriers all along our route, and we established communication before we crossed the river.

It took three more days to reach Bichana, his grandfather's old capital he is now rebuilding. As we approached the last ridge before Bichana, we were met, under a huge fig tree, by the Ras's head Chamberlain and a military escort of five or six hundred, with a Shankalla (slave Negro) band—eight one-piston cornets and six native two-toned flutes, which fell in ahead and conducted us to our camp site, where Hailu had erected a huge tent for our use, with vestibules fore and aft and rugs spread two thick all over the grass inside. He sent word that as it had rained and looked like more, he would postpone his call, but would we all come up tomorrow at 11:30, converse a while and stay to lunch? So, day before yesterday, we all slicked up, and the band was here to blow us up the hill. We passed right through the market and into the palace compound, a double sort of hour-glass shaped affair, with his whole army of 1,000 about equally divided and lined up in two facing rows. As we dismounted and walked up the compound, the rifles were raised and shouldered in advance of us, giving a curious wheely appearance quite impressive.

We had a strictly native lunch of barley-bread, hot sauce of gravy and red pepper that would burn out a steel pipe; champagne was the only European touch, which was added to *tej* and barley or wheat beer.

We took all kinds of pictures of him, and on leaving invited him to lunch the next day (yesterday). He came, and our cooks spread themselves and produced a marvelous meal, which he enjoyed hugely. Eight full courses, opened by rum cocktail (rum and pineapple juice and water.) After lunch we made a tour of the tents, each man showing his stuff and explaining it. He was much entertained, but really sparkled when the guns were put in his hands. Jack asked if he didn't want to shoot. 'Isshe,' (Yes) and with three strange rifles made three very good targets—took my shotgun and strolled out to the edge of camp and folded up five kites in five successive shots!! not so bad. After that we had tea in the big tent, and he stayed until nearly an hour after dark, promising a hunt for to-day.

We left camp this a.m. at 7:30 and rode an hour up the country and finally saw a huge crowd a mile up the road. It was Ras Hailu and his retinue, whom we joined, and the whole thousand of us went on, arriving in another half-hour at a very old church he has recently restored. I'll have to *tell* you about that, but it was a topnotcher among all our queer experiences. Here *all* the men and women of the village came out and danced (men together and women and children in another frenzied throng) and sang welcomes to their Ras. Then we went out, only 16 mounted men and about 30 attendants, to hunt reedbuck in the open valley. The Ras killed one—a very good shot, heart, at 75 yards. Approaching another village, more dancers came and danced and shouted before us all the way in, up to the church, and when we left, escorted us out of the village to a shady acacia grove on the hillside, where the 'hunt breakfast' was served—tej and barley bread—under a tent, with the entire village dancing and singing outside. We got home about 2 p.m., with the most colorful and bizarre of all our experiences back of us.

Every day since our arrival a procession of food-bearing slaves has come in with bread, bullocks, sheep, chickens, eggs, firewood, and feed for our 60 mules. At the present moment the men are squabbling and quarreling over the apportionment of the day's provender.

This will be our last camp all together.

> Near Jigga, a small town in
> s.w. Gojjam, Mar. 8, 1927.

A most unlooked-for chance to get a letter off to you by a runner from Addis bringing accumulated mail, including yours from Siena dated Feb. 6th. Your birthday greetings gratefully rec'd.

After leaving A.A. we spent a couple of days at Mulu, Col. Sandford's ranch, and then crossed the Muger River safely—a 3,000 foot cañon—three or four days over the plateau to the Blue Nile, and crossed that huge cañon, as I now remember writing you from Bichana, where we visited Ras Hailu. We got away from there about ten days ago, and stopped for a couple of days at Debra Markos, where we visited the Ras's daughter, the tragic wife of Lij Yasu, the deposed and now imprisoned son of old King Menelik— I drew her portrait, to her great delight. Hailu was wonderful to us, gave us gold, trinkets, a beautiful royal spear each, and topped off with two fine riding mules, and the same to the others, who left a few days earlier.

This camp is quite low—only 6,500 feet—and warm of evenings, unlike most of our camps. Hyenas and bush-buck are vieing with each other to-night, barking right near the tents; Dabba shot three big reed-buck this p.m., and the carcasses haven't been druggen away, but will be before a.m. probably. Dressy guereza monkeys are common in the nearby woods, as are great big jungle pigs and several kinds of antelopes—they dash right through camp! Eagles yelp around the carcasses of our game, waiting for a chance to scavenge. . . .

Tell Mary I gave her Venetian glass beads (the flowery ones) to Ras Hailu's thirteen year old grand-daughter, and both she and her mother (the one I drawed off) were much pleased, and that the beautifully made little basket she presented goes to her, naturally, with s'm'other things. I've quite a glum of plunder—and now our lamp is out, and this is being finished by the aid of a bug light. As I've hunted five hrs. to-day and skun 11 birds including two trogons, I'm about due for bed, especially as it's 9:15—nearly two hrs. past my usual.

This is the last letter from Abyssinia proper, but before finishing off the story of the expedition with a few notes written by Louis from Khartum, from the ship, and from Paris, I interpolate here a few reminiscent paragraphs written by Alfred M. Bailey.

Fuertes was constantly exclaiming in wonder, and occasionally pulled his horse to a stop as he watched a group of birds near at hand. When we came to a shallow lake with muddy shores where small white herons, two large blue species, lapwings, short-tailed and white-bellied ravens, and a large flock of white-winged pigeons were elbowing each other for room, Louis' delight overflowed. He sat back in his saddle, waved his hand toward the broad expanse of bird-filled country and exclaimed, 'Bill, this is the high-light of my ornithological career. Birds everywhere and every damned one is new.'

On one occasion, when we were camped in the high Arusi mountains in south Abyssinia, I crawled out of my blankets early in the morning and shot a buzzard high upon the cliffs with a .22. The camp boys swarmed up the mountain-side to retrieve the bird, and it was such a nice specimen that Louis decided to paint it. When the drawing was completed, I noticed he had marked five B's in pencil: B.B.B.B.B., and upon my inquiring what they stood for was told, 'Bill Bailey's Before Breakfast Buzzard!' I've always regretted [that] the lettering was removed when the plate was reproduced.

Fuertes was always a delight to us. He was one of those rare combinations of sportsman and sentimentalist. He delighted in making good shots, and a double—a bird with each barrel of the 20-gauge Ithaca—delighted him. If he ever bragged, it was of a quartering down-hill shot through heavy cover. Then after killing his feathered victim, he would, like as not, sit down and put all the feathers in their natural position, stroking the bird gently. On one occasion Louis had volunteered that one of his embarrassments was to come in from a collecting trip, and then . . . have some enthusiastic bird student gush, 'Mr. Fuertes, don't you just love birds?' Occasionally when we would catch Louis being a little sentimental, someone in camp was sure to start, 'Mr. Fuertes, don't you . . .' which would bring flying anything close to the artist's hand.

L.A.F. TO MRS. FUERTES

Khartum, Sudan, April 26, 1927.

We are out of Abyssinia, and on our way! The boys met us just before we got to Gallabat, on the *dot!* not an hour lost. We found no chance of a lion hunt or anything like that, and *all* want to get home as soon as possible.

You will get a wire, probably before you get this. But this is the first chance I've had to get in a letter I wouldn't beat to you.

We've been very successful . . . had *no* sickness nor serious trouble with the men; the Simien boys got thirteen ibex, including four fine bucks—one an inch short of the record.

I am awfully glad you're with Sheila and D. K. [Mr. and Mrs. David Kennedy-Fraser, in Milngavie, Scotland] and it is quite likely that O. and I will come up to Glasgow and sail from there. We shall be here a week, then right down to Cairo and out, overland to England, put in a few days at the Brit. Museum, and then Ho for Glesgie.

L.A.F. to Sumner Fuertes

On board ship, one day out
from Cairo, May 7, 1927.

Here we are, on our way out, and *home*. This will beat me by a week or ten days, at a guess.

Our second journey lay north, across the Blue Nile, to Bichana, in eastern Gojjam, where we visited Ras Hailu and had a very remarkable time, but it was hard to get any work done. Soon after Washington's Birthday we split up—Jack, Cutting and Bailey going n.e. on a month's trek to the highest Mts. in Abyssinia, in Simien, after ibex etc. (and got a plenty.) O. and I went to Debra Markos, and there saw Hailu's capital and spent a day or two very interestingly, on our way ever west and north to the west shore of Lake Tana, and then west on the long trek to Gallabat, on the Sudan border. We met the other party (left on Feb. 25) as if by appointment where their return trail met ours, half way to Gallabat, on the 13th of April. We got to the spot within six hours of each other, and are consequently about a week ahead of our schedule as we'd thought it would probably work out.

We crossed the upper Nubian semi-desert by Fords, two cars and two trucks, spending just half of the running time going, and the other half mending tires at 125° in the shade, if there had been any. Thus four days to Gedaref and Wad Medani, then a R.R. from W.M. to Khartum with all our stuff, which we shipped, including five live Gelada baboons, to Chicago. We came on down the Nile, R.R., boat between the cataracts (36 hrs.) to Asuan dam and the ruins of Philae, now up to their armpits in water, and R.R. to Cairo, whence we sailed yesterday on this Italian floating resteraw, with a lot of nice English people going home on leave. Brindisi tomorrow a.m., and a day or two at Rome, Flo., and I hope Siena, —then pop for London and pick up M. and M., and p.d. pronto home.

We had a lot of fun and interest—no great excitement—on the second journey. The whole trip netted 2,000 birds, 1,400 mammals and 100 'scattering' specimens—3,500 in all, all first class and of very valuable stuff. I painted more than I ever have, and have 100 studies, some of great interest, I think.

I wished you could have heard some of the musicians and minstrels of Ras Hailu's; marvelous old melodies on 'instruments of one string,' open tube flutes, etc. I tried to transcribe some of them, but the songs got entirely by me; in key, scale, tempo, and rhythm, stuff that I couldn't fathom, but that *had* all these qualities, being done, often by many in unison, and having a singularly catching swing to them. One flute orchestra was made up of seven men, each flute with but a single note, or at most an overtone added, and their melodies, endlessly repeated, were achieved by having each man (quite simply) play *his* note when it fell due. All sway and dance, and I was interested to see that these were *all* black, gourd-headed Negroes—Shankalla slaves—and not Abyssinians at all.

I have been delighted with your letters which Mother has sent on to me. If Ab. had had *any* kind of postal service I should have written you a lot more, but after leaving Addis there is no way of communicating except by a hired runner, and that was too expensive to be even considered, and in any case isn't very certain. News is sometimes six months getting from one town to another!

See you soon, good luck to you, and love to all the dear Brauners.

L.A.F. TO MRS. FUERTES

Paris, May 12, 1927.

Just got into Paris, having spent a day in Florence and Siena, and rather expecting to find you here with Gertrude [Baum.] . . . Of course I was bitterly disappointed, having you, as it were, already nestled on my sunburned chest—but (swallowing hard) I am truly awfully glad you and Mary got in your visit to Scotland. . . .

We are in fine fettle. I had to go and get a terrible attack of the 'hipness' which lasted from Khartum to Rome, now entirely gone. Thus I began and ended my long trip a cripple, but you can't hold a really good man down for more than a week, though he may be pretty far down for the time being.

I hope you have found something really nice for Katharine; she has been a perfect peach, and done (as I know) a *lot* of hard work. Of course I've been nowhere where I could get anything nice, and have only queer things, and not many of them. The Abyssinian ladies have no souls (by order of the church) and so aren't considered at all, and have no more embellishments than the dogs, and not as much as the horses. . . .

I know my long lapses must have seemed unnecessarily long. But I have truly not let a single possible chance to get a letter out go by. . . . There aren't even any telegraph lines where we were after my letter from Bichana, and I couldn't have communicated, as father would have said, with 'the holighost.'

21

Home Again

M Y FATHER MET US in London looking young, brown, excited. From our brief stay in the city I retain a few pictures: rhinoceros-hide shields, leather water-bottles, spears, and Abyssinian wearing apparel arrayed upon the satin bedspreads at the Savoy Hotel (expedition headquarters); my father being accosted in the lobby by a young man who said, 'Aren't you Hugh Breckenridge's Uncle Louis?' It was Mordelo Vincent, a Cornell student traveling with his parents, to whom Louis recounted then and there some of the high-lights of his trip. We ate plovers' eggs with Dr. Osgood at a restaurant, and my father bought a new top-coat. We boarded the boat-train, he put the tickets in the new coat pocket, laid it across the back of the seat, and promptly forgot it was his coat, so that when the conductor came by, the tickets were not to be found.

A few letters remaining from 1927 suggest the way in which he began to work back into regular life at home. He was determined to push through to its end his contract for the Birds of Massachusetts and thereafter to bind himself to no drudgery of that nature. Worthy and useful as the State publications might be, it was always distasteful to him to crowd onto one page birds of related species that do not associate in nature. He planned to give himself room for more free, original composition and also to write an account of the Abyssinian expedition.

One pleasant letter in his accumulated mail was from Daniel

Beard, who wrote: 'I think it bully that the Boy Scouts of America have selected you as one of the seventeen great outdoor men to be elected as Honorary Scouts.' The list included some acquaintances and several of Louis' very good friends: Frederick Burnham, Merion Cooper, Roy Chapman Andrews, Cap't. Bob Bartlett, Commdr. Richard E. Byrd, Lincoln Ellsworth, Stewart Edward White, Clifford H. Pope, George Bird Grinnell, Orville Wright, George K. Cherrie, Kermit Roosevelt, George Palmer Putnam, Donald Mac-Millan, Carl Rungius, James L. Clark. Charles Lindbergh was added later; we were at sea when he made his famous flight across the Atlantic.

L.A.F. TO T. GILBERT PEARSON

Ithaca, N. Y., June 2, 1927.

First of all, thanks for your welcome. . . . Sure, I'll do you a blue-jay (the surest sign of your degeneration in the north is that you say blue-jay instead of jaybird) just as P.D.Q. as I can get into my own house. We rented it last Sept. to one Martinez and his five sixteen-year-old boys (my son calls it the Mexican Revolution) and they have it till June 11, and besides that, my stuff is all packed away and I can't get at the *materia* for a few more days, while we are 'living around.' But it will be my first job. Do you want him (1) squawking, (2) with a robin's egg on his bill, or (3) looking like the Sunday School Superintendent that he is (or is not, according to your view of S.S.S.'s). I can make him like Simon Legree or Little Eva, just as you direct.

L.A.F. TO CONRAD ROLAND

Ithaca, N. Y., June 8, 1927.

My dear boy, I wish, more than I can tell you, that I could help you in the choice of your work, or throw a fine opportunity into your path. I'm at a loose end myself, with no idea, after all this long absence, of what is going on. There is no one I would rather be helpful to, yet I can't think of a thing. In my own case, things seem to turn up; just about as I close up one job another pops up. I will surely bear you in mind, and if anything does appear that you would enjoy doing I will certainly let you know and help you to land it. . . . In the meantime you might profit by L. H. Bailey's advice to the lady who asked him frantically, 'What *shall* I do about dandelions, they are spoiling my lawn,' to which he said, 'Learn to love them.'—A bromide, but what-the-hell? There they are, and you can make yourself sick over them or think they are pretty, as you prefer. So I'd try like the devil to make the stained glass interesting.

L.A.F. TO T. G. PEARSON

Ithaca, N. Y., June 22, 1927.

I am sending y'all your jaybird; I omitted eggs, but the obsequies seemed to call for flowers, so I went out in my yard and picked the first tulip that my tulip-tree (hand planted by self, 23 years ago) ever bore—all to decorate a jaybird that doesn't need it!

It is always hard to make a blue-jay 'stand out,' as the critics say. There is something about the chalky blue that simply will look like distance color, and it is my constant problem to overcome it. This is the chief fault, to me, in the sketch submitted—red is a positive color, and sticks right out; blue is a negative one, and fades right *into* the picture. But I've tried to make contrasty green do the trick, and I hope you will find the result satisfactory.

I'm *years* behind, hence my anxiety.

L.A.F. TO GEORGE SUTTON

Ithaca, N. Y., June 26, 1927.

Your letters were among those I found on my return recently from Abyssinia. Thank you for them and for the 'Notes on Birds of Southern Florida.' I am delighted to have it. I got a great thrill myself out of my brief visit at Cape Sable and Cuthbert Lakes, with the Würdemann's heron colonies on the keys. . . .

We had a marvelous trip in Abyssinia, and among other things I got far the best lot of field studies I ever did on one trip; a hundred color studies and a lot of drawings. Many of the birds most curious and bizarre.

I've so much now to do to catch up my neglected work that I

can't see which way to turn. But I must turn somewhere so have to sign off before I write you a book on Abyssinia. I've had no chance yet to talk to any but the home-town folks, interested mostly in the people and the country. I think I'd talk a bird man into an early grave!

L.A.F. TO WILFRED H. OSGOOD

Ithaca, N. Y., June 28 or so, 1927.

I'm mighty glad to know the *stuff* is all in the building. That's great, and *how* I'd like to be in it up to the shoulders, helping to unpack it. I've as yet conducted few conversations that haven't hinged on Addis Ababa, and have tried to fix it so that I haven't had to repeat much in the family's presence. What a lot of experience was jammed into those seven months! It becomes daily more evident, even in the rush and roar of other matters on all hands. . . .

Poor little monks—I hope they come through. Probably they're in Hamburg with Hagenbeck, waiting for a vicarious nurse to cross the Atlantic. We're all well, and still driving the old Rollin—doing pretty well, too, for her age and the shape she's in!

SIMON H. GAGE TO L.A.F.

Ithaca, N. Y., July 19, 1927.

It has almost always turned out in my experience that to follow one's good impulses was just the best thing to do. This was certainly true when you wrote to me that beautiful letter about the sketch of the life of our friend, John Henry Comstock.

I certainly join in your prayer that God send us always worthy heroes for the boys to worship. I suspect that a lot of them will feel the urge to follow your skilled hand in depicting the forms of strength and beauty that the world is so full of; and perhaps more will feel the desire to see with their own eyes the strange sights that Africa and South America and other distant lands hold for the traveler. I have envied you myself sometimes, but with the envy was satisfaction that you, who can appreciate so keenly all the wonderful things, were having the opportunity.

WILFRED H. OSGOOD TO L.A.F.

Chicago, Ill., July 20, 1927.

A box containing your personal trophies, guereza robe, koodoo horns, nyala horns, etc., is being shipped to you by express. Unfortunately it has to go collect, and I hope you can stand the pressure. . . .

It looks as if a single specimen of a guinea-fowl from the south rim of the Muger cañon might prove to be new. At least this suspicion was cast by Conover and one of his visitors a few days ago. Apparently, we did not save any guineas from north of the Muger which now seems too bad. Conover is also bewailing the fact that we saved only one specimen of the bluish-gray highland goose which is to be found only in Abyssinia. . . .

Perhaps you'd be interested to know that the big snake you dallied with on the escarpment trail is a mamba and probably the most poisonous species in Africa. Maybe there is a God, after all.

L.A.F. TO WILFRED H. OSGOOD

Ithaca, N. Y., July 27, 1927.

This is just because it's too dark (10 a.m. thunder showers) to work, and I presume you've nothing to do!

All the duffle came in perfect shape, as stated. I soaked the hide of the nyala and cleaned the bone base, and yoked up the kudu's corkscrews, based them both in clean plaster, and gave them a rub with floor wax; they now hang in state on my walls and look like 1,000,000 (count them) 1,000,000$. They are really great. Gosh, I'd forgotten what big things the nyala waves around on his head! That *big* pair you got must be soakers; I remember they were a lot bigger than my pair. Likewise Jack's kudus. Mine are just three feet, on a straight line, base to tip. Brehm gives three feet six inches as normal maximum, and three feet nine and a half inches as the record (many years ago, however). So mine are a good pair, and absolutely matched and perfect. They are really beautiful things.

The guereza robe makes an enormous hit—but *what* to do with it? It's too good for any practical use, and the bugs would eat it as a hanging. Give it away? No better fate.

Have you read *Trader Horn?* Get if, if you haven't. It's a remark-able book.

The rainy season is on here. It pours by the hour, and frowns and growls and spits something awful. . . .

I thought we saved more than one blue goose. As I remembered we had one made up and at least one (I thought two) in salt. I knew it was a peculiar endemic species.

Satdy. a.m.

I thought this had gone long ago, but I found it among the shuffle on my desk, so here it goes, with all its interruptions, breaks, discontinuity and all. It carries, dear professor, a burden of unseen regard and esteem. . . .

Yours over the hot sands and all.

Later in the summer Louis and Madge drove to spend a week-end with Dr. and Mrs. Chapman near Tannersville, New York, taking with them the Abyssinian pictures. They had a happy visit; Dr. Chapman examined the pictures and gave his opinion that they were the finest Louis had ever done.

On the twenty-second of August they started home. Near Una-dilla their car was struck by a train at a grade crossing, and Louis was instantly killed. An account in the Ithaca Journal News for August 25 described the accident as follows:

As the roadster approached the crossing, a heavily loaded hay wagon was coming toward the car, effectually screening the crossing and obscuring a car parked on the opposite side of the tracks. Intent on the task of passing the hay wagon the crossing was not seen, and the roadster, according to Mrs. Fuertes, was on the tracks before the train was seen.

Mrs. Fuertes was severely burned; the bundle of pictures was flung away from the car and escaped any injury. On August 25 there was a private funeral service in the studio and burial in a cemetery overlooking the city and the lake.

Louis' friends arranged an exhibition and sale of his pictures in the memorial room of Willard Straight Hall at Cornell University from the 21st to the 30th of October, and a memorial service was held there on October 30th at which Livingston Farrand presided and Romeyn Berry, Arthur Allen, and Frank M. Chapman spoke. This was the occasion when President Farrand answered someone who worried about the lack of precedent for such an event by saying: 'There is no precedent for Fuertes.'

Addressing the hundreds of people crowded into the room the speakers by instinctive agreement endeavored to make the occasion a happy one, recalling a joyous life. Said Dr. Chapman:

If the birds of the world had met to select a human being who could best express to mankind the beauty and charm of their forms, their songs, their rhythmic flight, their manners for the heart's delight, they would unquestionably have chosen Louis Fuertes.

Love of birds as the most eloquent expression of Nature's beauty, joy and freedom is the rightful heritage of everyone who hears the call of the outdoor world. But that instinctive, inexplicable passion for birds which arouses an uncontrollable desire to know them intimately in their haunts, and to gain a thorough understanding of their ways, and which overcomes every obstacle until in a measure, at least, this longing is gratified, is the gift of the gods which marks the true ornithologist.

Men to whom this priceless gift makes birds the most significant of living creatures are not numerous; but without it no one can become a really great painter of birds. When, therefore, one considers how small is the chance that the inherent attributes of the ornithologist and the artist will be found in one individual, it becomes clear why there have been so few famous painters of birds' portraits.

Here, then, we have the fundamental secret of Louis Fuertes' success. His inborn love of birds made him primarily a tireless, responsive student of their appearance, actions and habits, while his talents as an artist made it possible for him to portray what he saw and felt . . . Louis Fuertes was not only an artist, he was also a musician. . . . [He] wrote but little, but if the demands of his brush had spared him time he might with equal force have used his pen to express his love of birds. Where in the literature of ornithology will one find a more eloquent tribute to the power of birds' song than Fuertes' description of the emotions aroused by the call of the Tinamou. . . .

It was one of the marvels of Fuertes' nature that much as he loved birds he loved man more. . . . No one could resist the charm of his enthusiasm, his ready wit, and whole-souled genuineness, his sympathetic consideration and generosity of thought and deed. Everywhere he made new friends and everywhere he found old ones. We never seemed to get beyond the range of Cornell men. They appeared at most unexpected times and places. They might be classmates or recent graduates, but to them all he was 'Louis,' and the warmth of their greeting bespoke the depth of their affection. These meetings symbolized Louis Fuertes' contact with life. He brought only beauty and happiness into the world. Every memory of him is joyous.

Soon plans for permanent memorials began to take shape. The first of these was the Fuertes Room containing birds mounted by Louis Fuertes and a good collection of his drawings and paintings. A reading room originally set aside for students in the Laboratory of Ornithology, it was opened as a memorial May 31, 1928, in McGraw Hall, but it was later moved to Fernow Hall to be used by the entire Department of Conservation. The Fuertes Room was made possible with the assistance of Louis' fraternity brothers in Alpha Delta Phi; members of Psi Upsilon purchased and gave to the University two large water-color paintings.

The Louis Agassiz Fuertes Wildlife Sanctuary at Stewart Park, just south of Cayuga Lake, was a project of the Cayuga Bird Club and the Ithaca Rotary Club, made ready for the birds and the public in June, 1933. His name was attached for good and all (and for the confusion of future spellers) to the local council of Boy Scouts, to scholarships for students of ornithology, and to several new birds.

A detailed list of writings by and about Louis Fuertes, with a list of the publications he illustrated and the more important collections of his original paintings, appears in the appendix. The portfolio of Abyssinian pictures was published by the Field Museum with the generous assistance of C. Suydam Cutting in 1930; in 1936 the volume Artist and Naturalist in Ethiopia appeared. Dr. Osgood edited the book, which consists of the diaries that he and Louis wrote during the expedition.

Following the accident Louis' family was engulfed in a very tidal wave of kindness and messages. As soon as she was able Mrs. Fuertes acknowledged the letters, and then destroyed them all. She was sorting, filing, and discarding the apparently useless items in Louis' accumulated correspondence when Dr. Chapman came to Ithaca in October. He urged her to save everything that was left, and it was thanks to this advice, to Louis' habit of saving letters, and to the generosity of his friends that the present volume was made possible.

The announcement that it was in progress brought immediate response from people who had letters written by Louis. Dr. Chapman turned over his complete file at once; many others did likewise. George Sutton most graciously offered his invaluable set of letters although he had plans to publish them himself. By a combination of kindness, good luck, and diligence the family of Gladys Thayer Reasoner were able to find the letters Louis wrote to Abbott Thayer, without which the portrait would have lacked its proper depth. Some important letters have not been found, especially those to Gerald Thayer and Elliott Coues, and some written to his mother and sisters were carefully saved and then lost in a flood. Many people wrote regretting that they had not saved letters, many offered anecdotes and recollections of Louis Fuertes.

The years since his death had distilled their communications, removing expressions of shock and distress such as were contained in the earlier ones, retaining only the essence of the writers' feelings for Louis. In these letters phrases like the following abound: 'He was one of the very best men I have ever known and I loved him.' 'Louis had the greatest skill I have ever seen in winning and retaining friends.' Many people, young and old, felt about him as the artist Walter King Stone did, although they lacked his devoted modesty in expressing what they felt. 'I never thought I was Louis' best friend,' he said, 'but he was mine.'

He was another like Robert Louis Stevenson, whose biographer said: 'He was the only man I have ever known who possessed charm in a high degree whose character did not suffer from the possession.' His sister wrote, 'It was an unmarred life.' There was no youthful error, no grave mistake, no tragic flaw, and though his work might have gone on to still higher achievement he was spared even the suggestion of a decline.

And, Dr. Chapman to the contrary, opinion is not unanimous in maintaining that his last paintings were his best. In a sense he attained that high level of ability to create his kind of picture very early, and could at any time from 1898 or so—as soon in fact as he had absorbed the teaching of Abbott Thayer—produce incomparable portraits of particular birds. It is almost as if one could select Louis' best picture according to his own favorite bird and choice of medium, someone preferring a black and white wash drawing of a Sabine's gull from Coues' Key (1903), another, the water-color peregrine falcon of the Birds of Massachusetts (1922), a third, field studies of toucans made in the tropics (1910-13) or an undated pencil sketch of a kingfisher. I know a duck-hunter who prefers Fuertes' ducks, a crow-fancier his crows, a photographer the drawings that show characteristic postures, birds caught in the act of looking natural.

Much of his work was never seen by his teacher in painting, the man best able to give judgment, and he did not express a formal opinion at any time. But his son Gerald Thayer, writing in 1911, said:

Once more I have been smitten with amazement and delight by that work of yours. It comes so near being miraculous that it appears to me in a sense unique among human achievements of all sorts. Certainly it is inconceivable that such a genius as yours should be duplicated, ever, in all the circles of the years. No one has ever painted birds as truly and as intimately as you do, and it is inconceivable that anybody ever shall again.

We need not agree with this strong partisan voice, for certainly there have been good painters of birds since Louis Fuertes' day. Many of them learned from him—Roger Tory Peterson in Bird-Lore wrote of a 'Fuertes school' of bird-painting. Still art does not continuously improve, and the combination of traits in any human soul is unique. In Louis the artist was both born and made, the ornithologist as well, with the result that his pictures possess a high degree of truth and charm for those who have the eyes to see. But it is the great and complete man whose influence pervades and will not die. Like Louis Agassiz he taught men to observe. 'I am out here on this hill,' wrote one who speaks for an increasing number of amateur and professional watchers of birds; 'I am out here on this hill with a field-glass in my hand because of what your father did.'

Books and Other Publications Illustrated
by Louis Agassiz Fuertes

1895   The Annual *Cornellian* contains three black and white drawings by L. A. F.

1895–1898   The Cornell *Widow* (founded 1894) for these years contains many drawings, notably a series of cartoons known as 'Louis' Monks,' by L. A. F.

1896   L. A. F. was the 'Artistic Editor' for this number of the *Cornellian*, to which he contributed eight drawings.

1896   *A-Birding on a Bronco* by Florence A. Merriam. Pen-and-ink drawings by L. A. F.

1897   *Cornellian*. One drawing.

1897–1899   *The Osprey*. The first issue of this magazine, March 1897, contains four drawings: screech owl, American rough-legged hawk, long-billed marsh wrens, and snowy owl. In all it used twenty Fuertes drawings, some taken from other publications.

1897   *Citizen Bird* by Mabel Osgood Wright and Elliott Coues. 111 illustrations by L. A. F.

1897   *Song Birds and Water Fowl* by H. E. Parkhurst. 18 illustrations by L. A. F.

1898   *The Auk*. Between this date and 1920 Fuertes contributed ten illustrations. In 1913 he designed a new cover, and two years later improved on the design, which is still in use.

1899–1926   The federal government used designs and pictures by L. A. F. to illustrate many of its publications. They appear in Dep't. of Agriculture Year Books for 1901, 1903, 1906, 1907, 1908, 1909, 1914; in Farmers' Bulletins 497, 506 and 513; in Technical Bulletin 711; in North American Fauna 16 (1899), 25 (1905); and in Department of the Biological Survey Bulletins 21, 23, 24, 30, 32, 34, 35, 37, 38, 39, 44; Department Bulletins 185, 326, 862, 1091, 1196, 1249.

1899   *On the Birds' Highway* by R. Heber Howe, Jr. Color frontispiece by L. A. F.

1900   *Birdcraft* by Mabel Osgood Wright. 80 full page plates by L. A. F.

1900–1903   *Outing*. During this period L. A. F. contributed illustrations to five separate articles in the magazine, the last one, 'After Flamingos in the Bahamas' written by himself.

1901   *The Second Book of Birds* by Olive Thorne Miller. Eight illustrations in color by L. A. F.

1901   *Alaska*. Report of the Harriman Alaska Expedition. 2 vols. 16 colored plates and three black and white drawings by L. A. F.

1901   *The Woodpeckers* by Fannie Hardy Eckstorm. Five colored plates by L. A. F.

1902   *Upland Game Birds* by Sandys and Van Dyke. 5 black and white drawings by L. A. F.

1902   *Birds of the Rockies* by Leander S. Keyser. Eight full page plates (four in color) by L. A. F.

1902   *Handbook of Birds of the Western United States* by Florence Merriam Bailey. 33 full page plates by L. A. F.

1902   *Economic Value of Birds to the State* by F. M. Chapman. In Seventh Report of the New York State Forest, Fish and Game Commission. 12 plates by L. A. F. There are 14 in the combined 8th and 9th report.

1903   *Key to North American Birds* by Elliott Coues. Two colored frontispieces and more than 200 wash drawings by L. A. F.

1903   *The Water Fowl Family* by Sanford, Bishop and Van Dyke. 13 black and white drawings by L. A. F.

1903   *The Condor*. In this and the following years six Fuertes illustrations were used in the magazine, one of them to accompany his own article 'With the Mearns Quail in Southern Texas,' Sept.–Oct., 1903; another to accompany 'A Note on the Prairie Falcon,' Mar.–April, 1905. A drawing of the California condor by L. A. F. has appeared on the title page since Jan. 1904.

1903   *The Third Book of Birds* by Olive Thorne Miller. Nine plates by L. A. F.

1904   *A Guide to the Birds of New England and Eastern New York* by Ralph Hoffman. Four black and white plates by L. A. F.

1904–1927   *Bird-Lore*. Colored plates by L. A. F. formed the frontispiece of this magazine almost continuously. The National Committee of Audubon Societies published its educational leaflets in *Bird-Lore* and they carried illustrations by L. A. F. in 1904, 1910, 1913, and 1915. Six papers on 'Impressions of the Voices of Tropical Birds' were written and illustrated by him in 1913–1914, F. M. Chapman's 'Notes from a Traveler in the Tropics,' May–June 1919, had five pictures by L. A. F., and R. C. Murphy published a wash drawing by him of a strutting woodcock in July–Aug., 1926.

1905   *St. Nicholas*. In the department *Nature and Science for Young Folks* in the magazine for Dec. L. A. F. contributed a heading and five drawings for his article, *Winter Bird Visitors*.

1907   *The Warblers of North America* by Frank M. Chapman. Twelve colored plates (from *Bird-Lore*) by L. A. F.

1910   *Birds of New York* by Elon Howard Eaton. Memoir 12, New York State Museum, 2 vols. More than a hundred colored plates by L. A. F.

1910   *The Amateur Sportsman*, Sept. Cover by L. A. F.

1911   *Bird Stories from Burroughs*. 8 plates, four in color, by L. A. F.

1912   *Birds of Eastern North America* by Frank M. Chapman. Fifteen plates (eight in color) by L. A. F.

1913– Outline drawings of birds and animals by L. A. F. were commissioned at several times by Anna Botsford Comstock and published by the Comstock Publishing Company for the use of school children. They have been widely and often printed: in Mrs. Comstock's *Nature Study Review*, in the Cornell Rural School Leaflets, the Boy Scout Handbook, Arthur A. Allen's *Ornithology Laboratory Notebook* and his albums of recorded bird songs. E. L. Palmer purchased the plates in 1942 and has used them in *Nature Magazine* and in his *Fieldbook of Natural History* (1949). Some of the outlines appear in *Birds in Kansas* by Arthur L. Goodrich (1946). L. A. F. made black and white wash drawings also for the Comstock Publishing Company, used in Cornell Rural School Leaflets, and a set for *Nature Songs and Stories* by Katherine Creighton.

1913–1920 *National Geographic Magazine.* Articles illustrated in color by L. A. F. are as follows: 'Fifty Common Birds of Farm and Orchard' (originally prepared for U.S.D.A. Farmers' Bulletin 513) June 1913. 'Birds of Town and Country,' May, 1914. 'American Game Birds,' August, 1915. 'The Larger North American Mammals,' Nov. 1916. 'The Warblers of North America,' April, 1917. 'The Smaller North American Mammals,' May, 1918. 'Our Common Dogs,' March, 1919. 'Falconry, the Sport of Kings,' Dec. 1920. (This article and its companion in the same issue, 'American Birds of Prey—A Review of their value' were written by L. A. F.)

1915 *American Museum Journal*, May. Cover by L. A. F. 'A Great Portrait Painter of Birds' by Frank M. Chapman is illustrated by 11 plates by L. A. F.

1917 *The Country Gentleman*, March 3. Cover by L. A. F.

1917 *The Distribution of Bird Life in Colombia* by Frank M. Chapman. Bulletin of the American Museum of Natural History. Illustrated by L. A. F.

1917 *The Way to Study Birds* by John Dryden Kuser. Nine plates by L. A. F.

1918 *The Game Birds of California* by Grinnell, Bryant and Storer. 12 plates by L. A. F.

1919 *The Burgess Bird Book for Children* by Thornton W. Burgess. Color plates by L. A. F.

1920 *The Burgess Animal Book for Children* by Thornton W. Burgess. Color plates by L. A. F.

1920 *Trees, Stars and Birds* by Edwin Lincoln Mosely. 58 color pictures by L. A. F.

1922 *Monograph of the Pheasants* by William Beebe. Two colored plates by L. A. F.

1922 *Ants of the American Congo Expedition* by Wm. Morton Wheeler. Paper III, 'The Predaceous Enemies of Ants' by J. Bequaert, has a color plate by L. A. F.

1922 *A Natural History of the Ducks* by John C. Phillips. 25 plates by L. A. F.

1924 *Birds of Alabama* by Arthur H. Howell. Four drawings by L. A. F.

1924 *Herons of the United States* by T. Gilbert Pearson. Bulletin 5 of the National Association of Audubon Societies. Plates by L. A. F.

1925 *Birds of Massachusetts and other New England States* by Edward Howe Forbush. 67 plates by L. A. F.

1926 *Report on a Collection of Birds Made by J. R. Pemberton in Patagonia* by Alexander Wetmore. 3 plates by L. A. F.

1926	Catalogue of *First American Bird Art Exhibition*, Cooper Ornithological Club. Condor on cover and prairie falcon within by L. A. F.
1926	*The Distribution of Bird Life in Ecuador* by Frank M. Chapman. 5 plates by L. A. F.
1928	*The Heath Hen* by Alfred O. Gross. In Memoirs of the Boston Society of Natural History 6.4. One colored plate by L. A. F.
1930	*Album of Abyssinian Birds and Mammals* from paintings by Louis Agassiz Fuertes.

IN ADDITION L. A. F. designed many book-plates, letter-heads, posters, decorations for conservation projects in various states, and several handsome calendars with paintings of game birds. Beginning in 1922 he undertook some advertising orders: a picture of cardinals for the Parker Pen Co., about 100 small cards for Church and Dwight, to be distributed with baking soda, and 12 colorful drawings to be used with a series of Lincoln cars.

The list above does not take into account the re-use, both with permission and without, of countless Fuertes pictures, particularly those done for government and state publications.

Principal Collections of Original Works by Louis Agassiz Fuertes

The American Museum of Natural History in New York City.
    Besides birds painted into the backgrounds of some of the habitat groups, the museum owns several hundred field studies.
Cornell University. Additions to this large collection, now housed in the Fuertes Memorial Room in Fernow Hall, are constantly being made by gifts of former friends.
Museum of the State of New York in Albany. The originals for the *Birds of New York* are in this museum, gifts of Mrs. Russell Sage.
New York Zoological Society. Original paintings are in the Administration Building.
Museum of the Department of the Interior, Washington, D.C. Fifty small pictures are on display. In addition the Fish and Wild Life Department owns many Fuertes originals, some 90 of which have never been reproduced.
National Audubon Society. This society owns a valuable group of Fuertes paintings, which are sent out on Audubon Art Tours.
Private Collections. Mr. Frederick F. Brewster of New Haven owns a series of large panels in oils, possibly Fuertes' finest work. Dr. Donald Guthrie of Sayre, Penn. owns many drawings and paintings in watercolor and oil. The Estate of Louis A. Fuertes holds a large number of pencil sketches. Finally, there are many groups of pictures, or single pictures, privately owned.

Some Writings about Louis Agassiz Fuertes

1897   *The Osprey*, March, carries a portrait of L. A. F. and a letter to the editor about him by Elliott Coues. In the April issue Coues praises him in a brief article.

1908   *Camps and Cruises of an Ornithologist* by Frank M. Chapman contains narratives of expeditions taken with L. A. F.

1909   *Outing*, August. 'Drawing Wild Birds in their Native Haunts. A sketch of the personality and methods of Louis Agassiz Fuertes, the bird-artist.' By David T. Wells.

1915   'A Great Portrait Painter of Birds' by Frank M. Chapman.
    The American Museum Journal. Reprinted in *Bird-Lore*, July–Aug., 1915.

1927   *Bird-Lore*, Sept.–Oct. 'The Passing of a Great Teacher' by A. A. Allen.

1927   *Science*, Nov. 'Louis Agassiz Fuertes' by Wilfred H. Osgood.

1928   *The Auk*, Jan. 'In Memoriam: Louis Agassiz Fuertes 1874–1927' by Frank M. Chapman.

1931   *American Forests*, Feb. 'With Fuertes in Florida' by Alden H. Hadley.

1933   *Autobiography of a Bird-Lover* by Frank M. Chapman.

1937   *Natural History*, March 'Fuertes and Audubon' by Frank M. Chapman.

1939   *Bird-Lore*, Jan.–Feb. 'Memories of Louis Fuertes' by Frank M. Chapman.

1941   *Audubon Magazine*, Nov.–Dec. 'Louis Fuertes, Teacher' by George M. Sutton.

1942   *Audubon Magazine*, Jan.–Feb. 'Louis Fuertes at Work;' Mar.–April, 'Fuertes and the Young Bird Artist' by George M. Sutton.

1954   *The New York State Conservationist*, Feb.–Mar. 'Louis Agassiz Fuertes' by Mary Fuertes Boynton.

Some Autobiographical Writings by Louis Agassiz Fuertes

1903   *The Condor*, Sept.–Oct. 'With the Mearns Quail in Southwestern Texas.'

1903   *Outing*, April. 'After Flamingos in the Bahamas.'

1905   *The Condor*, Mar.–April. 'A Note on the Prairie Falcon.'

1905   *St. Nicholas*, Dec. 'Winter Bird Visitors.'

1910   *The Amateur Sportsman*, Sept. 'Louis Agassiz Fuertes, a Bird Portrait Painter.' (Not signed; attributed to an 'interviewer.' However the article in L. A. F.'s handwriting was found among his papers.)

1913–1914   *Bird-Lore*. 'Impressions of the Voices of Tropical Birds.' Six papers, printed together in the Annual Report of the Smithsonian Institution, 1915.

1936   *Artist and Naturalist in Ethiopia* by Louis Agassiz Fuertes and Wilfred Hudson Osgood.